Miscellany from Morley Green

Reverend Eric Chambers, FRPS. FRSA. FIOP. (FIP3)
Edited and Arranged by Clifford Higginson, MIOP (MIP3)

To the memory of Marjorie, ever a loving wife and mother,
a good companion in life for more than 53 years,
and to Paul, Sheila and Justine

Foreword

I first met Eric Chambers in 1957, when, as an 18-year old student, I attended the College of Printing, in Manchester, of which he was the Head. He was, at the time, an active, well-known, lay preacher in the United Reform Church. About 1974 he retired from the college and became an ordained minister in the URC Church.

On his 90th birthday a number of his former students hosted a dinner for him at which they presented him with a commissioned painted portrait as a token of their esteem. At that time he received numerous letters and e-mails of goodwill from his former students now resident in India, Australia, New Zealand and America. He is a Christian Freethinker, extremely well read, with an inquiring, sharp mind and an encyclopaedic knowledge of a variety of subjects including Philosophy. The respect, he engenders, whenever his name is mentioned, is self-evident and it has been my privilege to know him over many years.

CEH October 2004

Authors Preamble

A miscellany is an invitation to share other person's thoughts and aspirations. The Radio and Television have, to a marked degree, led to the neglect by many, of the influence of reading and literature. A good book is like a trusted friend and companion, always there, forever a help and provider. Knowledge is a power and reading supplies the source.

Michael de Montaigne observed four Centuries ago, that every sort of contradiction can be found in ourselves! The fact of life is that, at sometime, we are all sinners in thought, word or deed. James Elroy Flecker, in that lovely verse drama 'HASSAN' (1922), which is set to the music of Delias (now long forgotten and neglected) observed that: "We must ever make allowance for the purple threads of madness, woven into the camel cloth of our characters".

Life is not a vessel to be drained, but a cup to be filled, education, unlike schooling, is for life; and the longer we live, like John Ruskin, the author of some 35 books, in humility we realise that as far as knowledge is concerned, "we are forever as children, gathering pebbles on a boundless shore.

EC 2004

Preface

The author, born in 1909, retired in September 2002, after 69 years in Christian service and witness. At the age of 24 he was asked by the Manchester and District Congregational Board to take over the leadership of Tatton Street Congregation Mission Church, in Hulme, Manchester, on a voluntary basis. After 16 years there he transferred to Cheshire, serving a group of churches for 40 years, interspaced with a full-time ministry at Morley Green United Reformed Church for 30 years. This is a village church, situated near Wilmslow, Cheshire.

He was ordained to the URC ministry in 1979 and has always been non-stipendiary. In his professional career, apart from early responsibilities in management, he was, for over 20 years, Principal Lecturer and Head of Graphic Technology at the Manchester Polytechnic, now the Metropolitan University of Manchester. He was recognised as an expert in his subjects, the author of 4 technical books and a lecturer and consultant in many countries in Europe, Asia and America. He was Chief Co-ordinating Examiner and Chairman of the Graphic Reproduction Processes Advisory and Moderating Committee of the City and Guilds of London Institute, and a voluntary supervisor of student welfare, visiting and entertaining students and their families at home, and in many countries, in the past 35 years.

The Morley Green Newsletter was 'created' by the minister in 1973 for the benefit of the membership: the interest in it was soon apparent. Although the church membership was only 34, the newsletter eventually had a circulation to 250 families, and the request for an edited omnibus edition has received wide approval and support.

Contents

1974–79

1. 1974

The Good News of Christmas (1973)

The Christian year will soon pass into Advent and the time draws near when we celebrate the birth of Christ. The eyes of many – especially children – are turned in expectancy towards Christmas. One would like to feel that this change of direction and anticipation was no shallow observance of mere custom, but a rich and deep appreciation of the difference that Christ makes to our civilisation.

The threefold fact the He came, that in some real degree He abides, and that He grows, in spite of all opposition, constitutes a challenge to those who are heedless of Him. Christianity has been reported many times in history to be upon its last legs and tottering to its grave, only to confound its mourners with a new sudden outburst of life. Advent reminds us that Jesus is not a mere historic figure, but a present and powerful initiative and that he acts and works amid all the complexity of modern life. Nevertheless, He has a preference for working through men rather than independently of them – hence His choice of His disciples and His call to us.

When Robert Louis Stevenson came to Samoa, under the physical doom of death pronounced on him by his doctors, Christ came to Samoa! There was in Stevenson, such a charm of friendship that the Samoans, only a little removed from cannibalism, recognised in him the essential spirit of humanity and felt all its authority. When at last he was too weak to come down from his bungalow on the hillside to talk with them, they set to work to build a road up the hill to his house. While they were in the midst of road-making, a ship came into the harbour and an old Scots captain came ashore. He asked what they were doing and was told the story of the man who lived on the hill and what the road meant to them and their name for it – the Road of the Loving Heart. The tears trickled down the old captain's cheeks as, taking off his hat and coat he said, "I'd like to have a hand in a job like that!" He felt the dynamic impulse to worthwhile effort which the essential spirit of humanity always arouses. That essential spirit came on earth the first Christmas-tide and it has brought us thus far on the road of life, and it is that same Jesus Christ who, in fullness of time, will save and perfect this world of ours.

> Light looked down and beheld Darkness
> "Thither will I go," said Light.
> Peace looked down and beheld War
> "Thither will I go," said Peace.
> Love looked down and beheld Hatred
> "Thither will I go," said Love.
> So came Light and shone,
> So came Peace and gave rest,
> So came Love and brought Life.

2. 1974

God with us

Bonhoeffer, that outstanding German Christian and thinker of our age, wrote of God as 'the beyond in the midst of life.' An incident in the last war illustrates and gives this meaning. A long line of vehicles had become halted on a narrow road because of a truck at the head of the column which had become bogged down in the mud. Some walked up to the front to see if they could help, the majority stayed where they were. There were many already pushing and struggling to free the truck, including a vast and bulky figure shrouded in a gas cape, who heaved and pushed with great effort.

At last the truck was set in motion and the army column moved forward. It was only then that it was noticed that the big figure, who had worked so hard, was the divisional commander himself. Up to that moment he had been unrecognised and if any of the soldiers had been asked where the general was to be found, they would have answered that he was far behind the lines, comfortably secured at headquarters. In fact, he was nearer to them than they could have ever imagined. So it was in the first century. If the Jews had been asked where they could find God, they would have replied that He was 'beyond it all' in heaven. In fact, He was, in the person of Jesus, pulling and struggling with humanity in first-century Palestine, knowing and experiencing human troubles, sorrows and difficulties, with His shoulder to the wheel of the human predicament. For the Christian, God is to be found not at the end of life, but in the midst of it, perhaps unknown and unrecognised, but nevertheless present and aiding – a very present help in trouble. May our lives be charged with moments of awareness when we sense that the mysterious and ineffable is close at hand, challenging and encouraging us to persevere and to be of good cheer.

Discipleship

We are found – to find another!
We are told – to tell another!
We are won – to win another!
We are saved – to save another!

A Philosophy

To weep for what we cannot have
Gets no-one very far,
A pity to miss all the fun
While searching for a star;
He's wise who takes what each day brings,
And somehow makes the best of things.

3. 1974

A Thought

...all who joy would win
must share it – Happiness was born a twin.

Byron

I asked God for strength,
that I might achieve,
I was made weak,
that I might learn humbly to obey.
I asked for health,
that I might do greater things,
I was given infirmity,
that I might do better things.
I asked for riches,
that I might be happy,
I was given poverty,
that I might be wise.
I asked for power,
that I might have the praise of men.
I was given weakness,
that I might feel the need of God.
I asked for all things,
that I might enjoy life,
I was given life,
that I might enjoy all things.
I got nothing that I asked for –
but everything I had hoped for.
Almost despite myself, my unspoken
prayers were answered,
I am among all men, most richly blessed.

Henry Viscardi (who is without legs)

The Seven Modern Sins

Policies without principles.
Pleasure without conscience.
Wealth without work.
Knowledge without character.
Industry without morality.
Science without humanity.
Worship without sacrifice.

4. 1974

Council for World Mission

The work in the mission field is a vital part of the life and witness of the church. Look at this picture painted in a few brief and simple words, by an Indian peasant – "I couldn't afford to hire a bullock cart, so I put him on my shoulders and carried him here."

The patient was seventeen years of age and his village was ten miles away from Jammalamaduga Hospital in south India. The desperate poverty and lot of the Indian villagers is such that a father must carry his son ten miles to the nearest hospital. Here is poverty indeed. It doesn't cost much, by our standards, to hire a bullock cart but the peasants cannot afford an amount which it would take days to earn by heavy labour, and from wages already inadequate for the needs of the family. The poverty of the Indian villager (and the Bangladeshi peasant and many others throughout the world) passes our comprehension, because we have so little in our own experience to guide us in understanding. We and they live in different worlds. How can we, who may call an ambulance by telephone or who live on an island where a helicopter can be used to rescue a sick person in the snowy wastes of remote hill country during severe wintry weather, understand the necessity for carrying a seventeen-year-old patient ten miles along a hot and dusty track, to the only place where help can be obtained? Grinding poverty and inadequate medical service are the lots of millions of people in Africa, India and the East. To preach the Gospel by warfare on poverty and by relentless effort to meet medical and surgical needs, is an inescapable responsibility for Christian people – and that means us!

A Prayer
    Lord, make old folk tolerant
    Young folk sympathetic
    Great folk humble, busy folk patient
    Poor folk thankful, rich folk understanding
    Strong folk gentle, weak folk prayerful
    Religious folk thoughtful, clever folk kindly
    Bad folk good, good folk pleasant,
    – And make me what I ought to be!

5. 1974

Spring-Summer and Seeing

    To see a World in a grain of sand
    And a Heaven in a wild flower
    Hold Infinity in the palm of your hand
    And Eternity in an hour

William M Blake

William Blake in his 'Ideas of Good and Evil' as a Christian faces the hard facts of life with courage, faith and serenity:-

Every night and every morn
Some to misery are born;
Every morn and every night
Some are born to sweet delight;
Some are born to endless night.
Joy and woe are woven fine,
A clothing for the soul divine;
Under every grief and pine
Runs a joy with silken twine.
It is right it should be so;
Man was made for joy and woe;
And when this we rightly know
Safely through the world we go.

So wrote William Blake with poetic vision. Many have been away on holiday, seeing new sights and making new friends whilst others, perhaps not so fortunate, have remained at home. Nevertheless, all of us this spring and summer have had the opportunity again of looking at nature and observing the wonder of everyday things. Unfortunately, so often, familiarity breeds contempt and we look without seeing and fail to appreciate and give thanks for this wonderful world which God has lent us for our lifetime to use and appreciate.

Helen Keller, that wonderful American personality who was born blind, deaf and dumb, reminds us that we differ, 'blind' people and 'seeing' people, one from another, not in our senses but in the use we make of them, in the imagination and courage with which we seek wisdom beyond our senses. She says – "It is more difficult to teach ignorance to think than to teach an intelligent blind man to see the grandeur of Niagara. I have walked with people whose eyes are full of light but who see nothing in wood, sea, or sky, nothing in the city streets, nothing in books. What a witless masquerade is this seeing!

It were better by far to sail for ever in the night of blindness with sense and feeling and mind, than just be content with the mere act of seeing. They have the sunset, the morning stars, the purpose of distant hills, yet their souls voyage through this enchanted world with a barren stare.

6. 1975

The Pharisee and the Publican (St Luke, Chapter 18)

When we read this parable, told by Jesus to his disciples and the multitude, we despise the Pharisee and commend the publican. Yet, so often, we fail to see the 'beam in our own eye', and there is much of the Pharisee in us, in that we lack true humility and the spirit of true dedication and self-giving love. Like the Pharisee, probably none of us are as important as we like to think we are, and is there such a person as an 'Indispensable Man'?

> Some time when you're feeling important,
> Some time when your ego's in bloom,
> Some time when you take it for granted,
> You're the best qualified man in the room;
> Some time when you feel that your going,
> Would leave an unfillable hole,
> Just follow this simple instruction,
> And see how it humbles your soul.
> Take a bucket and fill it with water,
> Put your hands in it up to your wrists,
> Pull them out – and the hole that remains,
> Is a measure of how you'll be missed.
> You may splash all you please when you enter,
> You may stir up the water galore,
> But stop, and you'll find in a minute,
> That it looks just the same as before.
> The moral of this is quite simple;
> Do just the best that you can,
> Be proud of yourself, but remember,
> There is no Indispensable Man.

Values (True and False)

> Wisdom is the right use of knowledge, not the scheming of men's mind.
> Prayer is communion with God, not pious exercises.
> Love is sacrificing devotion, not idle sentiment.
> Conviction is steadfastness of purpose, not obstinacy of will.
> Victory is the defeat of an enemy, not shirking the contest.
> Humility is forgetting oneself, not underestimating oneself.
> Compassion is sharing the burden, not pitying the burden-bearer.
> Greatness is intensity of purpose, not aimless publicity.
> Power is the might of God, not human energy.
> Peace is calm in a storm, not the tranquillity of an unruffled sea.
> Unselfishness is living for the good of others, not extravagant liberality.

7

7. 1976

The Salt of the Earth

Many years ago now, a fine Christian said, 'Religion means work. Religion means work in a dirty world. Religion means peril; blows given, but blows taken as well... The world is to be cleansed by somebody; but you are not the called of God if you are ashamed to scour and scrub.' Never were these words more needed than today. This is an age when lovers of materialism, when the politics of defiance and the followers of false ideologies, are striving zealously to attain their ends. Christians must watch their dedication if the things they believe in are to survive. We cannot survey the continuing decline in the figures of membership in our churches without a sense of alarm. As the strength of the church in this land declines, we witness the moral and spiritual disintegration of the nation. Douglas Stewart, some years before his death, wrote:

> Europe no longer goes to church. The common spiritual heritage of the Christian religion is disregarded but you cannot say that despite this, Europe has remained 'decent' or 'clean' or 'just'. The silent spiritual collapse has been followed by an open and thunderous collapse which exhibits itself in campaigns of lying, treachery, violence, injustice and brutality on an unimagined scale.

The worsening of the situation, since those words were first written, calls for greater consecration on the part of all Christians. If the world is to be cleansed by somebody, it is we who are to do it, as we are true to our role of being 'the salt of the earth'. What if the salt has lost its savour? But if the world cannot afford the removal of the church, it does require its revival. "Revive Thy Church, O Lord, beginning with me." Only so, can our Christianity do its cleansing work in the world. For this purpose, and to this end, we exist as a fellowship within the locality that this part of the nation may be affected by the vigour and health of our Christian presence.

Togetherness

A minister once went into the home of one of his members who had stated, loud and clear, that it wasn't really necessary for him to attend church on Sunday, as he could find God in his garden or anywhere in the open air! He sat in silence before the open fireplace with his friend, who had been absent from the Sunday service for some considerable time. The man knew that his pastor had come to discuss with him his absence from worship and the remarks that he had made. The minister knew that he was expected to say something, yet they both sat there for a long time in silence. At last the minister arose from his chair and went to the fireplace. Taking the tongs, he lifted a single piece of coal from the embers and placed it alone on the hearth. He waited in silence as this single piece of coal glowed and burned and then burnt itself out and was extinguished, whilst the fire in the fireplace continued to burn brightly and give out heat and warmth. The man of the house looked at him and said, "You need not say a word, the moral is that I cannot keep the fire of my faith burning alone – I'll see you in church next Sunday."

8. 1976

Bible Study

It is a good thing, in the midst of the rush and bustle of life, to be able to withdraw and study or read a good book – especially when the book is the greatest of all books – the Bible. In this modern world, we are the objects of a ceaseless assault upon our privacy. So often we are the slaves of circumstances and not the masters. The radio and television dominate and occupy so much of our time away from our work.

We have so little time or inclination for reading. Books are quiet things; they serve our bidding; they fall into our pace and speed. We can lay them down or we can put them aside. A wise man once said that the best books are those which are open in your lap while you think over what they have told you. They are still the best nourishment for the mind. Something like 300 books are published every week in this country alone. Most of us will never know the names of a fraction of them and they are books on every subject under the sun. To discuss a serious book from time to time with a friend, can lead to a revelation about the deepest problems and mysteries of life. To know how people of the past lived and thought and suffered, can be an inspiration to our own living. Those who wish to take their Christian faith seriously, should consider whether they are sufficiently acquainted with the literature of their faith. Many of us read the technical, trade and home journals which concern us in our daily work and life; but should we not pay at least the same attention to the material which awaits us in the greatest of all things, the study how to live in Christian faith? We are called to fight the good fight of faith, and good living is helped by good thinking, and good thinking by good reading. And the greatest of all books is one – the Bible, which is in reality a library of 613 books. In this connection, the annual IBRA (International Bible Reading Association) Notes on Bible Readings, are most helpful.

Just a Thought (From an old stone in a country cemetery)

If your nose is close to the grindstone
And you hold it there long enough
In time you'll say there's no such thing
As brooks that babble and birds that sing.
These three will all your world compose
Just you, the stone and your poor old nose!

Recipe for Living

Take equal parts of kindness, unselfishness and thoughtfulness,
Mix with an atmosphere of love,
Scatter a few grams of cheerfulness,
Season with smiles,
Stir with a happy laugh and dispense to everyone.

To err is human but to really foul things up requires a computer.

Paul Ehrlich

9. 1977

The Preaching of the Word

In many instances these days, the sermon is out in public worship and replaced by a variety of substitutes. Customs change; not many years ago *The Sunday Times* and *The Observer* gave free advertising space to publishing the Sunday services to be held in a number of London churches. Apparently they feel it is a service no longer required today as most visitors would not dream of looking for a place of worship – music, theatre, exhibitions, pubs perhaps, but not churches! A century ago, people were feverishly putting up buildings all over Britain for worship, now there is an abundance of redundant church buildings. Times have changed and the buildings have outlived their usefulness. Perhaps, as Solzhenitsyn has said of Russia, the empty buildings and stones cry out proclaiming the word of Christ. He goes on to say, 'People were always selfish and often unkind. But the evening chimes used to ring out, floating over villages, fields and woods, reminding men that they must abandon the trivial concerns of this world and give time and thought to eternity. Our forefathers put all that was finest in themselves, all their understanding of life, into these stones, into these bell-towers.' Solzhenitsyn was remembering not the social events of his childhood, but the celebrating of the Christian faith in the Russia of a bygone era.

Here many church buildings in use are not adequately used, and the modern idea of an all-purpose church has much to commend it. It is good that a church should be used as a place of fellowship; a meeting place for the whole community. Nevertheless, it must always be recognised as a sign and symbol of the heart of the Christian faith, and this has been its character throughout history. It is the place fundamentally where the Word of God is proclaimed and the sacraments given, whatever other uses may be applied.

The criticism of the pulpit and its alleged position six feet above contradiction, has increased in recent years. We don't like being preached at! Who does he think he is? It's a feature of modern life. Magistrates with elongated forefingers tell people how they ought to behave, as though their own lives were above reproach. Politicians indulge in endless criticism of opponents, for sins which nestle in their own minds. Trade unionists complain about employers and management and these in turn scold the workers – preaching at each other has become the most common form of human speech!

The one constant theme of true preaching – from Paul the Apostle to Bonhoeffer, and Paul Schneider in our own generation (and all three lived and died in the practice of their faith), is that if we obey God, we disobey ourselves – we change our lives according to the example set by Christ Himself. The modern alternatives to preaching and responsibility for the spoken word are found in 'dialogue' and 'happenings' (drama, etc.) and it is conceivable that they could provide an acceptable alternative to a preacher garrisoned in a pulpit, offering a stream of platitudes and clichés to a bored congregation.

Essentially, we have to remember that the preacher and the church, do not witness to themselves. Always there is the life beyond, which is given and nourished by God in Christ. Thus we celebrate in word and sacrament. The Christ who is head of the church is the centre and heart of the universe and the church lives in the glory of God and for the love of man.

10. 1977

Exit One Lime Tilia Platyphllis

All followers of Gardeners' Question Time will know that this refers to a lime tree – and to us, one particular lime tree which has stood in the churchyard protecting us from the cold blasts blowing from Wilmslow for over 100 years! Alas, it is no more and we mourn its passing. Our good friend 'Dr' R. Boyer, the son of our church treasurer, kindly visited the patient and gave us his professional advice, which was to terminate its life forthwith, as it was in an advanced state of decay. This was done speedily and efficiently by Mr Ward and our old familiar friend is no more – and in memory we shed a silent tear – hail and farewell!

> I think that I shall never see;
> A poem lovely as a tree;
> A tree that may in summer wear;
> A nest of robins in her hair;
> Upon whose bosom snow has lain;
> Who intimately lives with rain;
> Poems are made by fools like me;
> But only God can make a tree.

Money and Giving

One of the most mis-quoted sayings of St Paul is that 'money is the root of all evil'. What he said was that the love of money is the root of all evil, a very different thing when money is acquired selfishly as an end in itself and not as a means of service. Archbishop Temple used to insist that Christianity is the most materialistic of all the great religions. The doctrine of Creation, no less than that of the Incarnation, teaches that the Lord, who made and redeemed the whole of life, is concerned with the whole of life. There can be no sphere of human activity which must not be consciously sanctified by His praise. Christ certainly wishes from us a spiritual sacrifice, but the matter and medium of which the sacrifice is made, is in material things.

When a Catholic lights a votive candle in the church, this is a symbolic action which is one of the approved sacraments of the Catholic Church. But it is also significant in that the person not only lights the candle, but pays for it also, and in so doing asserts an important principle of spirituality which is that we can pray with our pocket – with our giving.

As the Season of Goodwill draws near, may we be moved to remember others less fortunate than ourselves and may the Christmas spirit which is the Christian spirit, inspire and actuate our thinking, giving and serving.

Sermons in Sentences

Seven days without prayer makes one weak. Think of self and trouble grows, think of God and trouble goes.

A Prayer for Late-comers

It is said that the great preacher, Rowland Hill, was so troubled by late-comers to his services, that one Sunday morning he prayed, 'O Lord, bless those mightily who are in their places; give grace to those who are on their way; and have mercy on those who are getting ready to come, and will never arrive.'

Bible Holiday

Little Tommy was asked by his teacher which Bible story he liked best. "I like the one where everybody loafs and fishes," came the prompt reply.

11. 1977

Pentecost (Whit Sunday)

At this time we thank God for the worship, witness and fellowship of the Church and remember the great words of Andrew Reed which we sing at Whitsuntide:

Spirit divine attend our prayers,
And make this house they home;
Descend with all thy gracious powers;
O come, great Spirit come!

David was denied the privilege of building a temple for God in Jerusalem and it was left to his son, Solomon, to fulfil his father's aspirations and in due time it was declared open, with a great service of dedication. Yet, later it became, in the eyes of many of God's prophets, a hindrance to true religion, a place which had become an end in itself, instead of an avenue into the presence of Almighty God. The lesson of history is that unless we are very watchful, our churches can become like this too – ends in themselves instead of instruments for God to use.

At Morley, we trust and feel that our church is part of the community life, that it belongs to everybody and everyone is part of the church. Many who, through age, infirmity or sickness have been unable to attend worship for a long time still feel that they are part of the church family – and that is how we want it to be.

Nevertheless, we are saddened, sometimes, by the knowledge that there are many who could attend, who are always intending to attend, but who rarely manage to attend service on Sunday afternoon. We miss them and our prayer is they may heed our appeal to make that little extra effort to spare an hour on Sunday afternoon to worship with us.

It is said that the unconscious prayer of mankind is, "Lord, make me better but not just now," and there is an ancient legend which tells of the devil examining his minions before sending them into the world to do their work. "What will you tell men?" said he to the first. "I shall say there is no God," was the reply. "No good," said the master, "they will not believe you; and you?" he asked another. "I shall report that there is a God but that he does not love or care for them."

"That is not much better, for few will believe that," said the devil. "How about you, what will you say?" he asked a third. "I shall say that there is a God of Love, but that there is no hurry to seek Him."

"Splendid," said the devil. "Off you go, you will certainly succeed."

This 'putting-off habit' plays havoc with us all, for the simple reason that the longer we put off making a decision, the harder it becomes and the more easy it is to let things drift. This creeping paralysis of perpetual postponement does play havoc with all our good intentions! What about making the effort?

Just a Thought

Let us not be like porridge
Slow to boil, and hard to stir
Instead, let us be like cornflakes
Always ready and quick to serve

12. 1977

A Modern Parable

Now it came to pass that a certain parishioner invited his pastor to lunch at a popular restaurant. The waiter was very efficient and his food was good. As they rose to depart, the pastor observed that his host laid a number of coins under the edge of the plate. And the waiter who stood by, smiled happily – which meant the tip was satisfactory.

Now, with such customs all are familiar and this parable enters not into the merits and demerits of tipping. But the pastor began to meditate. Well, he knew that the usual tip must be in the region of ten per cent (a tithe) lest the waiter takes exception to your lack of generosity. And it came to him that few people so honour their God as they do their waiter. For they give unto the waiter the tithe due, but they give unto their God whatsoever they feel able to spare at the time.

Verily, does man respect his waiter more than he respects his God? And does he love God less than he loves the waiter?

Truly, a man and his money are beyond understanding!

Politeness

Somebody has observed that the only true source of politeness is consideration, a moral sense that never loses sight of the rights, the claims and the sensibilities of others. It is the one quality, over all others, which is the hallmark of a gentleman (or lady). "Politeness," says Montague, "costs nothing and gains everything" and, as Macaulay has well observed, "politeness is benevolence in small things."

There is a house in Poynton which has a printed notice on its gable end, which reads, Polite Notice, Private, No Parking. If some inconsiderate person parked there, they would effectively block the whole entrance. Politeness in life is like an air cushion, there may be nothing in it but it eases the jolts of life wonderfully. Eastern people, including the Arabs, are naturally courteous and polite. The Malayans also are a courteous people. At the entrance of the main street in Johore there is a notice which says, in big letters, 'DRIVE NICELY'. All of us in the UK would benefit if we did just that! If we all behaved nicely, politely and courteously to each other, what happiness and goodwill could we spread abroad, and how much closer would our lives relate to Him who 'went about doing good,' bringing joy and happiness wherever He went.

A Dilemma

A minister, after parking his car in a prohibited place, put a note on the windscreen – 'Clergyman in a hurry, seeking God – forgive us our trespasses.' Upon returning, he found a reply stuck on his windscreen – 'Traffic warden trying to do his duty – lead us not into temptation'.

13. 1978

Recipe for Happiness

There is a right and wrong way of doing everything. If you have been muddling along, doing a job in any old way, what a relief it is to be shown by the expert how the thing really should be done. Not only do we save ourselves much wear and tear, but we feel much more satisfied when we have learned the right way, even though it may hurt our pride to unlearn the method we were using before. Christians have always believed that there is a right way of doing the most important job of all – 'living,' and there are certainly plenty of wrong ways!

They believe that Jesus gave us the clue for the right way of living – the only Recipe for Happiness. It is a pretty revolutionary Recipe, but it is one that will bring real happiness (blessedness) when practised, and it is found in the Sermon on the Mount (St Matthew 5, verses 3–9).

Blessed are the poor in spirit; for theirs is the Kingdom of Heaven.
Blessed are they that mourn; for they shall be comforted.
Blessed are the meek, for they shall inherit the earth.
Blessed are they that do hunger and thirst after righteousness, for they shall be filled.

Blessed are the merciful; for they shall obtain mercy.
Blessed are the pure in heart; for they shall see God.
Blessed are the peacemakers; for they shall be called the children of God.

If we compare this Recipe with the generally accepted worldly recipe, what do we find?

Blessed are the 'pushers'; for they get on in the world.
Blessed are the hard-boiled; for they never let life hurt them.
Blessed are they that complain; for they get their own way in the end.
Blessed are the blasé; for they never worry over their wrongdoings.
Blessed are the slave-drivers; for they get results.
Blessed are the 'know-alls' of the world; for they know their way round.
Blessed are the troublemakers; for they make people take notice of them.

This latter is a recipe which many use, and the result is a world full of unhappiness, greed, cruelty and selfishness.

The first Recipe may not look very attractive, and it may not look as if it would work. But those who have made the effort to study it and put it into practice, find that life lived according to that Recipe is one of happiness and satisfaction – and it is the way life was meant to be lived by all of us.

Thoughts on Heaven

John Newton, the slaver, turned hymn writer and preacher, once said, "If ever I reach Heaven, I expect to find three wonders there. First, to meet some I had not thought to see there; second, to miss some I had expected to see there; third, the greatest wonder of all, to find myself there!"

14. 1978

Immigration

It is sometimes suggested that there is uncontrolled immigration into the UK and that it's making us an overcrowded island. This is not so, as under the Immigration Act 1971, very few categories of people can come and settle here.

The size of the 'coloured' population is 1¾ million – 3.2% of the total population. Since 1964 more people have left the UK each year than entered. In 1975, 190,000 people came to live in Britain and 230,000 left, a net loss of 40,000. Holland, Belgium and West Germany, all prosperous industrial countries, have more people per square mile than the UK. During the 1950s and 1960s, there was a worldwide shortage of labour and we, like many industrialised countries, looked to other countries to help us out. 11% of the total work force in West Germany and France, and 28% of that in Switzerland, are imported labour, compared with 7.5% of workers in Great Britain. At the present time, racial discrimination makes it harder for a 'coloured' man than for a white man, to get a job.

Miracle of Nature

Snowdrops are lovely little, fragile, flowers which, somehow, are capable of standing up to the snow and frost of the most severe winter. Why is this possible? Every evening as dusk begins to fall, the snowdrop's head droops a little lower and its petals close. In so doing, it imprisons within its bell, some of the daytime warmth and the amazing thing is that, even in the hour just before dawn, when the night is coldest, the air cradled in the snowdrop's petals can be several degrees warmer than the air surrounding it. This is why the snowdrop can survive the bitterest of winter nights and the coldest frosts. The moral for us is that when life is at its coldest and darkest, we must hold fast to the warmth and blessings that still surround us, and believe in the promise and hope of sunshine yet to be.

Tranquillity (A Japanese version of Psalm 23)

> The Lord is my pace-setter, I shall not rush
> He makes me to stop and rest for quiet intervals;
> He provides me with the images of stillness which restore my serenity.
> He leads me in the ways of efficiency through calmness of mind
> And His guidance is peace.
> Even though I have a great many things to accomplish each day,
> I will not fret, for His presence is here.
> His timelessness, His all-importance, will keep me in balance.
> He prepared refreshment and renewal in the midst of my activity
> By anointing my mind with His oils of tranquillity.
> My cup of joyous energy overflows.
> Surely harmony and effectiveness shall be the fruits of my hours
> For I shall walk in the pace of my Lord.
> And dwell in His house for ever.

Many years ago, a boy (now elderly) was walking home with an old gentleman. In those days the paths were laid with ashes and a new load had just been spread, leaving the way rough and dusty. "Let's walk in the road," the boy suggested, "it'll be easier."

The old man smiled and shook his head. "We'll walk on the path," he said. "If we don't tread it smooth, the folk who come after us will have to do it and they may be less able than we are to do it."

15. 1979

A Personal Reflection

The BBC series and the book 'Life on Earth' has, and is attracting, great attention and the book looks like being the best seller for many years – rivalling the Bible itself in sales. That great Christian scholar Dr Michlem, in his book The Creed of a Christian, observes that nature proclaims her great original and declares by every sign that she did not conceive herself, but is the expression of another. No blade of grass but is God's handiwork no human being but is someway in His image, no being exists but by sharing in His being, no will, no power, no life, no joy, no beauty, but has its source, its end, its process by His Word. All the visible things of the word show forth the glory and the wisdom and the power of His Creator.

Every child asks the question, 'Who made God?' For thousands of years people have wanted to know how everything began. How can we find out about the beginning of things? A child knows what happened in school last week because he was there. If he was absent, someone else who was there could tell him. But, in the beginning, no one was there so, therefore, no one can tell us. No one can help us to learn about the beginnings of all things but God. Can we think of a time when nothing anywhere at all but God? 'In Him was life.' It was God who began to make all things and He has told us part of the wonderful story in all the world – the story of creation. Every day He is telling us a little more of that story. One day, perhaps, He will tell it all. He tells us this story in many ways – in the Bible and this other book, the book of nature, a book that is still being written, and written by the very finger of God.

The word Genesis implies that it is a Book of Beginnings. Some people say that we ought to re-write Genesis in the light of modern knowledge and tell the story in the language of today. But the Bible is not a scientific text book. Its purpose is not to answer the questions that science can answer but the questions that science cannot answer. It does not tell us when, or how, the world was made; it tells us who made it. It does not tell us how man was created; it tells us who created Him and why he was created. It passes through the doors of mystery to which science has no key. Galileo put it like this, 'The Bible was not given to teach us how the heavens go, but to teach us how to go to heaven.' The Bible teaches us how God controls the destinies of all things. The distinguishing mark of the Bible, is the writer's ability to see God in the world. The subject of the first chapter of Genesis is not creation but the Creator. What it gives us is not a world, but a God. It teaches us that the God of the universe is a God of order. Thus no advance of science can make its teaching out of date. Science may fill in the details of the process; but only the Bible can declare with authority, that evolution is but the natural side of God's creation. The Bible, throughout its many pages and by different authors, teaches us that 'God has created all things by His hand, loving and almighty power.'

16. 1979

Working like the Rest of us

In the spring of 1978, Richard Syms resigned his job as a parish priest in the Church of England, and began work as an actor in the professional theatre. He had been a full-time minister for 10 years (aged 35) and his local butcher, when he heard the news, said, "Well, now you're going to be working like the rest of us." An interesting comment because the butcher knew that he was not a priest who spent life tending roses in the vicarage garden or a one-day-a-week vicar, invisible for six, incomprehensible for one. And yet he did not regard the priest as 'working'. Is this one of the many problems facing the church, in that ordinary people do not identify the minister with themselves, regarding him as separate and different? Yet Jesus was accepted always by ordinary folks – they received him gladly – as one of themselves. The decline in the number of ministers serving the churches, in all denominations, is a matter of grave concern, as is the decrease in suitable candidates seeking ordination. The reasons are complex and certainly not always concerned with salaries, stipends and cost of living. For example, with the Rev Richard Syms, it was a matter of principle between the church and himself. His church wanted to spend £3,000 on organ renovation. He expressed the view that half the world was starving to death, that £3,000 could be a deposit on a mortgage for a homeless family and that God cared more about people than organs. But the church didn't agree – "We like raising money for things like organs, it creates a sense of fellowship," and in any case a sister church was launching an appeal for £45,000 for its bell-tower, organ and windows.

Then there was the question of the harvest festival. The minister suggested an alteration for the evening service – to hold it as a service of thanksgiving in the local community centre and to invite the local shopkeepers' support and help, to auction the proceeds for Christian Aid and to arrange for elderly people, living near the community centre, to get to a harvest service. But this created a wealth of bad feeling in the church. "If these people want to come to church, they can always come. We like to have Songs of Praise on harvest evening in our own church."

What is the church for? Is it to keep the members happy and content, to give them what they want and expect. The minister can (if he wishes) go on about making the faith relevant, about ministry and mission and service to the local and worldwide community. These things are interesting – they make lively, controversial sermons that really make us think – but don't touch our traditional Harvest Festival. The Christian community cannot sit there using words about love and caring and just using its resources to raise exorbitant sums of money to spend on itself, on luxuries to project its own image. It has been said that you can tell a person's creed by the stubs in their chequebook.

So often the church's creed is solely self-preservation, to maintenance of its institutions and its plant, and these priorities are the exact opposite of the priorities of Jesus.

Here in the seventies, half the world is dying of hunger, there are the homeless, there is marriage breakdown, there are drugs, there is a god called growth, there is mental illness, vagrancy, youth unemployment and delinquency. There are millions of black people in Rhodesia and South Africa with no control over their own lives, and there is racial conflict here in our schools. These are facts, the real situations of many people in our generation. What are we doing for such people? The world, so often, has nothing to offer. Only the care and compassion found in Jesus Christ will suffice. A church, true to Him, must be prepared to lose itself in the salvation of the world.

Crisis in the Presbytery

In Bergamo recently a priest was found printing forged 50,000-lire notes. The reason he gave was that the collections at his church had fallen so low that he had difficulty keeping his parish running.

17. 1979

Hope

Most of us have seen copies of the picture, painted by G.F. Watts, which he called 'Hope'. It shows a woman sitting on a world floating through space; she is blindfolded and her head and shoulders are bent in grief and perplexity but she still clings to a crude harp, all of which the strings are broken but one. Some school children were asked to define the meaning of the picture's symbolism, suggested that "the woman was hoping she wouldn't fall off."

A closer study of the painting would have shown that one string was still taut on the broken lyre and that one little star was still shining in the dark, sombre and stormy, sky. Thus there was still hope! However bleak the prospect, or mute the music, life is still possible if one star shines or one string still vibrates.

Christianity has a monopoly of hope. Take this faith away and what is there to live for? Money? – you can't take it with you! Personal pleasure? – There's nothing more wearisome, or boring, than over-stimulated nerves. Sometimes we query the meaning of life and where is it leading to? Is it just a procession to the cemetery or crematorium? Shall we sit and play patience till the undertaker comes round? No! The programme and hope of the Christian way is to live to the glory of God by the service given to others. Joy and lasting peace can be ours, and death itself will be the gateway to a fuller life. No person is so sick as the one who is sick of themselves, and to turn from ourselves to God, the Giver of Life, is to find a meaning and purpose in life which always eludes the self-centred. God made us and cares for us. "Hope thou in God," says the Psalmist, "for I will yet praise Him' who is the Health of my Countenance, and my God".

Credo

Listening recently to the glorious music of Verdi's 'Othello' and contrasting the sublime beauty of Desdemona's 'Ave Maria' with the viciousness and worldliness of Iago's 'Credo' – "I believe in a cruel God who has created me in his image." I began to reflect whether I could state my creed – my belief? Well, here it is.

I believe that God is here, and now, closer than breathing, nearer than hands or feet. I do not believe that He created the world and went away and left it to run itself. I believe that the best way to prepare for a future life is also here and now, living, one day at a time, doing the work I can do best in kindness and love, doing it as well as I can. I believe that, as well as the Sabbath, I should remember the weekday to keep it holy. I believe that so often, particularly with young people, sin is misdirected energy and that in life there is no devil but fear and that no-one can harm me but myself. I believe that we are all sons and daughters of God and that the only way to reach the Kingdom of Heaven is to have the Kingdom of Heaven in my heart. I believe in the paradox of success through failure, of hope through despair – that death is the manifestation of life and that the universe was planned for good.

18. 1979

A Statement of Faith

Daniel Jenkins in his 'The Gift of the Ministry' writes a tremendous passage on the calling of the minister – "All the doubts and difficulties and terrors which confront mortal men as they face the temptations and hazards and ambiguities of existence, should be his familiar ground. Life, at its grimmest and harshest, should have an almost morbid fascination for him. Wherever there is trouble he should be found. He is the one man, among all men, who cannot be permitted the luxury of a sheltered life. Like Lear, he must experience the humiliation and agony. Like Abraham, he must know what it means to lift the knife against Isaac, his well-beloved son, at the commandment of God, and like Paul he must be prepared to wish himself accursed for his brethren's sake. Of all men, he has to be the freest thinker, allowing the most dangerous of facts to lead him where ever they will, without regards to personal safety or comfort, or professional prestige; offering himself on the altar of God's truth that God's glory might be made manifest in his weakness."

In the final analysis, Christianity does not depend upon going to church or even observing the Sabbath – although both are necessary. The Sabbath and the church were made for man, not man for the Sabbath. It is by love, service and sacrifice that we daily recapture the Spirit of Christ. The core of the Christian faith is that he who loses his life shall find it. From Jesus we learn that those who act on this principle have a capacity for real freedom. If as individuals we find life so dear that we will sacrifice anything – betray our friends, renounce the truth, grovel in the dust, in order to keep the heart pumping and the lungs breathing, we are already for all practical purposes as human beings, dead. The distinguishing mark of the Christian is the realisation that life at its highest and best, has nothing to do with the mere maintenance of the physical body. At the moment of saying goodbye to that body, we may for the first time truly live.

We have all heard of the little girl, well taught in her Sunday school, who defined faith as the capacity to believe what we know to be untrue! Many interpretations of the Christian religion need re-examining in the light of modern thought and knowledge. Faith, in the truest sense, is that by which we take a thing on trust in order to find out if it is true. Dean Inge reminded us that all faith consists essentially in the recognition of a world of spiritual values beyond yet not apart from, the world of natural phenomena. Change rules today and whether it shows itself in the process of breaking down or building up, change rules. No sphere of life and thought is exempt from the closest scrutiny and challenge of the modern mind – religion, theology, social and political instructions, are all subject to scrutiny and interrogation.

We have, sometimes, to distinguish between the Gospel and the Christian religion; the latter, a historical movement, has produced a rich variety of beliefs and practices. Dr L.P. Jacks has observed that if you take Christianity along with its entanglements, encumbrances and unnatural alliances, plus all the secular baggage which the ages have fastened upon it, you may find it a hopelessly perplexing thing which neither reason nor faith, acting singly or in combination, can accept. Fortunately alongside the authorised version, it has an inextinguishable spark of life – the unauthorised version, which has kept it alive through the ages, based solely on the Gospel as a Way of Life, revealed by Christ Himself.

Paul reminds us that we are all the children of God by faith in Jesus Christ and that Jesus is the first-born among many brethren. This conception is the essence of Christianity, distinguishing it from all that come before, or after, and vitally affecting our attitude to God, man and the world. In its essence, the Gospel is a call to make the experiment of comradeship, the experiment of fellowship, the experience of trusting the heart of things, throwing self-care to the wind, in the sure and certain faith that we will not be deserted, forsaken or betrayed and that our ultimate interests are secure in the hands of the Great Companion; Our Father. God, said Jesus, is Spirit, man is spirit no less, and when the two meet in fellowship, there is religion.

The essence of Christianity is the proclamation of a standard of absolute values – all the good and all the evil which defile us have their seat within us, in our own characters. We are sent into the world to suffer and to conquer suffering; to realise that it is more blessed to give than to receive; that love is the great revealer of the mysteries of life, that here we have no continuing city and must, therefore, set our affections and lay up our treasures in heaven, that the things that are seen are temporal and the things that are not seen are eternal. Herein is the essence of the Christian religion, seeking to enjoy and love God for ever and ever for it is in Him that we live and move and have our being.

Favourite Hymns?

Do we really listen to what we sing?

We sing, "Onward Christian Soldiers" – but have to be pressed-ganged into service.

We sing, "Tell me the old, old story" – but we are seldom there to hear it.

We sing, "Take my silver and my gold" – but put our small change in the offering.

We sing, "O, for a thousand tongues" - but we fail to use the one we have.

We sing, "I need Thee every hour" – but grumble about spending one in Church.

We sing, "What a friend we have in Jesus" – but turn to Him only when we're in a jam.

We sing, "I'm not ashamed to own my Lord" – but wouldn't dream of mentioning it outside the Church.

We sing, "Rise up, O men of God" – and lie in bed till 12 on Sunday mornings.

1980–89

19. 1980

Belief

Spring is the time of miracles – the miracle of the re-birth of life in nature after the long winter sleep. Easter is the time when Christians anticipate and expect miracles, and there are two from which the whole of our hope of eternal life derives – the resurrection of Jesus from the dead and the full implication of the meaning of forgiveness. They are both miracles and neither, as Our Lord says, is easier, nor more difficult, than the other. They both break through the natural orders, one of which we commonly call the law of nature, and the other the moral law – and both miracles proclaim that with God nothing is impossible. The Church of Christ is the one society which is not at the mercy of death and – verily, the gates of Hell have not and shall not prevail against her.

A recent survey, conducted by Marplan, on behalf of *NOW!* Magazine, produced some astonishing, and perhaps encouraging statistics about Britons' religious beliefs.

73% of the questioned believe in God
76% of all Britons claim to be Christians
82% claim to have a religious belief
16% claim to go to church every week (though this is not apparently borne out in practice)
52% of the public believe the clergy to be "complacent, old-fashioned and out of touch"
44% of Church of England clergy agree with the above
6% of all questioned claim to be atheist
7% claim to be agnostic

Throughout the survey, Roman Catholics show a strong grasp of points of fundamental doctrine, for instance whilst only 50 per cent of all those claiming C of E membership believe in an after-life, the equivalent Catholic figure is 80 per cent.

Sometimes we say, rather glibly, that the task of the church is to convert the world. But in reality the Church cannot convert anybody. It may evangelise; it cannot convert. Only God can do that. We can build an altar, lay the wood, prepare the sacrifice, but the fire must descend from heaven. In general terms the task of the church is to continue the work of Christ, she is His body, the means of His self-expression. The signs of the times are that the crisis for Christianity will not be resolved without profound changes. The time is ripe for a new reformation, in which many things of notable value in their day will be destroyed or transformed. This movement of the Spirit, which we remember at Eastertide and Whitsuntide, will restore in ways fitted for this age, the great gifts of the church of the New Testament – fellowship, freedom, service and love.

A Thought for the Future

Look not mournfully into the past – it comes not back again; wisely improve the present – it is thine; go forth to meet the shadowy future without fear and with courage, faith and manly heart.

Longfellow

20. 1980

Advice to Husbands, from the East (Recorded in the *Cyprus Anglican News*)

Tell Her So

Amid the cares of married life,
In spite of toil and business strife,
If you value your sweet wife,
Tell her so!
There was a time you thought it bliss
To get the favour of a kiss;
A dozen now won't come amiss –
Tell her so!
Don't act as if she's past her prime,
As though to please her were a crime –
If e'er you loved her now's the time;
Tell her so!
You are hers and hers alone;
Well you know she's all your own;
Don't wait to carve it on the stone –
Tell her so!
Never let her heart grow cold;
Richer beauties will unfold.
She is worth her weight in gold;
Tell her so!

Thoughts on Doing

If you think you are beaten, you are.
If you think you dare not, you don't.
If you'd like to win but think you can't,
It's almost certain you won't.
Life's battles don't always go
To the stronger or faster man:
But sooner or later, the man who wins
Is the man who thinks he can!

(Author unknown)

'Lost yesterday, somewhere between sunrise and sunset,
Two golden hours, each set with sixty diamond minutes.
No reward offered, for they are gone forever.

(Horace Mann)

A little more kindness, a little less creed;
A little more giving, a little less greed;
A little more smile, a little less frown;
A little less kicking a man when he's down;
A little more 'we', a little less 'I';
A little more laugh, a little less cry;
A little more flowers on the pathway of life,
And fewer on graves at the end of the strife.

(Anonymous)

21. 1980

Christian Responsibility

The Brandt Report (North–South. A programme for survival) is a major attempt to avoid confrontation between the rich and poor countries by means of reform and co-operation. Prospects for the world are bleak and alarming. If mankind is not prepared to act in solidarity now, its very existence and survival will be at stake. We see a world in which poverty and hunger still prevail in many huge regions; in which resources are squandered without consideration of their renewal; in which more armaments are made and sold than ever before; and where a destructive capacity has been accumulated to blow up our planet several times over. The Report, published by Pan Books at £1.95, should be read by all who are concerned about the future of mankind and the world God created for our use, benefit and enjoyment.

In the UK we face massive cuts in public expenditure and it is inevitable that the most serious effects of these cut backs will be felt by those least able to bear them, the poor, the aged and the very young. Many of the principles of the welfare state developed from Christian concern that those who enjoy good health and fortune should help to carry the burden of the sick and handicapped and disadvantaged. It has been estimated that arising from economies in the welfare services of the state, a person facing gradual loss of sight may not now be able to expect the training from a mobility officer to help manage their daily life. An elderly person, crippled with arthritis, may not now be able to expect the advice and aids provided through the occupational therapist or the service of a home help. A single parent facing stress after the death of a partner or the break up of the marriage may not now have the advice, support and guidance of a social worker. A child in care may not now be found the appropriate foster home, as his social worker has insufficient time and opportunity to find the right family. In every case, the lack of support in the community increases the risk of that person having to seek residential accommodation which is usually a less desirable and always a more expensive way of caring.

It is suggested that churches and individual members, as well as challenging policies and seeking to change them, have a role to play in alleviating distress wherever it is found locally either by supporting existing statutory and voluntary organisations, or by initiating their own caring services.

A Golden Rule

Bear ye one another's burdens, and so fulfil the law of Christ.

(Galatians 6 v2)

God was made humble that...
The pride of the human race might not
Disdain to follow the footsteps of God.

(Augustine)

22. 1980

Life's Basic Principles
What sort of people does God intend us to be?

Most people think:

Happy are the 'pushers'; for they get on in the world.
Happy are the hard-boiled; for they never let life hurt them.
Happy are they who complain; for they get their own way in the end.
Happy are the blasé; for they never worry over their sins.
Happy are the slave-drivers; for they get results.
Happy are the knowledgeable people of the world; for they know their way round.
Happy are the troublemakers; for people have to take notice of them.

Jesus Christ said:

Happy are those who realise their spiritual poverty, for they have already entered the Kingdom of Reality.
Happy are they who bear their share of the world's pain, in the long run they will know more happiness than those who avoid it.
Happy are those who accept life and their own limitations, they will find more in life than anybody.
Happy are those who long to be truly 'good', they will fully realise their ambition
Happy are those who are ready to make allowances and to forgive, they will know the love of God.
Happy are those who are real in their thoughts and feelings, in the end they will see the ultimate reality – God.
Happy are those who help others to live together, they will be known to be doing God's work.
And in doing they will find their greatest joy.

A small boy from a poor family wrote to God for help. His letter addressed to simply 'To God', asked if he could be sent £50 to buy food and clothing, badly needed for his family. He said his father was out of work and his mother was ill and they had no money.

A post office official intercepted the letter and read it. He decided to give it to the local Rotary club. The club investigated and found the family was indeed quite destitute. However, as they only had £40 in their benevolent fund they gave that.

Some weeks later the post office official noticed another letter addressed 'To God'. He opened it and read: "Dear God, thanks for the money you sent, but next time could you deal direct? Those Rotary blokes took a commission out of it.

There were glum faces in the church hall at the farewell party for the vicar. "Now, now," said the vicar, "don't be sad. The bishop is sending a good man, a much better one."

"But," they wailed, "that's what they told us the last time."

23. 1981

Queen's English (Author of Life's Problems)

> We'll begin with box, the plural is boxes.
> But the plural of ox is oxen not oxes.
> One fowl is a goose, but two are called geese,
> Yet the plural of mouse is never meese.
> You may find a lone mouse, or a whole nest of mice,
> But the plural of house is houses, not hice;
> If the plural of man is always men,
> Why shouldn't the plural of pan be called pen?
> If I speak of a foot and you show me two feet,
> And I give you a boot, should a pair be called beet?
> If one is a tooth and a whole set are teeth,
> Why shouldn't the plural of booth be called beeth?
> If the singular's this and the plural these
> Should the plural of kiss ever be keese?
> We speak of a brother and also of brethren,
> But though we say mother, we never say methren.
> Then the masculine pronouns are he, his and him,
> But imagine the feminine, she, shis and shim.
> So, what?

A Thought

> I regret often that I have spoken; never that I have been silent.
> (Publilius Syrus)

Life's Symphony

To live content with small means; to seek elegance rather than luxury, and refinement rather than fashion; to be worthy, not respectable, and wealthy, not rich; to listen to stars and birds, babes and sages with open heart; to study hard; to think quietly, act frankly, talk gently, await occasions, hurry never; in a word, to let the spiritual, unbidden and unconscious, grow up through the common – this is my symphony.

(W.E. Channing)

From an inscription on the clock in Chester Cathedral

When as a child I laughed and wept,
Time crept.
When as a youth I waxed most bold,
Time strolled.
When I became a full grown man,
Time ran.
When older still I daily grew,
Time flew.
Soon I shall find, in passing on,
Time Gone.
O Christ wilt thou have saved me then?

24. 1981

Conservation

Hundreds of thousands of 'Christmas trees' will be cut down to decorate our homes over the festive season. This has now become a very large, and profitable, industry. Everyday in the world trees, covering an area as large as Wales, are cut down to make paper and to supply building timber. Wood pulp for the paper industry accounts for the majority of this plundering of the earth's surface. The trees, in general, are not replaced and this leads to soil erosion and the eventual creation of vast deserts as in the Sahara and areas of America. Is the end product worth all this waste and despoliation of natural resources?

I think that I shall never see
Aught lovely as a pulpwood tree,
A tree that grows through sunny noons
To furnish sporting page cartoons.
A tree designed by providence
For classified advertisements.
A tree whose shady arms give scope
For reams of editorial dope.

A tree widespreading t'ards the skies
Will soon spread propaganda lies.
A tree whose friends die hour by hour
To give press barons wealth and power.
It always seems so strange to me
That only God can make a tree.
Yet, when it's into 'newsprint' made
The devil often plies his trade.

A worthwhile recollection from 1939–1945 – which still applies today

In a world that is seething with malice and greed,
When nations forget just one thing they need;
When skies are o'ercast, and your heart feels like lead;
When reason has vanished, and fear reigns instead,
I give you a motto – 'tis simple and straight:–
"Let the world turn to God – before it's too late."
When the Heel of Oppression is stalking around,
When truth seems o'erwhelmed and tramped to the ground;
When guns are a-booming and the world is at war;
When poor simple mortals cannot tell what it's for;
Yet He made the earth and our souls did create –
"Let the world turn to God – before it's too late."
There's a Cross that stood, long ago, on a Hill
That could change every heart and right every ill,
And doubting and fears could be all chased away
If we each turn to Him, and our part nobly play,
And that's all we need to change malice and hate.
"Let the world turn to God – before it's too late."

Who said this?

I expect to pass through this world but once. Any good thing therefore that I can do, or any kindness that I can show to any fellow-creature, let me do it now; let me not defer or neglect it, for I shall not pass this way again.

25. 1981

Easter Day

As always it is a day which produces emotions which defy analysis. It involves a sense of victory and achievement. It is the source of our personal salvation and also points to the creation of the church which is the community of the resurrection. It is clearly a day which speaks of Christ, but resurrection is also a life theme and has its echo in our own human experience. Each Easter Day says something different to us because its total message is too deep and potent for us to hear in one day of one year.

The Easter message gives hope and support to all who mourn, those who have loved and lost a while. William Penn the Quaker and founder of Pennsylvania, wrote, for posterity, some immortal words:

They that love beyond the world cannot be separated by it.
Death cannot kill what never dies.
Nor can spirits ever be divided that love and live in the same
Divine principle, the root and record of their friendship.
If absence be not death, neither is theirs.
Death is but crossing the world, as friends o'er the seas; they live in one another still.
For they needs must be present, that love and live in that which is omnipresent
In this Divine glass they see face to face; and their converse is free as well as pure.
This is the comfort of friends that though they may be said to die, yet their friendship and society are in the best sense ever present, because immortal.

With wide-embracing love
Thy Spirit animates eternal years,
Pervades and broods above,
Changes, sustains, dissolves, creates and rears.
Though earth and man were gone.

And suns and universes ceased to be,
And Thou were left alone,
Every existence would exist in Thee.

There is no room for death,
Nor atom that his might could render void;
Thou – Thou are being and breath,
And what Thou are may never be destroy'd.

(Emily Bronte)

Members of the Church of Scotland who have read the prayer, "O, Lord, grant that we may not be like porridge – stiff, stodgy and hard to stir; but like cornflakes – crisp, fresh and ready to serve," have suggested a revised version:

Oh, Lord, grant that we may not be like cornflakes – lightweight, brittle and cold; but like porridge – warm, comforting and full of goodness.

26. 1981

Our Children

The Bournemouth 1981 General Assembly of URC was held 27 April to 1 May in the Pavilion, Bournemouth. Amongst the many interesting statistics, in the course of the reports and discussion, was the fact that there are 70,000 children with 12,000 teachers in the URC. Sometimes parents wonder – what can we give our children? Love, a home, a secure background with a little bit of culture? But supposing we want to give them not just our love and worldly goods, but something that can give meaning to their lives, whatever may befall them. If only we could give our children faith! It is reasonably easy to teach children manners, even if they are sometimes difficult. We send them to school where they receive knowledge and information about the world they live in. But to teach our children to believe is far from easy! We are so uncertain of our own faith. And even if we believe, can we make our faith real in our lives for our children to see? With children this is what matters so much.

One wise parent has said, "I cannot imagine that my daughter would never look down at the toes of her shoes and ask herself – here I stand now, who am I and where am I going? And then I would feel guilty if I had never given her anything at all by way of an answer."

It is unfortunate that most parents have a tendency to run away from questions, which they have never answered for themselves. Our children's questions confront us with the immensity of our own immaturity and emptiness in knowledge and under-standing. We find religious education difficult and children ask for matter-of-fact information about God, heaven and death. How can we find the words in which to convey faith in sober and honest terms, which the children can understand? We some-times have the feeling that we have failed in this respect because we would rather do nothing than say something in which we do not ourselves understand.

Up to the present day the child has never been valued as a personality, as a member of society; he was only for the future, he was still becoming and did not count until he had 'grown up'. In the marriage books and household books of the sixteenth to eighteenth centuries, the duties of a parent were largely confined to discipline – the child's own will was regarded as a diabolical origin and had to be broken. In antiquity a father had the right to sell, or kill, a child. A child was completely without rights, as an animal or a piece of furniture. In the Middle Ages a child already had to work when he was four years old. A farmer would sooner get a veterinary surgeon to his sick cow than a doctor to his sick child. Even in the nineteenth century in many European coun-tries, small children of 4–6 years were sold to chimney sweeps, who lowered the poor creatures down hot chimneys and drove them up again with goads of burning straw.

The founder of Christianity knew with certainty how important it was that we should begin as children. A religion that every year gathers us about a crib has to be aware of this. One can say that a person is a believer when, in their deepest being, they become a child. All our life is the continuation of childhood, the constantly increasing fulfilment of it. Education is showing what life means. A child can only live in a world which is secure and fit to live in. The task is to make the child proof against the fact that good does not always triumph in the world. There is no faith without knowledge and education. A child possesses the points on to which faith can be grafted, but if religious education does not carry out the task of grafting, everything is left to chance. A child will believe anything, however improbable, from anyone he trusts. His universe at first is small but his trust is infinite – thus our responsibility.

We pray to you for our children and descendants, for all who are born after us, that we may give them bread and not stones, and not leave them an inheritance that breeds selfishness, hatred and strife, but one of love, freedom, joy and peace, founded in Jesus Christ.

27. 1981

Memory

My friend, my bonny friend, when we are old
And hand in hand, go tottering down the hill,
May we be rich in love's refined gold,
May love's gold coin be current with us still.
May love be sweeter for the vanished days,
And your most perfect beauty still as dear
As when your troubled singer stood at gaze
In the dear March of a most sacred year.
May what we are be all we might have been,
And that potential, perfect, O my friend,
And may there still be many sheaves to gleen
In our loves acre, comrade, till the end.
And may we find when ended is the page
Death but a tavern on our pilgrimage.
(John Masefield)

"A sermon by a negro preacher"

If all the sleeping folk will waken up, and all
The lukewarm people will fire up, and all the
Disgruntled folk will sweeten up, and all the
Discouraged folk will cheer up, and all the
Quarrelling folk will make up, and all the lazy folk
Will shake up, and all the gossiping folk will shut
Up, then we shall have a good church.

A Red Indian Prayer

O Great Spirit, whose voice I heard in the winds
And whose breath gives life to all the world, hear me
I am a man before you, one of your many children.

I am small and weak; I need your strength and wisdom.
Let me walk in beauty and my eyes ever behold
The red and purple sunsets
Make my hands respect the things you have made
My ears sharp to hear your voice.
Make me wise so that I may know the things you have taught my people.
The lessons you have hidden in every leaf and rock.
I seek strength, One Creator, not to be superior to my brothers,
But to fight my greatest enemy – myself.
Make me every ready to come to you with clean hands and straight eye,
So that when life fades as the setting sunset
My spirit may come to You without shame.

Count your obligations
Name them one by one,
And it will surprise you,
What the Lord wants done!

28. 1981

Loneliness

Many of the outstanding social services, which the Christian church pioneered, have now become the responsibility of the state. Education, the care of the sick and needy, the relief of poverty, are all part of the welfare state.

In the main, it is true to say that in this country, people no longer go hungry or barefoot. Hospitals and doctors are available for the cure of physical ills. In this affluent age, money buys all the amenities of a modern home – the fridge, electric heaters, central heating, the washing machine, the TV and the motor car. But material progress has brought other problems in its train and one of these is the problem of loneliness, which has become a major social problem which affects the mental health of many people.

An enquiry, held several years ago into this problem, revealed the fact that amongst the causes of loneliness was listed the loss of religious beliefs. It stated – "The consequent decline in churchgoing has meant the loss to them of an opportunity for corporate worship and fellowship in a community of like-minded people." It also stressed the loneliness of the two- to five-year olds who live "about the fourth floor in huge blocks of flats," and among the thousands of 'bed-sitters' and small flat dwellers who sit alone year in and year out. Companionship is a human need which, paradoxically, in this modern world of rapidly expanding communications, is in short supply. The new housing estates, urban and rural society devoid of all sense of community, the inevitable impersonal approach of the welfare state, have all accentuated the solitariness of the individual.

It is essential that the church should have this problem of loneliness very much on her conscience. It is one which money cannot solve. We must realise that the church's concern for people, which inspired her 'good works' in the past, has a new sphere of service today in meeting the universal need for friendship. There is much that we can do, and it is essential that we get to know the people concerned. Experience has taught that one of the most effective ways of helping is to involve lonely people in some worthwhile job of work, so that, in service to others, they forget themselves, their problems and their isolation, and find companionship and friendship. The teaching and life of Jesus ever reminds us that in helping others, we help ourselves.

Frances Ridley Havergal wrote her famous hymn, "Take my life and let it be," in 1874, but it was not until 1878 that it was printed. When she saw in print the stanza, "Take my silver and my gold, not a mite would I withhold," she was suddenly convicted of her failure to do just that. She had an amazing collection of exquisite jewellery, most of which had come by gift or inheritance, including an unusually fine jewel cabinet. Immediately Miss Havergal packed the jewel box full (except for half-a-dozen pieces which were special memorials of her parents and relatives) and sent it to her church missionary society. She also included a cheque to cover the monetary value of the jewels she had chosen to keep. "I don't need to tell you that I have never packed a box with such pleasure," she exclaimed.

29. 1982

Life's Blessings

The hardest arithmetic to master is that which enables us to count our blessings. As the New Year (1982) approaches we must look forward with keen anticipation – 'the best is yet to be.' Were 'the 'good olde days' as good as all they were made out to be? Recollect that our forefathers did without sugar until the thirteenth century, without coal fires until the fourteenth, without buttered bread until the sixteenth, tea or soap until the seventeenth, without gas, matches or electricity until the nineteenth, without cars, canned or frozen foods until the twentieth. So what are we complaining about?

A poem from Zimbabwe; Do you just belong?

Are you an active member? The kind that would be missed?
Or are you just contented that your name is on the list?
Do you attend the meetings and mingle with the flock?
Or do you simply stay at home and criticise and knock?
Do you take an active part to help the work along?
Or are you simply satisfied that you can just belong?
Do you ever visit a member who is sick?
Or leave the work to one or two and talk about a clique?
Think this over, member, you know the right from wrong,
Are you an active member, or do you just 'belong'?

A Thought

The expression "Don't let life embitter you" is a wise one, if we cannot believe in man we will never believe in God. In spite of all our shortcomings, we can never really draw near to God except through service. The story of the small boy at school is an interesting one. He was asked to work out, in his head, the following simple sum: If, at your table, you all had a pie to share, seven of you, mother, father and five children, what fraction of the pie would come to you? The boy immediately said 'a sixth.' The teacher told him to think again, but the boy still said 'a sixth', and went on to explain that "where there is a pie in our house, mother does not have any, her share comes to all of us."

Life without purpose is barren indeed –
There can't be a harvest unless you plant seed,
There can't be attainment unless there's a goal
And man's but a robot unless there's a soul...
If we send no ships out, no ships will come in,
And unless there's a contest, nobody can win...
For games can't be won unless they are played
And prayers can't be answered unless they are prayed...
So whatever is wrong with your life today,
You'll find a solution if you kneel down and pray
Not just for pleasure, enjoyment and health
Not just for honours and prestige and wealth...
But pray for a purpose to make life worth living
And pray for the joy of unselfish giving,
For great is your gladness and rich your reward
When you make your life's purpose the choice of the Lord.

(Helen Steiner Rice)

Look backward with gratitude
Look onward with hope
Look upward with confidence.

30. 1982

Some Reflections

Somebody once made the profound observation that the hardest arithmetic to master is that which enables us to count our blessings. It was Dean Inge who, reflecting on life, observed that the happy people are those who are producing something and the bored people are those who are consuming much and producing nothing. Boredom is a certain sign that we are allowing our faculties to rust in idleness. When people are bored, they generally look about for a new pleasure, or take a rest. There is no greater mistake; what they want is to be occupied, some task to do, some productive drudgery. Certain doctors in Harley Street are fond of sending their fashionable patients to take a rest cure. In nine cases out of ten a work cure, doing something for those less fortunate than themselves, would do them far more good.

It was the same Dean Inge who said that life for all of us is an adventure – "it starts as an experiment and ends as an experience." Those who have made the greatest achievements of history would not have won through it they have observed all the rules of caution and prudence and made a careful calculation of probabilities. We have to take uncalculated risks. This is true of history and of our own life. Your marriage for instance; the chances are that if you had played it right, you would not have married when you did. You couldn't afford it while you were getting so little pay, with a good chance of getting the sack next month. You were just a couple of babes in the woods. But what lovely woods! And in the end it was worthwhile taking the risk, you won! The same is true of babies. If a couple wait until the absolutely right time to have a baby, they find there is no convenient time. There never was. The greatest baby of all was born at a very inconvenient time; the parents were on a journey; there was no room for them in the inn. If parents play it absolutely right with 100% caution, they never win. "A bird in the hand is worth two in the bush," is the motto of all the faint-hearted and cowards in the world. If there is to be any winning, then we must be prepared to take risks.

The Essence of Christianity

What does being a Christian mean? This is a question to which there are many answers, most of which are partly correct. Perhaps part of the answer is that a Christian is one who believes the Christian faith and who belongs to the Christian church and who joins in Christian worship. But certainly for most of us, the essential is that we should make the following of Christ the guiding principle of our lives. If we continue that way, we may believe that the Holy Spirit will help and guide us into all the trust which we find in Him. We are summoned, not to mechanical repetition, but to creative living, and thinking in harmony with the mind of Christ.

No one would claim that imitating Christ is easy, but following Him is even more difficult. It demands the concentrated attention of the full personality. We must love Him or else we shall not wish to follow. We must exercise our imagination so that we may make real to ourselves the person of Our Lord. We must understand Him so that we are not deceived by false ideas of His significance. We must interpret Him so that we may bring His word to bear upon the conditions of our own life and times. Who could begin to do all this? We could not but that we have the Christ within us, because the Word of God has not left us without light and we have the support of the Christian fellowship, the church, to which He has promised the Holy Spirit. Only in the following of Christ, not only in the letter but in the spirit, is there any hope for the rebuilding of our divided world.

Jesus continues His ministry in the world through the church and through the whole people of God called and committed to His service and equipped by Him for it. This service is given by worship, prayer, proclamation of the gospel and Christian witness; by mutual and outgoing care and responsibility and by obedient discipleship in the whole of daily life, according to the gifts and opportunities given to each one of us.

Bible Reading – St Matthew 25 v 31–46; and 28 v 16–20

31. 1982

Speaking To and Of

Paul, in his short Epistle to the Colossians, writes – "Let your speech be always with grace, seasoned with salt" (IV. 6) and there is part of a remarkable Ms in Trinity College, Cambridge, dated 1530 which, translated into modern English, reads – "If you, your lips, would keep from slips, Five things observe with care: To whom you speak, of whom you speak, and how, and when and where."

It is no uncommon experience to be talking both to a person and of him. With so many of the people we meet, the easiest topic of conversation is themselves. In all these cases, of course, we know to whom we are speaking, but the situation is much more piquant when we talk to a person and of him, unwittingly. For instance, Sir Arthur Sullivan was standing at the back of the stalls at one of the D'Oyley Carte performances and began to hum one of the tunes being sung on the stage. An irritable old gentleman turned to him with the remark, "I paid to hear Sullivan's music not yours." James Agate, the writer and critic, once wandered into a bookshop at Leamington and found there a volume of his literary offspring. Feigning an airy unconcern he asked the bookseller whether he had much sale for this author. The answer came promptly and emphatically that there was no sale at all. "But yet you stock him?" said the crestfallen author, unwilling to believe the truth. Then came the knockout blow! "No, sir, we do not stock him. That is a copy ordered by a chance customer and never collected."

The Bible has many instances of talking to, and of, the famine-stricken sons of Jacob, when they went down into Egypt and had an interview with the Grand Vizier, told him of their long-dead brother, Joseph. They did not dream that this lordly person whom they were addressing, the controller of Egypt's corn, was he.

At the well of Sychar, a woman of ill repute fell into a talk with a stranger and referred in her casual way to the coming Messiah. "I that speak unto thee am He," was the astonishing revelation she received.

At Eastertide we recollect that in the Arimathean's garden in the half-light of dawn, Mary accosted the gardener and asked him where the body of Jesus had been laid. She found that the 'gardener' was the risen Lord Himself. Later that same day two wayfarers on the Emmaus Road fell into step with a stranger to whom they spoke of "a prophet mighty in deed and word." By evening they knew who their fellow-traveller had been.

Immortal Longings (Helen Keller, blind and deaf)

I believe in the immortality of the soul because I have, within me, immortal longings. I believe that the state we enter after death is wrought by our own motives, thoughts and deeds. I believe that in the life to come, I shall have the senses I have not had here and that my home there will be beautiful with colour, music, the speech of flowers and faces I love.

Mum – The Supremo!

The milkman had delivered the milk and was waiting for his customer to settle the account. It was near the end of the school holidays and whilst mum was getting her purse, her son, aged six, came to the door. The milkman asked if he was looking forward to going back to school. "No," was the reply. "But I bet your mum is," said the milkman. "Oh, no," answered the little boy very seriously, "my mum doesn't go to school, she's been and she knows everything."

Well, mums do, don't they?

32. 1982

Keeping up with the Records

A bout of 'spring-cleaning fever' has seen the demise of some old volumes of 'The Guinness Book of Records'. Those (like me) afflicted with acromania (Greek for being mad about records) will, of course, at this time of the Pope's visit to the UK, remember that the longest time anyone has yet taken to become a saint is 744 years. No one in this century has got within 29 years of the pole-squatting record of Simeon the Stylite, (nothing to do with Styal), who, in the fourth century AD, remained on top of a 50ft stone pillar for 30 years at Qualat-Seman in Syria. The world's heaviest human of over two decades ago, the 55½ stone Charles 'Tiny' Kinsey, needed to find another 19 stone before he could match the all-time record of 74st 5lb held by Robert Earle Hughes, the Illinois 'farm boy' whose round the waist measurement was 115 inches (9½ feet plus). Nevertheless, with the modern craze for television snooker, it is restful and comforting to know that in 1957, Mr Joe Davies, in achieving a perfect and unbeatable break of 147, reached the stage where from the record-breaking point of view, finality had been achieved and although equalled could never be surpassed.

This century has another 18 years to run, it has already broken many records and seen three new epochs. At 10:30 a.m. on 17 December 1903, near Kill Devil Sand Hill, North Carolina, the age of flight began. The morning of 16 July 1945, near Alamagordo, New Mexico, saw the dawn of the atomic era, and 4 October 1957, from a undisclosed site within Russia, man's agent first invaded outer space. The first lunar landing was on 20 July 1969, when Apollo 11's lunar module, Eagle, with Armstrong and Aldrin, landed on lunar soil – "That's one small step for man, one giant leap for mankind." (Neil Armstrong).

We ask ourselves the question, does every event have a cause? Few would deny it. An aircraft crashes because of engine failure, a tree grows because a seed was planted. Everything that happens seems to depend on something else. It is a principle, long used by theologians, to argue for the existence of God and by scientists to justify their belief in a rational, ordered, universe. As Einstein remarked "God does not play dice." Our prayer at Whitsuntide could well be, "Oh, God who art the Spirit of truth, lead us into all truth."

Excuses! (Not to be taken too seriously)

Some stay at home because it's cold,
And some because it's hot;
And some because they're getting old,
And some because they are not.
Some stay at home because their hat
The milliners not finished;
And some because their liking for
The parson has diminished.

True or False

The Bring and Buy Sale was rather like Heaven – many we expected to see there were absent.

33. 1983

Beware of the Cynic!

There never was a time when cynicism has been more persistent than it is today. One should think it to be almost a sin today to be in any degree, an idealist – to indulge hope for mankind or a belief in the individual. John Consadine, the millionaire film magnate of Hollywood, once read quite accidentally, the opinion of a Father Flannigan reported in the Press. "There is no such thing as a bad boy." The sentiment so outraged his common sense that he flew all the way to Omaha to quarrel with this 'mad priest'. But the believer overcame the cynic, with the result that 'boy's town' was created with Father Flannigan at its head, working out his belief in boys, and finally the famous film carried the truth round the world.

There was a time when the whole of Europe suffered from the cruel blight of the 'blood feud'. If a member of your family was injured by a member of another family, nothing could assuage the wrong, till one of you avenged it on one of theirs. Whole families would be wiped out in the seeking of an endless mutual vengeance. It was as strong a convention of society as slavery, or the making of war. Yet without human nature first becoming perfect, it has practically disappeared and is regarded as barbarism. At the time, many a cynic must have said "it will always be so."

Again when William Wilberforce proposed to abolish slavery from British dependencies, few could be found to agree with him. All the authorities of the day denied its desirability or its feasibility – they were a pack of cynics yelping defiance at him, "It could never work!" Stephenson's grandmother, also, still seems to live today. When her famous grandson told her that he had designed a locomotive she cried, "It will never go! It will never go." When he told her it was going, she cried again, "It'll never stop! It'll never stop!"

Cynicism dies hard in us all – but die it must, because we are men and women made in the image of God. The other Stevenson (R.L.) was also right when he said – "I hate cynicism a great deal worse than I do the devil: unless, perhaps, the two are the same thing."

Phobias

What are they? They are words for your fears! If you are afraid of dogs, it sound much better if you say, "I have cynophobia". Scientific terms give you fears (apparently), status and dignity. So enjoy your phobias. Thus:

Fear of cats – Ailurophobia
Fear of crowds – Ochlophobia
Fear of contagion – Mysophobia
Fear of being buried alive – Taphephobia
Fear of thunder – Keraunophobia
Fear of the dark – Nyctophobia
Fear of closed spaced – Claustrophobia
Fear of fire – Pyrophobia
Fear of thieves – Kleptophobia
Fear of men – Androphobia
Fear of the number 13 – Triskaidekaphobia

A Chinese Proverb

If there is righteousness in the heart there will be beauty in the character. If there is beauty in the character, there will be harmony in the home. If there be harmony in the home, there will be order in the nation. When there is order in the nation, there will be peace in the world.

34. 1983

"O Come all ye Faithful"

Sunday, 28 November is the fourth before Christmas and the first in Advent, when the first of the five Advent candles will be lit. On Christmas Day we light all five candles. One candle for our hope, the second for the prophets, the third for John the Baptist and the fourth for Mary. The fifth, and centre candle, is for Jesus, born of Mary and He is the Light of the World. To us the personality of Jesus, as portrayed in the gospels, is so vivid, His individual characteristics are so lively and unmistakable, He stands out so distinctively Himself and not anyone else, that the story leaves the intense impression of a real man, dealing with real people, in an actual historic situation. Nevertheless, and even at Christmas, many think that Jesus of Nazareth never lived – that He was only a myth and that Christmas is the survival of a pagan festival.

Some of the religions of the world have been built around mythological figures, while others have had historic founders. No reputable scholar today now doubts that Gautama founded Buddhism, Zoroaster Zoroastrianism, Mohammed Islam and that at the source of Judaism stands Moses. We know that Jupiter, Juno, Venus and Mars never lived as real persons; that Isis and Osiris, Adonis, Attis and Dionysus were mythological. Mithra was a mythical figure also, around whose legends and rituals a religion developed so powerful that, for a time in the third century, it threatened to out-do Christianity. To which category, then, does the Christian religious belong? Was Jesus a real, historic, personality or a myth? Modern scholarship and the evidence of history affirm that he was a real personality. Had Jesus not really lived, none would have known it better than the Jews and, had it been possible, they surely would have raised that issue. Upon the contrary, all Jewish attacks on Jesus take for granted His life and death in Palestine. Says the Talmud, "On the eve of the Passover, Jesus of Nazareth was hanged... no one came forward to speak in His defence and He was hanged on the Passover eve". The modern mind may have endless doubts and questions concerning the ancient frameworks of thought by means of which the first followers of Jesus interpreted him. Even when modern doubts are given full play, however, the personality in whose interpretation they were still remains – demanding explanation. Those who lived most intimately with Him stood most in awe of Him, with mingled love and adoration acknowledged in Him a divine authority, felt in Him the very presence of their God, gave Him the supreme name they knew to express transcendent greatness, Messiah, and, after Calvary, they were victoriously confirmed in their adoration of Him by their faith in His resurrection and their experience in His living presence. That is the astonishing fact with which the Christian church began – and in which we continue to believe and proclaim.

Church History

The church records of St Matthew's, Bethnal Green, records that – "In 1792, a special meeting in the vestry was summoned to decide how to prevent grave robbers from stealing freshly buried corpses from the churchyard. It was decided to employ a night-watchman in the churchyard at a wage of 10s and 6d per week, and he was to be armed with a blunderbuss and a rattle. In addition, the churchwardens announced that they would pay a reward of 2 guineas to any person apprehending a body-snatcher."

The Blind leading the Blind

An elderly lady, blind but very independent, was 'bowling' down the high street one Saturday morning in search of weekend provisions and was asked, on separate occasions, by three consecutive people, "Have you ever thought of having a blind dog?" Her sense of humour and grammar eventually got the better of her and, to the third person, she replied, "Well, I have thought of it, but frankly I'd rather have a dog that can see!"

35. 1983

Food for Thought

About 200,000 people were added to the world's population yesterday. Another 200,000 will be added today and still another 200,000 tomorrow. This is not news because it is happening every day. Someone may say 200,000 isn't much anyway, is it? Well, it is close on the combined population of greater Stockport, plus Wilmslow and district, and if you take the next five days, the total will add up to that of the Greater Manchester area. But it is still not news because it is not happening here. This population explosion is, in what we have come to call the Third World, a deceptive term because it can be taken to imply that their problems are not ours. The advanced industrialised rich countries, of which we are one, represent one fourth of the world's population, and this rich minority has settled for a consumer style of high living which demands a disproportionately large slice of the planet's resources. For example, one Swiss person consumes 40 times the resources needed to support one Somali and the annual average income in Bangladesh is £53 per annum. Overall, the rich quarter of the world consumes about two thirds of the earth's resources.

This makes it difficult to say The Lord's Prayer and really mean what we say. I cannot say "Our" if I live in a watertight spiritual compartment; if I think a special place in Heaven is reserved for me and my denomination. I cannot say "Father" if I do not demonstrate the real relationship of fatherhood in my daily life. I cannot say "Which art in Heaven," if I am so occupied with the earth that I am laying up no treasure there. I cannot say "Hallowed be Thy name," if I, who are called by His name, am not dedicated and holy. I cannot say "Thy Kingdom come," if I am not doing all in my power to hasten its coming. I cannot say "Thy will be done," if I am questioning, resentful of, or disobedient to His will for me. I cannot say "On earth as it is in Heaven," if I am not prepared to devote my life here to His service. I cannot say "Give us this day our daily bread," if I am living on past experience and favours. I cannot say "Forgive us our trespasses..." if I harbour a grudge against anyone. I cannot say "Lead us not into temptation," if I deliberately place myself, or remain in a position where I am likely to be tempted. I cannot say "Deliver us from evil," if I am not prepared to fight it in the spiritual realm with the weapon of prayer. I cannot say "Thine is the Kingdom," if I do not accord the King the disciplined obedience of a loyal subject. I cannot say "Thine is the power," if I fear what men may do, or what my neighbours may think. I cannot say "For ever and ever," if my horizon is limited and bounded by the things of time. I cannot say "Amen," if I do not also add, "cost what it may" – for to say this prayer, honestly and sincerely, will cost everything that I have to give in time, talent and service.

Things Overheard

Old lady to her butcher – "Two nice whale steaks and please could I have the head for the cat?"

First lady– "I bought this dress for a ridiculous figure."
Second lady – "My dear, they must have seen you coming."

When I asked him how much he'd give me for my car, he said he hadn't any change.

36. 1983

Much is Little

Most of us, in these vitamin conscious days, are well aware that there are many substances needed by the healthy body, in very small amounts. Iodine is a good example. Little more than one 3-millionth part of the human body consists of iodine – about as much as there is present in a few drops of ordinary tincture of iodine. Yet, without this trace of iodine, we could not keep alive. Nature has even gone to the trouble of providing a special gland to deal with our iodine metabolism. This is the thyroid gland, situated in the front of the neck, and iodine which enters the body in our food finds its way to the thyroid gland. It becomes concentrated there and forms a complex chemical called thyroxin, which is a hormone helping to control the body temperatures and to regulate essential bodily activities. A lack of iodine can cause goitre and in regions of the world where iodine supplies are insufficient in the food or water, goitre becomes a problem of disease proportion. Severe lack of iodine can result in serious disorders such as the physical and mental upset of myxoedema. Almost all our iodine comes from Chile and is a by-product in the manufacture of saltpetre or sodium nitrate, a salt deposit that forms part of a desert plateau, 3,000 feet high up in the Andes.

Thus another instance of our need to co-operate with each other and to share the resources of our 'ONE WORLD'.

Spring-time and Seeing

To see a World in a grain of sand
And a Heaven in a wild flower,
Hold Infinity in the palm of your hand,
And Eternity in an hour.

So wrote William Blake with poetic vision. Many have been, or are going, away on holiday, seeing new sights and making new friends, whilst others have remained at home. Nevertheless all of us this spring have had the opportunity again of looking at nature and observing the wonder of everyday things. Unfortunately, so often familiarity breeds contempt and we look without seeing and fail to appreciate, or give thanks for, this wonderful world which God has lent us for our lifetime to use and appreciate.

Helen Keller, that wonderful American personality who was born blind, deaf and dumb, reminds us that we differ, 'blind' people and 'seeing' people, one from another, not in our senses but in the use we make of them, in the imagination and courage with which we seek wisdom beyond our senses. She says – "It is more difficult to teach ignorance to think than to teach an intelligent blind man to see the grandeur of Niagara. I have walked with people whose eyes are full of light but who see nothing in wood, sea, or sky, nothing in the city streets, nothing in books. What a witless masquerade is this seeing! It were better by far to sail forever in the night of blindness, with sense and feeling and mind, than to be thus content with the mere act of seeing. They have the sunset, the morning stars, the purple of distant hills, yet their souls voyage through this enchanted world with a barren stare".

In Swansea, there is a well-known firm of solicitors, W G Christians & Sons. A letter was sent to them from abroad, addressed simply: W G Christians, Solicitors, South Wales. It eventually arrived at their office with a little note pencilled on the envelope by the Post Office. This said, "No Christians in Cardiff, try Swansea."

37. 1984

The Squint (The Beam in our own Eye)

Since God loves people, He must often find us funny, some of us are so skilful that we deceive ourselves. We stand on our dignity when it is not there. We battle strenuously for truth, without knowing exactly what it is. We air our wisdom eloquently whilst we are, in fact, babes in understanding. How quaint and childlike we must seem to God! All of us claim to be rational beings. If we have enthusiasms we seem to hide them. If we are deeply moved – unless it be something tremendously important – like body-line bowling or supporting Manchester United – we control ourselves. Other folks may get sentimental but our conduct is always the result of calm reasoning and sober judgements. It is a pity we cannot laugh at ourselves sometimes. If we get to Heaven we shall have lots of fun when we remember our past life.

The fact is our conduct is almost completely directed by our emotions. In women this is regarded as a virtue. We call it their sublime gift of intuition. Men feel, then act, and later produce (very cleverly) reasons for their actions. Often they seem very good reasons – even then women usually see through them! Our feelings harden into opinions with the result that we are prejudiced about almost everything and everybody. The last stage of this insidious disease comes when we begin to call our prejudices principles. Sometimes we are so blinded by our prejudices that words almost cease to represent ideas. They stand for emotions. Mention words like Capitalist, Bolshevist, Catholic or Socialist, and the blood pressure of many of us is affected by our prejudices that words almost cease to represent ideas. Yet all the time we keep up our pose of rationality. We surround our pet fallacies with logic-tight barriers and refuse to face facts.

Fortunately we live in a rational universe – we may ignore facts but facts will not ignore us. Sooner or later we have to face them. Why not now? Prejudices poison life. Why not get without them? We never have the whole truth on our side; almost always we have prejudiced the issues. If we could curb our tongues and keep our minds open (at one end) the world would be a sweeter place. Good things have been known to come out of Nazareth. Someday in a better world, we shall wonder how we have managed to get there.

Most of us, unfortunately, look at others and at life with a squint, thus we see things rather twisted. The glasses are available to correct this – but we don't need them we are sure we don't squint. It is a good job God can see straight. We know He can, for we have seen Jesus moving among men. If we were more like Him we should find that the world is peopled with interesting and loveable folk, few of whom agree with us. It might be a good thing to include in our prayers, this simple prayer – 'O God remove our squint. Give us clear, straight, vision, that we may see Thy beauty in all whom we meet,' Amen.

Progression or Retrogression!

The Red Indian chief, introducing himself to the paleface visitor said: "I am Brave Eagle." Then he added, "This is my son, Fighting Bird; and here is my grandson, Four-Engined Bomber."

Running Commentaries

Mary's mother wrote to the schoolmistress, "I am sorry Mary cannot come to school today. Her face has come out in spots through her stomach."
John's mother wrote to the schoolmaster, "I'm afraid John can't come to school today as his nose is running through holes in his boots."

38. 1984

Good News "As cold waters to a thirsty soul, so is good news from a far country" (Proverbs 25 v25)

"What's the news today?" is a question that is familiar to every one of us. We have all asked it, and we have all heard it asked. Every human heart is eager for news and every human being is also ready to impart news. How our spirits rise and fall with the news! If the news is good, we are optimistic to the point of recklessness. If it is bad, we are down-cast and depressed. Most of the news we read, or hear, is, unfortunately, bad. The press, radio and television, inform us each day of wars and rumours of wars; they tell us of mur-der, crime, disease, highway accidents and the like until we are sick at heart. Editors of newspapers seem to assume that there is nothing interesting in good news that people only want to hear of the scandalous, the evil and the perverted. Yet all the time glorious things, stirring things, brave and magnificent things go unrecorded and unannounced. It used to be (and perhaps still is) the practice in the primary department of the Sunday school for the little ones to have their News Time, during which they told of all the good and pleas-ant things that had happened to them and their family, during the week. It was a very exciting and informative experience – especially for the teachers! Why should we not continue this practice? If anything good has happened to you, if you have found a good joke or heard a good story, pass it on. If you know anything that will bring a smile to someone's face that will lift their load, go out of your way to pass on the good news.

Good news is something that can be shouted across the street, or road, like, "It's a grand day," "the baby's born," "John has passed his examination," "Mary's out of danger." The best of all good news came nearly 2,000 years ago and has not yet gone out of date. Many people have never taken it in at all. At Christmas time they listen to the story and they may be lifted for a moment on a gentle tide of wellbeing and good-will. But it never really gets home. It rings no bell of joy in their heart. Yet the news of Christ's coming remains the best of all good news. As the old Christmas carol says, "Good Christian men rejoice..." News! News! Jesus Christ is born today.

Christmas is the time of good tidings. Why do we so often, unlike the early Christmas, hold our peace? If you know Christ, if He has been strength to your weakness, comfort to your sorrow, light to your darkness, you hold in your possession the tidings for which the world is waiting. If the Gospel is not worth passing on, let us give it up; but if it is the hope of the world, let us give it out. Christmas is the time of good tidings. One thing is needful. The world cries for it. Christ commands it. Send the good news on, "We have heard the joyful sound: Jesus saves! Spread the gladness all around: Jesus saves! Bear the news to every land, climb the steps and cross the waves: Onward! 'Tis our Lord's command: Jesus saves!"

A joyous and happy Christmas to all and a healthful and peaceful New Year.

A Japanese Version of the 23rd Psalm

The Lord is my pace-setter, I shall not rush
He makes me to stop and rest for quiet intervals;
He provides me with the images of stillness which restore my serenity.
He leads me in the ways of efficiency through calmness of mind
And His guidance is peace.
Even though I have a great many things to accomplish each day,
I will not fret, for His presence is here.
His timelessness, His all-importance, will keep me in balance.
He prepared refreshment and renewal in the midst of my activity
By anointing my mind with His oils of tranquillity.
My cup of joyous energy overflows.
Surely harmony and effectiveness shall be the fruits of my hours
For I shall walk in the pace of my Lord.
And dwell in His house for ever.

39. 1984

Spiritual Resources

The late, greatly revered, William Barclay reminds us that in discussions about health, there is a word which has become increasingly common. It is the word 'psychosomatic'. This word is compounded of two Greek words psyche, which means the soul and soma which means the body. So the word psychosomatic describes something which comes from, or affects, both soul and body at the same time. Today it is commonly said that illness is psychosomatic. There was a time when illnesses were divided into two classes, those which affected the body and the causes of which were physical; and those which affected the mind or the spirit, and the causes of which were mental or spiritual. That distinction is less and less made nowadays. Illness is not only either of the body or mind, rather the whole person is ill. We have come to see that it is not possible to make a clear division between body and soul, or body and mind, or body and spirit. They are so intertwined and interwoven and connected that nothing can happen to the one without affecting the other. The mind can affect the body. We can think ourselves into illness. If we think we are ill, we will be ill. Nervous tension can literally raise the blood pressure to produce, for example, a stomach ulcer or open the way for the coming of a coronary thrombosis.

The word 'religion' is fundamentally a surgical term. It comes from the two Latin roots 're' – again and 'ligure' – to unite. We are reminded of the fact that the word ligature is used to describe any tissues used by the surgeon for sewing up a wound, and the word 'religion' essentially means those spiritual factors used by man to reunite himself with God.

Before any rational treatment can be organised for any illness it is essential to make as accurate a diagnosis as possible, but it is very often overlooked that a purely scientific diagnosis, while it may explain the bodily mechanisms involved, very often leaves out of account the underlying significance of the illness or disease. There are really two diagnoses in every physical and mental illness – an objective diagnosis – such as rheumatoid arthritis – which describes the pathology affecting the particular part of the anatomy, and a subjective diagnosis which seeks to answer the question, "Why has this person developed this affliction at this time?" Until this question is fully answered it can be argued that the illness can only be treated symptomatically and even if surgical and medical treatment brings relief, the real problem – "Why did the illness develop?", requires an answer. It is now increasingly recognised that behind and beneath many organic diseases there are emotional and spiritual upheavals that can undermine the general bodily resistance, so as to make it a prey to all kinds of infection. The Bible and science are not really opposed. The Christian believes that there are spiritual values and resources to be considered when facing the problems of illness and healing. Paul Tournick relates a patient saying to him, "You prevent us from dying, but you don't help us to live." For most doctors and surgeons the treatment ends when the patient has got over the immediate upset, whether it be operation or treatment of an infection, or dealing with some variety of mental illness. This is where religion, which involves belief and faith and trust in Christ, can help and sustain.

Schoolboy Howlers

The population of London is a bit too thick.
A herbaceous border is a vegetarian lodger.
A nightmare is a milkman's horse.

40. 1984

Facts of Life

If the world were a village with 1,000 inhabitants, its population would be made up of: 60 North Americans, 80 South Americans, 86 Africans, 210 Europeans and 564 Asians. Again if the world were a village with 1,000 inhabitants, 700 of them would be coloured, 300 would be white, and there would be 300 christians (nominally) in this total. Furthermore, 60 people would own half the total wealth, 500 would not have enough to eat, 600 would live in slums and 700 would be illiterate.

If this village were our village, we would want it to change... but in fact, this village is our village, since it is the world, the planet earth on which we live!

Effort

> Do what you can, being what you are;
> Shine like a glow-worm, if you cannot like a star.
> Pull like a pulley, if you cannot like a crane,
> Be a wheelgreaser if you cannot drive the train.

God in Us

Railway stations, nowadays, have a new contraption which has replaced the old porters' barrow. It is a small motor truck with a driver, and he attaches a whole train of loaded trucks to his motor and pilots his miniature goods train through the litter of packages and the crowds of people who throng the platform, making as much noise and clatter as a goods train usually does. At any rate, it is much more speedy and efficient than the porter who used to push his barrow crying, "Gangway please!" The difference between something which is motor driven and a wheelbarrow, is interesting. The difficulty with a wheelbarrow is that it will only move when there is someone to push it, and it will only go as far as it is pushed. Some of us are often like that too. We can be relied upon to carry a fair load, the trouble is that unless someone is pushing us along, we never get a move on. We have to be kept reminded or persuaded, or nothing is done. We lack push or go, have no energy in ourselves – just wheelbarrow people.

Of course there are some who are like the motor truck on the railway platform – they have power and energy in themselves. They have started up and they keep chugging along, they have such energy and perseverance and we envy them, and sometimes they get us hitched on to them and bring us along too. The motor truck person has a built-in power, he gets a move on, makes things go, never needs pushing or persuading. The power in ourselves to keep things moving and to get things done is based on what we call enthusiasm. It is an interesting word, made up of two Greek words, en, meaning in and theos meaning God. So it really means God in us. Thus it follows that the power in which we are able to do things and keep on doing things, is not our own power, but the power of God in us. That is the power which makes all the difference between being a wheelbarrow and being motor-driven – between being one who only goes when pushed, and one who keeps on going and bring others along with them.

The Apostle Paul said, "I can do all things through Christ which strengtheneth me." That was the secret of Paul's enthusiasm – "Not I, but Christ who liveth in me."

An Easter Thought

God hath not promised skies ever blue,
Flower-strewn pathways always for you;
God hath not promised sun without rain,
Joy without sorrow, peace without pain;
But God hath promised strength from above,
Unfailing sympathy, undying love.

Agreed! (Schoolboy howlers)

"The Royal Mint is the stuff the Queen puts on her roast lamb."
"They could not get wheat to grow in Egypt so they irritated it."
"Dead heat is the fire when it is out."

Hopeless

Sign in the chemist's window – "Try our cough cure – it is the best – you'll never get better."

41. 1984

Food for Thought

The new 'school year' has just commenced and much responsibility is placed on teaching staff for the care, wellbeing and development of our children. But this does not limit, or absolve us from, our responsibilities. The Book of Proverbs says "Bring up a child the way it should go, and when it is old it will not depart therefrom." The Police Department in Houston, Texas, published, some years ago, a set of rules for parents, which, if followed, guaranteed that delinquency in children would continue to persist and develop:–

Begin with infancy to give this child everything he wants. Thus he will grow up to believe the world owes him a living! When he picks up bad words, laugh at him. This will make him think he's cute, it will also encourage him to pick up 'cuter' phrases! Never give him any spiritual training, wait until he is 21 and then let him decide for himself! Avoid the use of the word 'wrong'. It might develop a guilt complex! Pick up everything he leaves around – books, shoes and clothes. Do everything for him so that he will be experienced in putting all responsibility on others! Let him read any printed matter he can get his hands on. Make sure that all utensils are sterilised, but let his mind feed on garbage! Quarrel frequently in front of your children. In this way they will not be shocked when the home is broken up later! Give the child all the spending money he wants. Never let him earn his own. Why should he have things as tough as you did? Satisfy his every craving for food, drink and comfort. See that every sensual desire is gratified. Denial may lead him to harmful frustration! Take his part against neighbours, teachers and the law. They are all prejudiced against your child! When he gets into real trouble apologise for yourself by saying "I never could do anything with him." Prepare for a life of sorrow. You will be likely to have it!

It is a bitter experience for parents when their children go wrong. That great Methodist the Revd Dr W.E. Sangster recalls seeking to comfort a father whose son had broken his heart. Socially, morally and spiritually, the lad had made a mess of things, and ended by taking his own life. "I can't make it out," said the distraught father, "I never denied him anything – I even sent him to church." Is it a good thing not to be denied anything? Doesn't our stubborn nature require at times the discipline of denial? Is part of the reason why the sons of many successful men often disappoint their fathers, the fact that they have had it too easy? Can you give people things so readily that you take away something more precious than you can give – independence, the necessity of effort, the satisfaction of having done something worthwhile 'by myself'? Sent to church – note not taken. Perhaps that father felt too busy himself to spare an hour a week for worship. There is an enormous difference between sending a child to church and taking him. If you go with him, he realises that it means something to you. If you never go yourself, he comes to think that church is just 'kids stuff,' and takes it as a sign of maturity when he is allowed to give it up. We don't go to church primarily to be made moral. We go to worship God. But sincere worship has glorious consequences – when rightly directed our mind and conscience is assisted and sound morality is underpinned. We must ever do our best for our children and remember that the conscience needs education and help, as well as the mind.

An Irishman down on his luck, called on a house in a prosperous suburb (obviously Wilmslow) to ask for a chance to earn some money, "All right," said the lady of the house. "Go round to the shed, pick up a pot of white paint, and paint the porch." An hour later the Irishman was back. "I've done that," he said "but I should tell you, it isn't a Porsche, it's a Mercedes."

42. 1985

Contentment

La Rochefoucauld, somewhere in his Maxims, observed that few things are necessary to make a wise man happy, but nothing can make a fool contented, and that is why nearly all men are miserable! One of our oldest proverbs says that "Content is the true philosopher's stone," and Burns, in one of his less quoted passages, says, "Hope not sunshine every hour, Fear not clouds will always lower. Happiness is but a name, make contentment thy aim." When a human being is paralysed by discontent, the trouble is not with the circumstances, but with his reaction to those circumstances. Thus in life one poor lad becomes a millionaire and another stays right where he is, so depressed over his circumstances and 'bad luck' that he does not make the necessary effort to progress. One woman keeps so cheerful and bright, even when the family income goes down and circumstances are adverse, that she is welcomed everywhere she goes, while another bemoans her fate until her friends avoid her because she has lost the will to persevere and face life with courage and faith. The discontented person thinks he wants to get away from where he is, to change his environment, his unsatisfactory job, his tiresome relatives and friends, and to somewhere else where he is confident that he will find success and convivial companions. But so often his intense dislike of his circumstances fills his thoughts to the exclusion of qualities which make for progress, activity, adaptability and interest outside of himself. All the time he blames his surroundings, but it is his own mental attitude which claims and restricts him.

Emerson states the case remarkably well – "Discontent," he says, "is the want of self-reliance; it is infirmity of will." With confidence and the will to go forward, no adversity, no obstacle can continue to obstruct progress. Every trial of strength only adds to confidence, increases determination, prepares for victory. None of us should be content with poverty or insecurity, but bitterness, jealousy and boorishness are no help in overcoming them, and confidence, energy and courage are the factors which will eventually win through and change our circumstances and outlook. Contentment is a quality of mind and spirit. St Paul, writing to the church in Philippi (Chapter 4 vii and 13) says, "I have learned, in whatever state I am, there with to be content... I can do all things through Christ which strengtheneth me". May we also, in His Grace, face the Challenge of 1985 likewise.

Agreed

The secret of being miserable is to have leisure to bother about whether you are happy or not. (George Bernard Shaw).

Mixed Blessing

A schoolteacher asked her class to give an example of 'mixed emotions'. One eleven-year-old girl wrote, "Seeing the headmistress ride over the edge of a cliff on my new bicycle."

True or False

In a London tube station an advertisement read: "75% of all top clergy take *The Times*." Scrawled below it was written, "The other 25% buy it."

"The subject of my sermon today," said the minister to his congregation, "is the milk of human kindness." A voice came back, "Condensed, I hope."

43. 1985

A Happy New Year to All

As I write this, my diary reminds me that Summer Time begins at 1:00 a.m. on Sunday, 31 March! How the days and weeks fly!

All through the Bible, there runs the idea of the fleeting nature of time – and of its preciousness. It teaches us to value time, to see it as a trust from God and to use it wisely and well, as He would have us use it. Francis Ridley Havergal put this truth into a great hymn, "Take my moments and my days: Let them flow in ceaseless praise." These words are a simple reflection of what Jesus, Himself, so often said. He knew the preciousness of time, "I must work the works of Him that sent me, while it is day, the night cometh when no man can work." As the years go by, there comes a note of urgency to our living – "so much to do, so little done."

Rudyard Kipling, in his famous poem which we all learnt as children, tells us to "Fill the unforgiving minute with sixty seconds' worth of distance run." Life for all of us should be a thing of joyous anticipation and not a matter of counting the days only, but of eager looking forward to the days ahead.

Every day is a day which God has made, and we ought to be able to say of every day, "This is the day which the Lord has made, let us be glad and rejoice in it." We are constantly reminded of the swift passage of time and must ever learn to 'number our days' using them eagerly as they come, looking forward to all their opportunity and challenge. The days that were, the days that are, all belong to God and we must use them wisely and well.

Junk

Perish the thought – spring-cleaning time is here – that annual virus which gets into a woman's blood and causes her to turn the house upside-down – to the discomfort of we poor men!

I suppose, on reflection, we should junk something every day! Junk our worries, our fears, our anxieties, our little jealousies, envies and hatred. Whatever interferes with our getting up and progressing in the real things in life – junk it!

Every night before going to sleep we should put in the junk heap, all our disappointments, grudges, desires for revenge and our resentments. Tomorrow is a new day, a new beginning – so junk everything which will in any way hinder our character and progress in the Faith.

The trouble with most of us is that we do not have such a junk heap, more's the pity. We are afraid to scrap anything for fear we shall need it someday. Consequently, our aberrations, our handicaps, discouragements, losses, misfortunes, troubles, worries, trials and tribulations, journey with us. All this huge load of rubbish requires more than 50 per cent of our energy and vitality to accommodate, so that we have only a relatively small amount of strength remaining with which to tackle the real achievement in life – going places, doing things, living dangerously for God in service to man.

So often we are weighted down with excess baggage and the beauty of life is befogged by the heaps of junk which clutter up our days. Now's the time for a spring clean. If there is something in our lives which should be discarded and is a burden – let us junk it – that's what trash piles are for!

Your manuscript is both good and original. But the part that is good is not original and the part that is original is not good. Samuel Johnson to a hapless author.

I return the book to you because I do not wish to soil my dustbin with it.

44. 1985

Snowdrops and Spring

When we come to think about it, we often wonder how snowdrops – these lovely little, fragile, flowers – stand up to the snow and frosts of the winter. It has been observed that every evening, as dusk begins to fall, the snowdrop's head droops a little lower and its petals close. In so doing, it imprisons within its bell, some of the daytime warmth and amazingly, even in the hour before dawn when the night is coldest, the air cradled in the snowdrop's petals can be several degrees warmer than the air surrounding it and thus it is that the snowdrop survives the bitterest of winter nights and the coldest frosts. This is surely a parable of life and of nature, for it is when life is at its coldest and darkest, that we must cling to the warmth of memories and blessings that have been, and believe in the promises of sunshine yet to be. In the Song of Solomon (Chapter 2 v 11–12) we read, "For lo, the winter is past, the rain is over and gone, the flowers appear on the earth; the time of the singing of birds is come and the voice of the turtle is heard in our land." Hope, trust and faith are the greatest sustaining forces of life. The cynic may say that only youth is a time for looking forward, old age is a time for looking back and middle age is a time in which you merely looked worried! An old song by Goldsmith says:

Hope, like the glimmering tapers light,
Adorns and cheers the way.
And still, as darker grows the night
Emits a brighter ray.

For all, hope springs eternal. There are some paintings which like certain stories, are also eternal. The reason is that they have a message that appeals to the heart at all times. G F Watts; picture 'Hope' is in this category. He shows the figure of Hope sitting on a world floating through space. She is blindfolded, but still clings to a crude harp, of which all the strings are broken but one. That one string and a solitary and tiny star in the dark and gloomy sky, convey the message of the picture. Hope ever remains while there is one tiny ray of light in the sky above, and one string from which a note of music can be obtained. Thus a painter's conception of the poet's thought – "Hope springs eternal in the human breast." Harold Begbie, the author of that masterpiece of Christian faith 'Broken Earthenware' wrote, thinking about this picture in The Children's Encyclopaedia:

One star, one string, and all the rest,
Darkness and everlasting space.

Save that she shelters in her breast, The travail of the race.
Borne through the cold and soundless deep,
With ruin riding down the air.
She bows, too heavenly to weep,
Too human to despair, And even on her lonely string,
Expects the music from above,
Some faint confirming whispering of Fatherhood and Love.
One star, one string, and through the drift,
Of aeons sad with human cries,
She waits the hand of God to lift
The bandage from her eyes.

True

The British consist of the Scots, who keep the Sabbath and anything else they can lay their hands on: the Welsh, who pray on their knees and their neighbours: the Irish, who don't know what they want but are willing to die for it: and the English, who pride themselves on being self-made men and thereby relieve the Almighty of an awful responsibility.

Advert on Newsagent's Board

"I do housework 80p per hour, please ring" (followed by the phone number). Underneath someone had written, "I do it free, but don't ring me, I'm a busy wife."

45. 1985

Whitsuntide – The Holy Spirit

As these words are written, Whitsuntide approaches, and when they are read it will have been and gone. It is an event in the church calendar worthy of reflection as it is the traditional occasion for special remembrance of the Holy Spirit. Whitsuntide is a happy time, the long winter is over, nature's flood-tide of colour has begun to appear again – witness the marvellous display of blossom on the trees. Perhaps the spiritual significance of this festival is less meaningful to us than Easter or Christmas. This ought not to be so, for whilst the doctrine can carry us into the deep waters of theological discussion, there are certain basic things which we can appreciate.

We often treat the Spirit as if He were a kind of magic, or a sort of celestial masseur whose sole job is to cheer us up when life is a bit hard. It is more than that. The Papuans say that the Holy Spirit "makes holes in our difficulties for us to squeeze through." He brings the grace of courage, gaiety of heart and the quiet mind. He is comforter and helper because one meaning of the doctrine of the Holy Spirit is that God never forsakes us. He is always present in a world that tries so desperately to get rid of Him and He is comforter and helper because He gives us what we need most.

When Mallory and Irvine, following Somervell and Norton's great climb in the 1922 expedition to Mount Everest, set out for the summit, the last person to see them was Odell. He tells us that he last saw them going well for the top. They never returned and in the morning, after spending an anxious night, he looked for them in vain and tried shouting, "But," he said, "only the wind replied." Only the wind replied. This is the position many find themselves in today, calling into the unseen from the tempests and storms of life. Whitsun, in its witness to the Spirit, should mean for us that when we 'shout' in our fears and troubles, more than the echo of our own voices comes back to us. When we call it is not just the wind that replies, for God is always with us in the Spirit – this is the good news of Whitsun – which can sustain us through all the days ahead.

Speak to Him thou for He hears
And Spirit with spirit can meet
Closer is He than breathing.
Nearer than hands or feet.

True and False Values
Wisdom The right use of knowledge, not the scheming of man's mind
Prayer Communion with God, not pious exercises
Love Sacrificing devotion, not idle sentiment
Conviction Steadfastness of purpose, not obstinacy of will
Victory The defeat of an enemy, not shirking the contest
Humility Forgetting oneself, not underestimating oneself
Compassion Sharing the burden, not pitying the burden bearer
Greatness Intensity of purpose, not aimless publicity
Power The might of God, not human energy
Peace Calm in a storm, not the tranquillity of an unruffled sea
Unselfishness Living for the good of others, not extravagant liberality

Too True!

A smile costs less than electricity and gives more light (Scottish proverb)

There is so much good in the worst of us, and so much bad in the best of us, that we need law and religion for all of us. (Louis Nizer)

It would take 50 people, working day and night for 200 years, to make the same mistake that an electronic computer could make in two seconds.

46. 1985

"Confession" and "The City of God"

These are the titles of the two best known books by Augustine of Hippo (St Augustine). They stare at me daily from my bookshelves – inviting me to read them. I must confess that I have tried many times, but their very richness and profundity gives me 'mental indigestion' and I can take them only in small doses or limited amounts! Hippo's in modern Algeria, on the coast of North Africa, and Augustine, the son of the saintly Monica, was born of African parents in AD 354. A great and brilliant scholar, he delved into various faiths and philosophies, probed the depths and degradations of life, but nowhere could he find satisfaction until he was eventually converted to the faith he had first been taught by his saintly mother. The following passage from his 'Confession', describes his experience of conversion.

"I probed the hidden depths of my soul and wrung its pitiful secrets from it, and when I gathered them all before the eyes of my heart, a great storm broke within me, bringing with it a great deluge of tears... For I felt that I was still enslaved by my sins and in my misery I kept crying, "How long shall I go on saying tomorrow, tomorrow?" Why not now? Why not make an end of my ugly sins at this moment.

I was asking myself these questions – weeping all the while with the most bitter sorrow in my heart, when all at once I heard the singsong voice of a child in a nearby house. Whether it was the voice of a boy or girl I cannot say, but again and again it repeated the chorus, "Take it and read, take it and read." At this I looked up, thinking hard whether these was any kind of game in which children used to chant words like these, but I could not remember ever hearing them before. I stemmed my flood of tears and stood up, telling myself that this could only be God's command to open my book of Scripture and read the first passage on which my eyes should fall. For I had heard the story of Antony, and I remembered how he had happened to go into a church while the gospel was being read and had taken it as an instruction addressed to himself when he heard the words, "Go home and sell all that belongs to you. Give it to the poor, and so the treasure you have shall be in heaven; then come back and follow me." By this message from God he had at once been converted.

So I hurried back to the place where Alypius was sitting, for when I stood up to move away I had put down the book containing Paul's Letters. I seized it and opened it, and in silence I read the first passage on which my eyes fell, "No orgies or drunkenness, no immorality or indecency, no fighting or jealousy. Take up the weapons of the Lord Jesus Christ, and stop giving attention to your sinful nature, to satisfy its desires." I had no wish to read more and no need to do so. For in an instance, as I came to the end of the sentence, it was as though the light of faith flooded into my heart and all the darkness of doubt was dispelled."

A Prayer of St Augustine

> O Thou, who are the light of the minds that know thee;
> The life of the souls that love thee;
> And the strength of the wills that serve thee;
> Help us so to know thee that we may truly love thee;
> So to love thee that we may fully serve thee;
> Whom to serve is perfect freedom. Amen

47. 1985

Reflection

We have recently read about research being carried out successfully in which the human brain is being controlled by the push of a button! Day by day we read of almost unbelievable experiments taking place in the world of science and technology. On the one hand we shudder at the potential they hold for evil; on the other hand, we thrill at the power they could have for good. We seem to have reached a point where, unless we look upon our minds and talents not just as gifts of God but actually belonging to Him and to be used by Him, we will destroy ourselves. Obviously we should not get the idea that God does not want us to develop our minds and brains, which also does not mean that the Kingdom of God is a special organisation suitable only for the intellectuals. The person who can do only the most menial work is just as important in God's sight as the man with the Ph.D. They come into the Kingdom in the same way, by simple childlike faith. Nevertheless, whatever the mental powers may be that God has given a person, He wants them to be developed to the fullest for service to all creation.

Since the time of Solomon, when he asked God for "an understanding mind... a wise and discerning mind," innumerable highly educated persons have used their minds for the glory of God. We read that Moses was instructed in all the wisdom of the Egyptians and was mighty in words and deeds, as a part of God's preparation for his leadership. Paul, the apostle, was a great scholar and Luther, Calvin and others, too numerous to name, have all used their great minds for the glory of God. It is a fact that many of the recent accomplishments in science and technology have been phenomenal, so much so that some may feel that science has the capacity for the achievement of any wish. Their trust is in things and they feel they have become self-sufficient – that they can live without God. Surely in this connection, J.B. Priestly was right when he said, "It is good for man to open his mind to wonder and awe, without science we are helpless children, but without a deep religion we are blundering fools, reeling in our new and terrible cocksureness into one disaster after another."

When Thoreau went into the woods of Walden, near Concord, to live on his own and by his own labours for two years, he borrowed an axe. Strange and egotistical man that he was, he was proud to the end of his days that not only did he return the axe but he gave it back to its owner sharper than he had received it in the first place. In some respects we are all Thoreaus. The gifts and powers with which we are endowed enable us to make our way in the world. But even if we do not have to hand them back to anybody, how often do we allow them to become blunted?

By the Way

A mother who scolded her little girl for being cross and ill-tempered got this retort – "All I can say, mummy, is that it's ill temper when it's me and migraine when it's you."

Overheard

"The wife who drives from the back seat isn't any worse than the husband who cooks from the dining-room table."

Church No-Parking Notice

"No Parking except Sundays. Violators will be given sermons."

Correct!

Gravity was discovered by Isaac Newton. It is chiefly noticed in the autumn, when the apples fall off the trees.
Lumbago is a mineral used for making pencils.
A Father is a person that is forced to endure childbirth without an anaesthetic.

48. 1986

A Christmas Meditation – He was born in a manger in another man's stable. When He died He was buried in another man's grave

Yet though He never wrote a book, all the libraries in the world could hardly hold all the books that have been written about him. Though He never founded a college, His teachings have influenced more students than all the schools put together. Though He never commanded an army, no leader has ever had so many volunteers or won more victories. Though He was never wealthy, He has given riches beyond compare to millions the world over.

Recruitment – Job Evaluation and Potential

The Probable Report

If Jesus had utilised 'modern techniques' for the selection of the Twelve Disciples:

Jordan Management Consultants
Jesus, Son of Joseph
Carpenter's Shop
Nazareth

Dear Sir

Thank you for submitting the details of the twelve men you are considering for management positions in your new organisation. All of them have now taken our tests and we have not only run the results through our computer, but also arranged personal interviews with our psychologist and vocational aptitude consultant.

The profiles of all tests are included herewith. As part of our service, and for your guidance, we make some general comments. These are given as a result of staff consultation and come without any additional fee.

It is the staff opinion that most of your nominees are lacking in background, education and vocational aptitude for the type of enterprise you are undertaking. They do not have team concept. We would recommend that you continue your search for persons of experience in managerial ability and proven capability.

Simon Peter is emotionally unstable and given to fits of temper. Andrew has absolutely no qualities of leadership. The two brothers, James and John, the sons of Zebedee, place personal interest above company loyalty. Thomas demonstrates a questioning attitude that would tend to undermine morale. We feel it is our duty to tell you that Matthew has been blacklisted by the Greater Jerusalem Better Business Bureau. James, son of Alphaens, and Thaddaeus, definitely have radical leanings and they both registered a high score on the manic-depressive scale.

However, one of the candidates shows great potential. He is a man of ability and resourcefulness, meets people well, has a keen business mind and has contacts in high places. He is highly motivated, ambitious and responsible. We recommend Judas Iscariot as your controller and right-hand man.

We wish you every success in your new venture.

Sincerely yours

Jordan Management Consultants

Discipleship 1986

We are found – to find another!
We are told – to tell another!
We are won – to win another!
We are saved – to save another!

Holy Rite

A teacher, puzzled when a pupil brought a note from home asking to be excused from school for a religious holiday, phoned the mother to ask, "What is the religious holiday?"

"Oh," the mother explained, "that's the day we go to the circus – we go every year, religiously."

Well observed

The cannibals who said when the saw the missionary on a bicycle, "Ah, meals on wheels."

49. 1986

Peace Within

"He that is slow to anger is better than the mighty: and he that rulest his spirit, than he that taketh a city." How to have peace within while living in a noisy world, is a question which religion claims to answer – not only religion but every teaching which aims at spiritual development. The soul grows in quiet. As our civilisation becomes progressively more noisy and distracting, the need for inner peace is more apparent. In a familiar passage in the New Testament, St Paul states this need in the form of a blessing, "The peace of God which passes all understanding shall guard your hearts." (Phil. 4 v 7). There is a peace which does not "pass understanding" but consists of understanding. Philosophers who, in former times, tried not only to define the Good but to help men to be good, thought that to understand the world and man's place in it, even though imperfectly, was a way to achieve peace and tranquillity. Spinoza was one who furthered this stoic tradition and, of course, it is a fact that anyone who believes that all things are ordered on natural and unalterable principles, will not be concerned with vain regrets or futile rebellion, but will accept the peace of acceptance and resignation.

But Paul surely meant that the "peace of God" in the life of the Christian is not negative but positive – not static but active and not gained by human reasoning or self-discipline, but is the gift of God – a grace which may be granted to all. The difference between the Christian's kind of peace within and that of the devout humanist, or atheist, would seem to arise from the different beliefs about the source of peace. St Paul's peace and serenity came from his knowledge of God in Christ, his trust in a God who loved him and he thought of his soul, his inner personality, as a city guarded by a friend, joining together peace and joy as gifts or grace. The peace within of the non-Christian who does not believe in a personal God, may lack the note of joy and triumph which sustained St Paul, but it is, nevertheless, one which we can respect. We are called to exercise charity in all things and we should respect all who seek to be fair in their judgements and benevolent in their conduct to others and who face up to misfortune and the travails of life with courage and without self-pity. We all serve God in serving our fellow men and women and that can bring a peace within.

Albert Schweitzer has said, "I don't know what your destiny will be, but one thing I know, the only ones among you who will be really happy are those who will have sought and found how to serve."

A Fact

A driver is safer when the road is dry;
The road is safer when the driver is dry.

A Church Notice

We need ladies who will sing in the choir very badly.

Excuses

Some stay at home because it's cold.
And some because it's hot;
And some because they're getting old,
And some because they're not.
Some stay at home because their hat
The milliner's not finished;
And some because their liking for
The parson has diminished

A Thought

Today I pray for one thing
Tomorrow quite another.
I am afraid that I give God
An awful lot of bother.

50. 1986

Sunday and Resurrection

What a wonderful day Sunday ought to be! Full of Hosannas and Hallelujahs, and Songs of Praise, for it is the Resurrection Day, no other; the first day of the week, the day which brought such joy to the fellowship of disciples, that showed it to be God's great gift to the world. Just as Jesus brought new life, new hope to the world by the Resurrection, so Sunday, the first day of the week – which had never been recognised as anything special before – was to be the day of joyful worship and fellowship to make a good start to each week; a day to remind the church, the fellowship, of the new life in Christ which was ours, a life of joy because He, by His perfect life of love even to the most cruel death, had won the victory of love and had shown that love was the only principle which ruled the world, God's very nature; and that the church was to be at one with God by living and proclaiming that love.

Hallelujah! Jesus lives! We are more than conquerors when we try to live the life of love with Him; and we rejoice to get together, not only on Easter Day but on every Sabbath day. They are days of joy and renewal – hallelujah.

In the year AD 627, Edwin, King of Northumbria, pressed hard by the missionary Paulinus, was in two minds whether to accept Christianity or not. He called a council of his wise men and asked them what they thought of this new faith. Coifi, the head of the heathen priests, spoke in a cynical vein and recommended rejections. In the silence that followed, one of the warriors addressed the company in these now famous words, "The present life of man upon the earth, O King, seems to me in comparison with that time which is unknown to us, like to the swift flight of a sparrow through that house

61

wherein you sit at supper in winter, while the fire blazes in the midst and the hall is warmed, but the winter storms of rain or snow are ranging without. The sparrow flying in at one door and immediately out at another; whilst he is within is safe from the wintry tempest, but after a short space he immediately vanishes out of sight, passing from winter into winter again. So this life of man appears for a little while, but of what is to follow or what went before, we know nothing at all. If, therefore, this new doctrine tells us something more certain, it seems justly to deserve to be followed."

This moving utterance proved decisive. It persuaded Edwin to accept the Christian faith, a decision which was to have consequences of incalculable significance for all of us. St Augustine knew the meaning of uncertainty and anxiety, and no one has analysed it more profoundly than he did in his 'Confessions'. But after his conversion, he came to know the peace that God alone can give and he could, therefore, write, "Thou hast formed us in Thine own image, and our hearts are restless till they find rest in Thee."

In the Spring a Young Man's Fancy...

Charles Haddon Spurgeon was not only the prince of Victorian preachers but was also a wise and witty advisor, whose knowledge and wide humanity enabled him to answer with insight and understanding, every question which the young people of his day put to him. His advice to students, before they went on vacation, is on record as follows: "Now you will have a brief holiday. If you talk at meetings, talk sense. Don't go courting – that is not good for students. Keep yourselves to yourselves. Come back with your hearts and manners uncracked. Walk in the fields, like Isaac, by all means and meditate, but don't lift up your eyes for Rebecca, – she will come soon enough!"

Fact or Fiction

A herbaceous border is a vegetarian lodger.
A nightmare is a milkman's horse.
The Matterhorn is a horn blown in Switzerland when anything's the matter.
Gross darkness is 144 times darker than ordinary darkness.

Impossible

Teacher – "Now, Tommy, if you put your hand in one pocket and pulled out 10p, and then put your hand in the other pocket and pulled out 50p, what would you have? Tommy – "Somebody else's trousers."

51. 1986

The Great Debate

Seventy years ago Sir Edward Grey, commenting on the Anglo–German naval arms race said, "Great armaments lead inevitably to war. The increase of armaments... produces a consciousness of the strength of other nations and a sense of fear." This observation gained immense authority with the subsequent onset of World War 1. He seemed to have identified a virtual Law of International Relations and, according to this law, those who wished to prevent further war must prevent further arms races. The key to this was disarmament; fixing the armed forces of all countries at the lowest possible level. Will we ever learn the lessons of history? Once again, it is apparent that an arms race must inevitably end in catastrophe. The warnings are given even greater urgency by the fact that the weapons involved are nuclear and the consequences of their use would move beyond mass slaughter to the destruction of whole civilisations. More arms do not make mankind safer, only poorer. For the price of one jet fighter, one could set up about 40,000 village pharmacies (Brandt Report, 1980).

It is vital that we see modern weapons of war for what they are – evidence of madness. This is a world where children are dying of hunger, while we continue to pour our best efforts into preparing for Armageddon.

Famous Last Words (Dr Schweitzer in "The Quest of the Historical Jesus")

He comes to us as One unknown, without a name, as of old, by the lakeside, He came to those men who knew Him not. He speaks to us the same word, "Follow thou me!" and set us to the tasks which He has to fulfil for our time. He commands, and to those who obey Him, whether they be wise or simple, He will reveal Himself in the toils, the conflicts, the sufferings which they shall pass through in His fellowship, and, as an ineffable mystery, they shall learn in their own experience who He is.

Reflections

The Evergreen Club for the 'over sixties' continues to grow in numbers – and enjoyment. Its many activities and interests makes one realise that senility doesn't set in with the arrival of the pension book or thereabouts! It is never too late to make a fresh start, or to take a new zest or interest in life. History testifies to this. Cato learned Greek when he was eighty. Sophocles wrote his grand Oedipus and Simonides carried off the prize for verse from his compeers, when each had numbered more than four score years. Theophrastus, at four score and ten, had begun to write his "Characters of Men". Chaucer, at Woodstock with the nightingales, at sixty wrote the Canterbury Tales and Goethe, at Weimar, toiling to the last, completed 'Faust', when eighty years were past and gone. For all of us 'the best is yet to be!'

> Forget each kindness that you do
> As soon as you have done it;
> Forget the praise that falls to you
> The moment you have won it;
> Forget the slander that you hear
> Before you can repeat it;
> Forget each slight, each spite, each sneer,

Whenever you may meet it;
And you will find through age and youth
True joy, true love and everything within it.

Count One

In 1645 one vote gave Cromwell control of this country.
In 1649 one vote decided the execution of Charles I.
In 1776 one vote gave America English, instead of German, as the national language.
In 1923 one vote made Hitler leader of the Nazi Party.
How important one person is – and it could be you.

52. 1986

Science and Religion

In "The Creed of a Christian" Dr Nathaniel Micklem writes – "Nature proclaims her great Original and declares by every sign that she did not conceive herself, but is the expression of another. No blade of grass but is God's handiwork, no human being but is in some way in His image, no being exists but by sharing in His being, no will, no power, no life, no joy, no beauty, but has its source, its end, its process by His word. All the visible things of the world show forth the glory and the wisdom and the power of their Creator.

Every child has asked the question, "Who made God?" For thousands of years people have wanted to know how everything began. How can we find out about the beginning of things? We know what happened last week, because we were there, or someone else was there who could tell us. But in the beginning, no one was there and therefore no one can tell us. No one can help us to learn about the beginning of all things but God. In Him was life and He has told us part of the most wonderful story in all the world – the story of creation. Everyday He is telling us a little more of that story. We find it in Bible and also in His other book, the book of Nature and Life, a book that is still being written, and written by the very finger of God in the modern world of science and technology. It is said that we ought to rewrite Genesis in the light of modern knowledge and tell the story in the language of today. But the Bible is not a scientific text book. Its purpose is not to answer the questions that science can answer but the questions that science cannot answer. It does not tell us when, or how, the world was made; it tells us who made it. It does not tell us how man was created; it tells us Who created Him and why He was created. It passes through the doors of mystery to which science has no key. Galileo long ago put it like this, "The Bible was not given to teach us how the heavens go, but to teach us how to go to heaven."

Whilst science cannot disprove God, the scientific impact of recent centuries has set in motion powerful repercussions that reach out to the limits of human thinking and one major consequence of this revolution is that God has become increasingly remote. Before the medieval cosmology was shattered by the emergence of modern science, this earth was thought to be at the centre of God's providential care. Earthquakes and floods and volcanos might, from time to time, raise awkward questions, but did not shake the conviction that this little planet was the special object of divine solicitude, supported and sustained by the strong everlasting arms of the Almighty. These discoveries initiated by Copernicus (1543), Newton (1687), Darwin (1859) followed by that branch of science, named Astrophysics, which revealed countless universes, multitudes of planets, mysterious nebulae and computed distances in light years, reduced our earth to an infinitesimal size, like one solitary leaf in a vast forest or a single grain of sand on the seashore.

Secure in the knowledge that we live in a law-abiding universe, where the vast majority of events are predictable and even ascertainable, God is pushed out to the very circumference of things and for many, is only called upon when the clockwork of normal events cease to function. For many, religion is the last ditch recourse, something to turn to in desperation when nothing else offers any hope. It is apparent that science has harnessed the powers of nature to human use. Once when drought spelt death for millions, men stormed heaven with their prayers in vain. Today we know that irrigation, not prayer, is the answer to the problem. Australians no longer pray for water – they build hydroelectric plants and carry it thousands of miles through pipes – thus the desert rejoices and blossoms as the rose. The same applies to many pestilences and diseases. In medieval times plagues and sickness decimated entire populations and were regarded as visitations and punishment for sins by an angry deity. We know now that they were due to septic drains, faulty hygiene and neglect. Science hasn't mastered all disease, but it has alleviated much pain and suffering. It has conquered space with the aeroplane, radio and television, so that in all real sense we are living in one world. Thus the verdict of the man in the street, "science deals with the rational and the measurable, religion preoccupies itself with the romantic and the mystical." As Christians we give full credit to these magnificent achievements. But science, far from diminishing the mysteries of the universe, has increased them and science is forced to assume the rationality of the universe and the competence of the human mind to correlate the available evidence and to draw therefore, the correct conclusions. The inner core of human existence and the personal problems of life are not solved by science. Moral and human problems do not relate to the symbols formulae of science. Faith, trust, love, forgiveness, renewal, do not conform to abstract laws but find their solution in religion. Science cannot lift a single despairing and defeated human being out of the abyss of self-loathing and despair. In this religion and faith can dynamically succeed. The New Testament, from beginning to end, is pre-occupied not with a God who is becoming increasingly more remote and less essential in the struggle of life, but with a Saviour whose resources are always available and in every crisis, more than adequate. Faith, not science, is the power of God unto salvation.

53. 1986

Reading and the Bible

It was the scholarly Fuller who made the observation that books, like friends, should be few and well chosen and John Milton, of blessed memory, has said that a good book is the precious life-blood of a master spirit, embalmed and treasured up on purpose, to a life beyond life.

We find ourselves here on Earth to live out the span of our lives, and inevitably we have to take conditions as we find them on arrival. For most, those conditions do not leave much time for very extensive reading, but at the same time many of us are conscious of the desire for a wider knowledge of life and of the finer thoughts, aspirations and experiences of others. We seek for a guidebook as we traverse this difficult tract of existence called Life. Few of us can share the experience, or privileges, of Alex Smith who said, "In my garden I spend my days; in my library I spend my nights. With the flowers I am with the present; with my books I am in the past. I go into my library and the past with all its history and knowledge unrolls before me."

It is a good thing, in the midst of the rush and bustle of life, to be able to withdraw from it for a while and study a book – especially when that book is the greatest of all books – the Bible.

In this modern world we are the objects of a ceaseless assault upon our privacy. So often we are the slaves of circumstances and not the masters. The radio, television and video dominate and occupy so much of our time away from work. We have so little time or inclination for reading. Books are quiet things, they serve our bidding, they fall into our speed. We can lay them down or we can put them aside. A wise man once said that the best books are those which are open in your lap while you think over what they have told you. They are still the best nourishment for the mind. About 300 books are published every week in the UK alone. Most of us will never know the names of a fraction of them and they are books on every subject under the sun. To know how people of the past lived and thought and suffered, can be an inspiration to our own living. Those who wish to take their Christian faith seriously should consider whether they are sufficiently acquainted with the literature of their faith. Many of us read the technical, trade and home journals which concern us in our daily work and life, but should we not pay at least the same attention to the material which awaits us in the greatest of all things, the study how to live in Christian faith? We are called to fight the good fight in faith, and good living is helped and inspired by good thinking, and good thinking by good reading – and the greatest of all books is one – the Bible.

Too True

Asked what her father did to earn a living, a little girl replied, "Overtime".

On an application form that asked, "Age, if you don't mind telling it," a woman wrote, "Sixty-five, I don't mind telling it, I just mind being it."

If you were on trial for being a Christian, would there be enough evidence to convict you?

54. 1986

Alternatives to Preaching – Are They Relevant?

We seem to like "a talk" as part of the service at Morley – as long as it isn't too long or theological! In many instances these days, the sermon is cut in public worship and replaced by a variety of substitutes. Customs change; not many years ago the *Sunday Times* and *The Observer* gave free advertising space to publishing the Sunday services to be held in a number of London churches. Apparently they feel it is a service no longer required today as most visitors would not dream of looking for a place of worship – music, theatre, exhibitions, pubs perhaps, but not churches! A century ago, people were feverishly putting up buildings all over Britain for worship, now there is an abundance of redundant church buildings. Times have changed and the buildings have outlived their usefulness. Perhaps, as Solzhenitsyn has said of Russia, the empty buildings and stones cry out proclaiming the word of Christ. He goes on to say, "People were always selfish and often unkind. But the evening chimes used to ring out, floating over villages, fields and woods, reminding men that they must abandon the trivial concerns of this world and give time and thought to eternity. Our forefathers put all that was finest in themselves, all their understanding of life into these stones, into these bell-towers." Solzhenitsyn was remembering not the social events of his childhood, but the celebrating of the Christian faith in the Russia of a bygone era.

Here many church buildings in use are not adequately used, and the modern idea of an all-purpose church has much to commend it. It is good that a church should be used as a place of fellowship; a meeting place for the whole community. Nevertheless, it must always be recognised as a sign and symbol of the heart of the Christian faith, and this has been its character throughout history. It is the place, fundamentally, where the Word of God is proclaimed and the sacraments given, whatever other uses may be applied.

The criticism of the pulpit and its alleged position six feet above contradiction has increased in recent years. We don't like being preached at! – who does he think he is? It's a feature of modern life; magistrates with elongated forefingers tell people how they ought to behave, as though their own lives were above reproach. Politicians indulge in endless criticism of opponents, for sins which nestle in their own minds. Trade unionists complain about employers and management and these in turn scold the workers – preaching at each other has become the most common form of human speech!

The one constant theme of true preaching – from Paul the Apostle to Bonhoeffer and Paul Schneider in our own generation (and all three lived and died in the practice of their faith), is that if we obey God, we disobey ourselves – we change our lives according to the example set by Christ Himself. The present alternatives to preaching and responsibility for the spoken word are found in 'discussions', and video presentations and the like and it may be conceivable that they could provide an acceptable alternative to a preacher garrisoned in a pulpit, offering a stream of platitudes and clichés to a bored congregation.

Nevertheless, we have to remember that the preacher and the church, do not witness to themselves; always there is the life beyond, which is given and nourished by God in Christ. A wise preacher of a bygone age used to say to his congregation, "I tell you these things, not because you know them not, but because you know them." Perhaps it is that all living instruction is nothing but corroboration of intuitive knowledge.

Sound Advice

Please make sure brain is engaged before putting mouth into gear.

Limitations

Lady to tramp, "Are you really content to spend your life walking around the country begging?" "No lady," answered the tramp. "Many times I wish I had a car."

55. 1987

On Looking Forward

The New Year begins with January, which means "door". The name would have no significance of any value unless it referred to an open door – a locked door would have simply no meaning. This is an encouragement to us to greet the New Year as a golden opportunity, a high and noble adventure, a thrilling exploration, an entry to be anticipated with hope and confidence. The best is yet to be!

As we enter again the "season of goodwill," it is appropriate that we should remember that the Church of the New Testament is, above everything else, a fellowship, a community, and a brotherhood. The great problem of today, in a divided society, is learning how to live together and to share and care for each other. In this spirit, only can the church accept and face the challenge of the days ahead, and in so doing God will bless the church in all its hopes, aspirations and endeavours. The church can never be a religious coterie around which high and artificial walls may be built. It is an embassage charged with the task of claiming the whole world and every aspect of human activity for Christ.

Quality of Life

"Life," said Seneca, "is like a tale; which makes it of value not in its length, but in its goodness," or, again, "It matters not how long you have lived but how well." Our own Shakespeare made the point that the web of our life is of a mingled yarn, good and ill together, and the Guinness saga with its sordid story of greed, dishonesty and corruption in high places, can shake our faith in human nature. Sir Wilfred Grenfell, that great Christian gentleman, reflecting on life makes a point that it is not life that is the failure, it is the pessimist; it is the quitter and the rich profiteers who are the failures. John Galsworthy, a great writer and also a trained lawyer, reminds us that values are queer in this world. We are accustomed, he says, to exalt those who can say "Boo," to a goose, but that gift of expression which twines a halo round a lofty brow is no guarantee of goodness in the wearer. The really good are those plucky folks who plod their silent, often suffering, generally exploited, ways from birth to death, out of the reach of the music of man's praise. He also recommends that we must learn to forget ourselves and to do our little best to ease the suffering of others. "For goodwill towards his fellow creatures, is all that stands between man and death in life". St Paul knew something of the travail and problems of life – "Now we see through a glass, darkly; but then face to face."

John Keble wrote:

The world's a room of sickness, where each heart
Knows its own anguish and unrest;
The truest wisdom there, and noblest art,
Is his whose skills do comfort best.

You and I have the predominating characteristics of an optimist or the predominating characteristics of a pessimist. We, then, are making hour by hour, our own heaven or our own hell; and in the degree that we are making the one or the other for ourselves, are we helping make it for all the world as well. The word Heaven means harmony. The word Hell is from the old English hell, meaning – to build a wall around, to separate – to be 'helled' was to be shut off and isolated. To be in right relationship with something, means to be in harmony of mind and spirit and that is the relationship we must seek with ourselves and God. It was Wordsworth who reminds us that, "Lifted on the breeze of harmony, we are beyond all earthly care."

Quote

LXXX means love and kisses.

The imperfect tense is used in France to express a future action which does not take place at all.

I live by this code – "You can't have bread – and loaf." (Louis Armstrong)

56. 1987

Requiescat in Pace

My favourite Indian author and mystic is Rabi Ndranath Tagore. He wrote, "When I go from hence let this be my parting word, that what I have seen is unsurpassable. I have tasted the hidden honey of this lotus that expands on the ocean of light and thus I am blessed – let this be my parting word. In this playhouse of infinite forms I have had my play and here have I caught sight of Him that is formless.

My whole body, my limbs and my soul, have thrilled with His touch who is beyond touch; and if the end comes here, let it come – let this be my parting word."

This quotation, from Tagore, came to mind when I received the sad and unexpected news early in February, of the passing of my cousin, Frank Douglas Chambers, who lived with his wife and two teenage daughters in Port Elizabeth, South Africa. He was a native of Liverpool, a man of splendid faith integrity, erudition, charm and ability (MA Hons. Cantab). He was 63 years of age and two years ago was given, by his doctors, a life expectancy of not more than 6 months. He knew death would not be long delayed and was thankful, though in pain, for the extended time. A few weeks before his death he presented his wife with a sonnet which he had written and which he called Last Sonnet. Here it is:

> Like creeping rust the insidious cancer spread,
> Invading and corrupting parts once whole.
> Till he who'd relished healthy life lay dead
> And mortal flesh released immortal soul.
> Before he died he'd oft in memory gaze
> On parents, brother, home in which he grew,
> His schools and college, church, his flying days,
> His travels, business life, the friends he knew.
> But most he thought of those he'd leave behind –
> His wife and daughters in the warmth of home;
> Might they through life fulfilled contentment find
> And peace enfold the land to which he'd come.
> Forgive his faults, his sins, but do not grieve –
> Death holds no fear for who in God believe.
>
>   FDC

Darkness is powerless before the onslaught of light. And so it is with death. We allow ourselves to think of death as a dark door, when actually it is a rainbow bridge spanning the gulf between two worlds. This is the message of Easter – one of hope and joy – the best is yet to be!!

Life's Challenge – Which are You?

> There are two kinds of people on earth today
> Just two kinds of people, no more, I say.
> Not the sinner and saint, for it's well understood
> The good are half bad, and the bad are half good.
>
>
> Not the rich and the poor, for to rate a man's wealth
> You must first know the state of his conscience and health
> Not the humble and proud, for, in life's little span,
> Who puts on vain airs is not counted a man.

Not the happy and sad, for the swift flying years
Bring each man his laughter, and each man his tears.
No, the two kinds of people on earth I mean
Are the people who lift, and the people who lean.

In which class are you? Are you easing the load
Of overtaxed lifters who toil down the road?
Or are you a leaner, who lets others share
Your portion of labour and worry and care?

A Thought

Fear not that thy life shall come to an end, but rather fear that it shall never have a beginning.

(Cardinal Newman)

57. 1987

Cuckoo!

Listening to a pair of ringed doves, which are driving me mad cooing and billing from 5 o'clock in the morning, and continuing all the day with monotonous regularity! – reminds me that I haven't heard the cuckoo this year! An old saying is , "Turn your money when you heard the cuckoo, and you'll have money in your purse till he comes again!" (Probably the reason why I'm hard-up?) There are many old folk rhymes about this bird; one says, "In April the cuckoo shows his bill, in May he sings all day; in June he alters his tune; in July away he'll fly; in August go he must." The expression "Don't be a cuckoo!" means don't be a silly ass, don't make a fool of yourself. Cuckold refers to the husband of an adulterous wife, so called from cuckoo, the bird which deposits its eggs in other birds' nests – and the Romans used to call any adulterer a 'cuckoo'.

Come to think of it, I've often heard, but never seen, a cuckoo! It has apparently a silvery grey body, a gliding flight, shimmering wings and a long barred tail – and a rich bell-like call. Why is it that this one bird forgoes the marvellous business of nesting and feeding its young and takes shrewd and unfair advantage of the labours of other birds? Is it a deliberately reasoned or calculated thing? Darwin couldn't explain it, such a satanically clever thing to do – was it a strange fantastic whim of the Creator in originating it? We are expected, by people of conventional and orthodox minds, to base our conception of God on the writings of frail and fallible men, and to accept their testimony to the occurrences of abnormal events as the best revelation of God that the world contains – often disregarding God's own patient writing upon the wall. We are constantly confronted with marvellous things which, God forgive us, we call natural. Centuries before our rude forefathers had learned even to scratch a few hillocks into earthworks, while they lived a crude, brutish, life herding in dens and caves; the cuckoo,

71

with her traditions faultlessly defined, was paying her annual visits, fluting about the forest glades and searching for nests into which to intrude her speckled eggs. Does she reveal the patient witness of God, a revelation of the Creator's mind hidden in the mystery of her instincts? Had Jesus drawn human breath in our bleaker northern air, surely he would have had something to say concerning the homely cuckoo, with her punctual obedience, her unquestioning faith for the future of her offspring, as He did for the beasts and flowers on the hot hillsides and pastoral valleys of Palestine. Life is full of mystery. God creates the frozen peak and the blue sea, here the tiger, there the cuckoo; here a Virgil, there a Jeremiah, here a St Francis of Assisi, there a Napoleon or Hitler or Schweitzer. The interpretation is left to us. We progress from the relative to the absolute, under His guidance using the gift and power of our intellect and understanding, "Seek" says Jesus "and you will find, knock and the door will be opened!"

The latest thinking on the cuckoo is that we should never judge the actions of birds, or of other wild creatures, by human standards of behaviour as this gives an utterly distorted view of nature. Animals are neither 'good' nor 'bad', neither 'moral' nor 'immoral'. They are simply amoral. Cuckoos are polyandrous. The female is known to be courted by two, three or more males. This would seem to be because there are considerably more males than females. Thus cuckoos do not pair in the way widely prevalent among birds, and nature has her own way of solving the problem presented by the numerical disparity of the sexes. One bird lays four or five eggs in a clutch, and more than one clutch is produced each year, and each egg, laid at intervals of some days, is deposited in a separate nest. Where one sex numerically exceeds the other so heavily, the bringing up of a family in the ordinary way is not possible. Domestic life, to be satisfactory, demands monogamy, one husband and one wife, both to share the tasks and obligations of rearing the young. Perhaps one day the biologist will provide the answer and the solution to the conundrum of the cuckoo. Meanwhile, who was it who observed that, "To know all is to forgive all?"

58. 1987

Prayer

Certain lines, once heard or read, are never forgotten, such as Tennyson's, "More things are wrought by prayer than this world dreams of," or Coleridge's Ancient Mariner –

> He prayeth best who loveth best
> All things both great and small:
> For the dear God who loveth us,
> He made and loveth all.

My own feeling about prayer is that it should not be relegated to certain seasons, or attended by certain postures; or even couched in definite language. It should rather be a constant uplifting of the heart, a stretching out of the hand of God. I do not think we should ask for definite things that we desire; as I am sure that our desires, fears, plans, schemes and hopes that visits one a hundred times a day, our cravings for wealth, success or influence, are as easily read by God, as a trained mind can discern the tiny atoms of filaments that swim in a crystal globe. But I think we may ask to be led, to be guided, to be helped; we may put our anxious decisions before God, ask for strength to fulfil hard duties and bear pain; our desires for others' happiness, our compassion for sorrowing or afflicted persons, our horror of cruelty and tyranny before Him. Here lies the power of prayer, that by practicing this sense of aspiration in His presence, we gain strength to do our own part. If we abstain from prayer, if we limit our prayers to our own small desires, we grow petty, self-absorbed and feeble. We can leave the fulfilment of our concrete aims to God: but we must ever be stretching out our hands and opening our hearts to the high and gracious mysteries that lie all about us. Prayer is an attitude of soul and not a ceremony: it is an individual mystery and not a piece of venerable pomp. The secret lies in the fact that our aim should be a relation with the Father, a confident humble waiting upon God. He alone knows why He has set us in the middle of such a bewildering world, where joy and sorrow, darkness and light, are so strangely intermingled. All that we can do is to follow wisely and patiently such clues as He gives us and to face the cloudy darkness in His strength. A humble and obscure poetess, Miss M.L. Haskins has so well written: "Go out into the darkness and put your hand into the hand of God. That shall be to you better than light, and safer than a known way."

Which Choice?

On the table side by side;
The Holy Bible and the TV Guide
One is well-worn but cherished with pride (not the Bible, but the TV Guide)
One is used daily to help folk decide.
No! It isn't the Bible; it's the TV Guide
As pages are turned, what shall we see?
Oh, what does it matter, turn on the TV.
So they open the book in which they confide, (no, not the Bible, it's the TV Guide).
The word of God is seldom read,
Maybe a verse ere they fall into bed.
Exhausted and sleepy and tired as can be,
Not from reading the Bible; from watching TV.
So, then back on the table, side by side,
Is the Holy Bible and the TV Guide.
No time for prayer, no time for the Word,
The plan of salvation is seldom heard.
Forgiveness for sin so full and free
Is found in the Bible, not on TV!

Quote

The fact that people are born with two eyes and two ears, but only one tongue, suggests that they ought to look and listen twice as much as they speak.

59. 1987

An Acknowledgement

Future days will always be happier when we experience happiness now. Happy days now make happy days in the years to come by the memory of them.

Marjorie and I had a wonderful 'Golden Anniversary' on Friday, 11 September, made memorable by the super party meal and cheque presentation, at Morley, on Saturday evening, 12 September; and again by the super get together of friends, old and new, and the marvellous entertainment, cheque presentation and supper, at Long Lane, on Wednesday evening, 16 September. On each occasion the food was stupendous and the atmosphere, warmth and friendship were 'out of this world'. We received almost one hundred cards, greetings and personal gifts. To all who contributed to these wonderful and memorable occasions, we say a humble, sincere and heartfelt "Thank you and God bless you all."

I suppose it's not difficult to give you a ready answer to the question, "To what do you attribute your happy life together over 50 years?" The following well-proven recipe combines all the main ingredients for happiness in family life and, indeed, in any relationship:

4 cups of Love, 2 cups of Loyalty, 3 cups of Forgiveness, 1 cup of Friendship, 1 cup of Understanding, 2 spoons of Hope, 2 spoons of Tenderness, 4 quarts of Faith, 1 barrel of Laughter. Take Love and Loyalty, mix thoroughly with Faith. Blend it with Tenderness, Kindness and Understanding. Add Friendship and Hope, sprinkle abundantly with Laughter. Bake it with Sunshine and serve daily in generous portions.

Reflections

Some years ago Jean-Paul Sartre wrote a novel called "The Age of Reason". In it he records the behaviour and reactions of those who have discarded not only the dogmas of traditional faith, but also the canons of conventional morality. Following the dictates of 'free will' and 'pure reason' they pride themselves on being completely emancipated from the restraints imposed by a so-called civilised society. Faith, according to Sartre, is old-fashioned, a thing of the past; in the UK an outmoded legacy, a pious Victorian anachronism which has ceased to command the allegiance of intelligent people – "The tide of knowledge sees the sea of faith on the ebb." Like a clear-cut mathematical formula, it is a simple case of inverse ratio. This is a myth, ours is the age of beliefs – unfortunately non-Christian and even less capable of rational proofs, demanding of the individual something akin to blind credulity. Our age is superstitious rather than scientific. There are literally millions of people who look not to science, certainly not to religion, but to astrology to forecast the future. Gambling, whether on the totaliser, stock exchange or football pools, has now developed into a major industry. It is based on the assumption that if we persevere long enough our luck is bound to turn.

Christians are also living in a collectivist age in which so many of our human relationships have become depersonalised. Thus people write, and think, about God in impersonal terms. They talk of A Just Cause, an Absolute Principle, or a Realm or Sphere of Values. Preachers wax eloquent about the Relevance of Christianity, but have little to say about the claims of Christ revealed in the Gospels, and abstractions can never satisfy the hunger of the human soul. The God revealed by Jesus is intensely personal. He is one to whom we turn in time of need. Jesus did not talk about something behind phenomena, Paul didn't subscribe to a number of abstract propositions defining the nature of ultimate reality. He said, "For I know Whom I have believed, and am persuaded that He is able to keep that which I have committed unto Him against that day" (2 Timothy 1 v 12). For the Christian, intellectual assent to a creed is secondary. The essence of our faith is trust in a personal God revealed in Jesus Christ. Christianity is the religion, not only of a book, but of a person. Jesus commissioned His Apostles and established His Church before there were any written records of His earthly ministry. In essence, Christians are asked to give their allegiance, not particularly to any dogma or abstract article of belief, but to the Living Lord, who still speaks and communes with His faithful, believing and trusting children.

60. 1988

Facing Life's Problems

Everywhere today the word 'problem' confronts us on the radio, television and in the morning papers, we face a jungle of huge and complicated and seemingly unsolvable problems which somehow have to be resolved. But suppose these were no problems at all: God might have made this universe like Aladdin's palace, all complete for our lazy occupancy, no difficulty to face, nothing required but to settle down and luxuriate. After even a few weeks of that, can you imagine anything more boring and soul-destroying. Instead, God has introduced us into this wild, raw, unfinished world to bear a hand in its completion – which means that human life's very essence is facing problems and being awakened by their demand. Only in this way has our growth in intellect and character been possible. We are all in the thick of life's struggle, participants in its winning or its loss. The tragedy at King's Cross Station makes us ask the question, "Are we part of the problem or part of the answer?" We have a traffic problem; millions of cars and vehicles, death and worse than death takes a dreadful toll of maimed and mutilated lives, constituting a cruel and needless sacrifice of health and happiness. Many of us are car drivers – are we part of the problem or of the answer? There are family problems, broken homes, neglected and ill-used children, which are a public menace, moral standards cracking and marital infidelity a national disgrace; yet we accept it and make a joke of it on radio, television and bestselling novels. Are we part of the problem or of the answer?

Jesus is the final answer to life's problems. Born in a manger, died on a cross, no wealth, no prestige, nothing to count on except those intangibles of character that cynics belittle, and yet across the centuries towering still, the life concerning whom more and more people know that He is the answer. Where His Spirit comes, that is the solution. Just as in science, we think a disease incurable until somebody finds a remedy, so the Christian is sure about Jesus Christ who, in the long run, has the solution to all the world's evil and its problems. The recently published autobiography of young Christopher Nolan (Under the Eye of the Clock) is an inspiration to all of us as we face life in 1988. A spastic who very nearly died, at birth, from asphyxiation; but survived with severe brain damage, cut off in his own silent world, restricted by a mute and paralysed body, yet he has managed to break the barriers of that impossibly cocooned existence to express the thoughts and realities of a state of existence nobody has ever know about. The spirit that stays undefeated, in spite of everything, is part of the solution to life's problems, and it should help us, who have so much to be thankful for, to take another notch in our belts and go to our tasks again with fresh zest and courage, "My grace is sufficient for thee, for my strength is made perfect in weakness." (2 Corinthians 12 v 9).

Face the Future – with Longfellow

Look not mournfully into the past – it comes not back again; wisely improve the present – it is thine; go forth to meet the shadowy future without fear and with courage, faith and a manly heart.

61. 1988

Easter

The Christian faith stands, or falls, on the Resurrection – either we have a Living Lord who has the mastery over sin and over death or we had best shut up shop without more ado. Whatever may be our personal reaction to Matthew's account of the earthquake, the angel and the empty tomb, (Matthew 28 v 1–10), the inescapable evidence of the Resurrection is the new life that came to broken and dispirited disciples; the renewal that has come again and again when the church has looked moribund and finished, we worship a Lord who meets us in the daily business of living, to renew our life and who will bring yet another resurrection in his church when we are really ready to let Him have his way with us.

Dietrich Bonhoeffer, who was martyred by the Nazis in 1945, wrote the 'Cost of Discipleship' in 1937 and wrote of God as "the beyond in the midst of life." Bonhoeffer stood for what is called Christian Humanism today. He offered his life for a new understanding of the personal life which has its roots in the Christian faith.

Great Thoughts

Tao is a Chinese word meaning way, path or road and is used, metaphorically, to indicate a line or principle of conduct. Confucius spoke of the doctrine, which he preached as The Way, and throughout history other philosophers and teachers have done likewise, with Jesus outstanding. One of my treasured thoughts from Taoism is the following:

"Among men, reject none; among things, regret nothing. This is called comprehensive intelligence. The good man is the bad man's teacher; the bad man is the material upon which the good man works. If the one does not value his teacher, if the other does not love his material, then despite their sagacity they must go far astray. This in life is a mystery of great import."

A modern follower of 'The Way' is Mother Theresa. This is what she says:

"The biggest disease today is not leprosy or tuberculosis, but rather the feeling of being unwanted, uncared for, deserted by everybody. The great evil is the lack of love and charity, the terrible indifference towards one's neighbour, assaulted by exploitation, corruption, poverty and disease. What the poor need, even more than food, clothing and shelter, – is to be wanted".

Our old friend 'Anonymous' is worth remembering, here is a long standing favourite of mine:

> A little more kindness, a little less creed;
> A little more giving, a little less greed;
> A little more smile, a little less frown;
> A little less kicking a man when he's down;
> A little more 'we', a little less 'I';
> A little more laugh, a little less cry;
> A little more flowers on the pathway of life,
> And fewer on graves at the end of the strife.

Supreme Optimist

> Cannibal (to captured missionary) – "Have you any particular wish before you are dished up?"
> Missionary – "I should like to deliver one more lecture on the advantages of a vegetarian diet."

Dead Right

The teacher was trying to persuade the children to buy a copy of the recent class photograph – "Just think how nice it will be when you are grown-up and say, "There's Rose, she's married," or "That's Billy, he's a sailor." A small voice piped up, "And there's teacher, she's dead."

62. 1988

Myth or Reality – Fact or Fiction

To which category does the Christian religion belong? – was Jesus a real historic personality or a myth? The legendary accretions surrounding the story of the Nativity may cause some heart searching, but had Jesus not really lived, none would have known it better than the Jews and, had it been possible, they surely would have raised that issue. Upon the contrary, all Jewish attacks on Jesus take for granted His life and death in Palestine. Says the Talmud, "On the eve of the Passover, Jesus of Nazareth was hung.

During 40 days a herald went before Him crying aloud – He ought to be stoned because He has practised magic, has led Israel astray and caused rebellion. Let Him who has something to say in His defence come forward and declare it. But no one came forward and He was hanged on the eve of the Passover."

Santa Claus has returned to Lapland. Over the past fifty years, I have kept my children and grandchildren informed about his homeland, his mode of transport, his acrobatic skills and his merchandising practices and they have gone on loving the friendly old fellow long after they noticed him appearing on two street corners at the same moment! Father Christmas, I assured them, is as real as I am – and it was the fairies who put 3d/5p under your pillow in exchange for your tooth! And Jesus lived on earth 2,000 years ago and is alive today! Difficulties arose, of course, when they saw the tooth being removed, and when they reach the age of 10 or earlier, they will write fairies out of their universe. They see Santa Claus every December and by the seventh visit, they know that he is clean-shaven and has a pension book!

The question is, "What will they decide to do about this other MAN whom they have met in book and ritual?" I could, of course, take the line of least resistance and tell myself not to worry – God can look after Himself and He will find ways to tell them His Son is real. But I look at the youngsters around me (fewer and fewer in church) who were once happy to believe in fairies and Santa Claus – and Jesus? – and I have these awful doubts whether God can make it stick – because He works through such as me! I would like to be reassured that the way we teach our children who Jesus is, is quite different from the way we teach them who Father Christmas is. It concerns me that many of us parents, and grandparents, find it more possible to enthuse and describe Father Christmas, than we do describing Jesus and His Life and Message.

We now enter the season of Advent in the Christian year, and the time draws near when we celebrate the birth of Christ. The eyes of many – especially children – are turned to expectancy towards Christmas. One would like to feel that this change of direction and anticipation was no shallow observance of mere custom, but a rich and deep appreciation of the difference that Christ makes to our civilisation.

The threefold fact the He came, that in some real degree He abides, and that He grows, in spite of all opposition, constitutes a challenge to those who are heedless of Him. Christianity has been reported many times in history to be upon its last legs and tottering to its grave, only to confound its mourners with a new sudden outburst of life. Advent reminds us that Jesus is not a mere historic figure, but a present and powerful initiative and that he acts and works amid all the complexity of modern life. Nevertheless, He has a preference for working through men rather than independently of them – hence His choice of His disciples and His call to us.

63. 1988

Random Thoughts in Spring – May 1988

This question of happiness! Our nature is to be happy. When happiness is absent there is something wrong, yet happiness is not the end of everything. Those who seek it do not find it. Happiness is to be earned; was it Aristotle who said it is a bi-product of activity, the wages paid when work is well done? Perhaps not a very good definition, because happiness is a crown rather than wages. It is a free gift. We have a right to happiness as we have a right to sunlight, no more, no less. But happiness cannot be enjoyed by snatching at it, any more than by waiting for it to turn up. The other word for happiness is joy, and it is a product of service and experience. Children are happy in innocence; we are happy when we find peace and serenity through victory. The happiness of children passes, because innocence has to be surrendered; but the tranquillity of wisdom nothing can destroy.

> To see a World in a grain of sand,
> And a Heaven in a wild flower
> Hold Infinity in the palm of your hand
> And Eternity in an hour.

So, with poetic vision wrote William Blake. To all of us this Spring and Summer presents the opportunity of again looking at nature and observing the wonder of everyday things. Unfortunately, so often familiarity breeds contempt and we look without seeing and fail to appreciate, or give thanks for, this wonderful world which God has lent us for our lifetime to use appreciate and develop.

Helen Keller, who was born blind, deaf and dumb, reminds us that we differ, 'blind' people and 'seeing' people, one from another, not in our senses but in the use we make of them, in the imagination and courage with which we seek wisdom beyond our senses. She says – "It is more difficult to teach ignorance to think than to teach an intelligent blind man to see the grandeur of Niagara. I have walked with people whose eyes are full of light but who see nothing in wood, sea, or sky, nothing in the city streets, nothing in books. What a witless masquerade is this seeing! It were better by far to sail for ever in the night of blindness, with sense and feeling and mind, than to be thus content with the mere act of seeing. They have the sunset, the morning stars, the purpose of distant hills, yet their soul's voyage through this enchanted world with a barren stare."

Her credo was – "I believe in the immortality of the soul because I have within me immortal longings. I believe that the state we enter after death is wrought by our own motives, thoughts and deeds. I believe that in the life to come, I shall have the senses I have not had here and that my home there will be beautiful with colour, music, the speech of flowers and faces I love."

"I do not want the peace which passeth understanding. I want the understanding which bringeth peace."

Today (Matthew 6 v 25–34)

> Look to this day, for it is the very life of life. In its brief course lie all the verities and realities of your existence: The glory of action, The bliss of growth, The splendour of beauty. For yesterday is but a dream and tomorrow is only a vision: But today well lived makes every yesterday a dream of happiness; and every tomorrow a vision of hope. Look well, therefore, to this Day.

Little Tommy was asked by his Sunday school teacher which Bible story he liked best. "I like the one where everybody loafs and fishes," came the prompt answer.

64. 1988

"This Treasure in Earthen Vessels" (2 Cor. 4 v 7)

Fundamentalism to many does appear to offer an objective authority in the midst of conflicting voices; offering a line of least resistance in the midst of conflicting views concerning which parts of the Bible to accept and which to reject? Whilst in South Carolina in June, the Southern Baptist Convention was being held – over a thousand delegates and the main topic of debate was not poverty, inequality, unity etc, but 'Fundamentalism' – and this split had divided the conference from top to bottom, with far-reaching results and problems for the continued unity and witness of this great church. Many interpretations of the Christian Religion need re-examining in the light of modern thought and knowledge. Faith in the true sense is that by which we take a thing on trust in order to find out if it is true. All faith consists essentially in the recognition of a world of spiritual values beyond, yet not apart from, the world of natural phenomena. Change rules today and whether it shows itself in the process of breaking down or building up, change rules. No sphere of life and thought is exempt from the closest scrutiny and challenge of the modern mind – religion, theology, social and political instructions are all subject to scrutiny and interrogation.

We have to make the effort to distinguish between the Gospel and the Christian Religion; the latter, a historical movement, has produced a rich variety of beliefs and practices. It was Dr L.P. Jacks, no mean scholar in theology and philosophy, who observed that if you take Christianity along with its entanglements, encumbrances and unnatural alliances, plus all the secular baggage which the ages have fastened upon it, you may find it a hopelessly perplexing thing which neither reason nor faith, acting singly or in combination, can accept. Fortunately, he observed, alongside the authorised version, it has an inextinguishable spark of life – the unauthorised version, which has kept it alive through the ages, based solely on the Gospel as a Way of Life, revealed by Christ Himself. Our ultimate interests are ever secure in the hands of the Great Companion; our Father. God, said Jesus, is Spirit, man is spirit also, and when the two meet in fellowship, there is religion – the essence of the Christian Faith.

Facts and Figures

Last year there were over 1,200 deaths from drunken driving: 95% committed by men, 5% by women. For every teenage in the United Kingdom who dies from abusing other drugs, 100 die from alcohol-related causes, mostly in driving accidents.

On average men smoke 115 cigarettes and women 97 each week in the United Kingdom.

Nearly one in four of all households in the United Kingdom were occupied by one person in 1986, compared to one in ten in 1951.

We live in an increasingly criminal society. Total number of recorded crimes in 1893 – 86,000. In 1986 – 3,847,000 to the police – only one quarter of all notifiable offences were actually recorded.

65. 1988

Discontent

A French proverb says, "Pills are to be swallowed, not chewed," and it was Fielding who observed – "Some folks rail against other folks because other folks have what some folks would be glad of." Discontent is like a canker and when a human being is paralysed by it, the trouble is not with the circumstances but with the reaction to those circumstances. One poor lad eventually becomes a millionaire and another stays right where he is, so unhappy over his 'bad luck' that he does not make the necessary effort to go forward. One woman keeps so cheerful and bright during sickness and loss of family income that she is welcomed and invited everywhere, while another moans and groans until her friends avoid her because she has lost her joy.

The discontented person thinks he wants to get away from where he is, to leave his poverty, his unsatisfactory position, his tiresome relatives and friends, and to go somewhere else where he is confident that he will find success, riches and admiring companions. But his intense dislike of his circumstances fills his thoughts to the exclusion of qualities which make for progress, activity, adaptability, and interest outside of himself. All the time he blames his surroundings and environment, but usually it is his own mental attitude which claims and restricts him.

Emerson states the case remarkably well – "Discontent is the want of self-reliance; it is infirmity of will." With confidence, and the will and purpose to go forward, no adversity, no obstacle can continue to obstruct progress. Every trial of strength only adds to confidence and increases determination to overcome and succeed. None of us should be content to accept poverty, but rebellion and jealousy are no help in overcoming it. While effort, energy and courage will eventually break down and improve circumstances, contentment is a quality of mind, and those who have not sought and found it will never acquire it even if they eventually get wealth or fame. "Happiness," said Aristotle "is a by-product of activity," and La Rochefoucault, in one of his many wise maxims, observed, "Few things are necessary to make a wise person happy, but nothing can make a fool contented. That is why nearly all men are miserable." Perhaps as always, the solution can be found in the Scriptures – for example in the life and teaching of St Paul... "for I have learned, in whatsoever state I am, there with to be content." (Philippians 4 vii).

Too True!

God and the doctor we alike adore,
But only when in danger, not before;

The danger o'er, both are alike requited,
God is forgotten, and the doctor slighted.

Flight to Egypt

The Bible story was "The Flight to Egypt," and the expression work that followed free drawing. One small boy drew a modern version showing an aeroplane. Inside were four figures. Three had haloes, one had not. Teacher asked who the three figures were. Mary, Joseph and the Baby Jesus, was the reply. "Then who is the fourth?" she queried. "Pontius, the Pilot," came back the prompt answer.

66. 1989

A Christmas Meditation

On 14 July 1789 Jean Lenoir, a cobbler living in Paris, wrote in his diary, "Nothing of importance happened today." A short distance away was the Place de la Bastille. On that day a mob had stormed the old fortress, massacred the garrison, freed the prisoners, razed the building to the ground and started the French Revolution, which changed the life of France and of so many other countries. It is often the same at Christmas. We are so preoccupied shopping, card- and letter-writing, parcel sending or receiving, food preparation, etc. that we are apt to forget the fact that Christmas marks the birthday of Jesus – the most revolutionary event in the world's history. Christmas survives for people only as a secular holiday and not as a sacred festival. The word 'holiday' means 'holy day' and in times past, the holy days of the Christian church were the only days when the working person was free for rest and recreation. Thus the church conferred secular benefits upon humanity, but now this value is lost and severed from its sacred source for the great majority of people. But Christmas will not survive as the happiest festival of the year if it ceases to be celebrated as the feast of the Nativity of Our Lord. We need, always, to put Christ into Christmas. Then we know the meaning of Joy, our hearts are revived by a renewed sense of the Divine at the heart of life.

We read in history that when Charles VIII demanded a huge ransom from the free city of Florence, Capponi, the mayor, refused to pay. Charles threatened "I will have my trumpets blown and attack the city." Capponi's reply was, "Blow your trumpets and we will ring our bells." That silenced the King, for he knew that at the ringing of the bells the hidden army of Florence's burghers would spring into action. At Christmas the bells of joy ring in our hearts. In life there is so much to weigh us down, to burden our souls, to depress our spirits. We can answer the trumpets of gloom and defeat by the ringing of the bells of joy that come from the heart when we put Christ into Christmas. All the hymns we sing at this time have, as their dominant note, the note of joy – "Rejoice, rejoice, Immanuel," "Joyful all ye nations rise," "Glad tidings of great joy I bring," "With them the joyful tidings first began," "Good Christian men, rejoice with heart and soul and voice." There is nothing dreary in our faith when Christ is at the centre. "Love came down at Christmas, Love all lovely, Love divine, Love was born at Christmas, stars and angels gave the sign." Let us put

Christ at the centre of not only Christmas but all the days in the New Year. Let us refuse to be so engrossed in presents and parties and plum puddings that we suffer the fate of the innkeepers who shut Him out. We can keep the festival and yet miss the treasure. Nothing could be more sad than to pass, unthinkingly, the stable where the holy child is, and neither see Him or the star of hope and salvation that shines brightly over head.

Expectation of Life

"Why did you want to go and insure my life again?" demanded an angry husband. "It's quite likely that I shall live longer than you."
"There you go again," said his spouse, "always looking on the black side of things."

67. 1989

Useless Information!?

To count a billion – at a pretty fast rate of two hundred a minute – would take 9,512 years, 34 days, 5 hours and 20 minutes! This reminds me of the occasion when, as a small boy, I was playing hide-and-seek with two, even smaller, boys, and rashly agreed to count up to a million when I was 'on'. I started looking for my companions after a few minutes (a long time for a small boy to wait). Fortunately my companions (and myself) did not realise that it should have taken me more than three days to fulfil my promise! Information has little value unless it is applied, and this is true of biblical knowledge as well as secular facts and figures. We are called to practise what we preach – to be not only readers and hearers of the word, but doers. The words of the Lord's Prayer trip easily off the tongue, but to be honest with myself and my Creator, I cannot say our if I live in a watertight spiritual, compartment; if I think a special place in Heaven is reserved for me and my denomination. I cannot say Father if I do not demonstrate the relationship to my daily life. I cannot say which art in heaven, if I am so occupied with the earth that I am laying up no treasure there. I cannot say hallowed be Thy name, if I, who are called by His name, am not holy. I cannot say Thy kingdom come, if I am not doing all in my power to hasten its coming. I cannot say Thy will be done, if I am questioning, resentful of, or disobedient to His will for me. I cannot say on Earth as it is in heaven, if I am not prepared to devote my life here to His service. I cannot say give us this day our daily bread, if I am living on past experience. I cannot say forgive us our trespasses as we forgive them that trespass against us, if I harbour a grudge against anyone. I cannot say lead us not into temptation, if I deliberately place myself, or remain in a position where I am likely to be tempted. I cannot say deliver us from evil, if I am not prepared to fight it in the spiritual realm with the weapon of prayer. I cannot say Thine is the kingdom, if I do not accord the king the disciplined obedience of a loyal subject. I cannot say Thine is the power, if I fear what men may do, or what my neighbours may think. I cannot say for ever and ever, if my horizon is limited and bounded by the things of time. I cannot say Amen, if I do not also add, cost what it may for to say this prayer honestly and sincerely will cost everything.

Harry Emerson Fosdick recalls (On Being Fit to Live With) a wealthy woman sight-seeing in the slums of a large city, noticing a particularly filthy child playing on the pavement, "Why doesn't that child's mother clean it up?" she demanded. The guide replied, "Well, ma'am, it's like this. The mother loves the child but doesn't hate the dirt. You hate the dirt but don't love the child. Until love for the child and hate for the dirt come to the same heart, the child will remain as it is."

68. 1989

The World is Better

Macaulay stated, with certainty, that the history of England is emphatically the history of progress and whilst, as Burke observed, the march of the human mind is slow his famous dictum is ever relevant – "Nothing in progression can rest on its original plan. We might as well think of rocking a grown man in the cradle of an infant." It is often said, and repeated parrot-fashioned by those who would pose as being sophisticated, that human nature does not alter, that the heart of man cannot be improved, that as things have ever been they remain. Some newspapers, seeking sensationalism, even infer a deterioration of standards and an increase in callousness and inhumanity. There are, of course, always exceptions, which modern publicity and communications systems exploit and we have to be eternally vigilant. As Gilbert Murray warned there can be, thank God only in isolated instances, a "homesickness for the slime." But for the majority, hope and progress for a better world springs eternal and with Tennyson (In Memoriam) we say, "Ring out the darkness of the land. Ring in the Christ that is to be."

Those who are pessimistic concerning human nature should read the record of history. Count Raymond, of Toulouse, was one of the most chivalrous and forbearing of the crusaders, yet he put out the eyes and cut off the noses of his prisoners, and sent them thus mutilated to their homes, as a warning to their neighbours not to molest 'the soldiers of the Cross'! King Henry I, of England, put out the eyes of his brother, Robert, and of his two grandchildren. Would any person, be he king or commoner, remain in high office today, in Europe, after having committed such acts? Most certainly he would not. Public feeling would clamour for his deposition. The 'greatest' of the counts of Anjou (Foulques, the Black) was pious enough to go on a pilgrimage to the Holy City, but did not scruple to burn at the stake his young wife, decked, for her doom, in her finest and gayest clothes. He also forced his own son to be bridled and saddled like an ass and to crouch and grovel on all fours at his feet.

Thank God the whole moral and spiritual sensitiveness of the community has been sharpened and alerted. A century or so ago in this Merrie England of ours, domestic chimneys were regularly swept by the device of sending up small boys and even girls to remove the soot as they climbed up inside the chimney. Their hands and knees were rubbed with brine before a hot fire to harden the skin against the abrasions that the rough brickwork inevitably caused. Sometimes the child stuck in the crooked flue, whereupon a fire would be lighted in the grate to give him or her more agility. In the library of Fulborne Asylum, the records show that at least one boy died from the soot which he swallowed and many others succumbed to the disease which was called 'sooty cancer'.

Granted, isolated cases of cruelty, neglect and abuse still occur to our everlasting shame, and the work and service of the NSPCC and social services is still vital and necessary. Nevertheless, and thanks be to God, the human race, under the influence and example set by Jesus, has slowly and painfully – "moved upwards, working out the beast, letting the ape and tiger (in us) die."

Quote

If you realise that you aren't as wise today as you thought you were yesterday, you're wiser today.

A good sermon leaves you wondering how the preacher knew all about you.

69. 1989

Face Value I

Thomas Carlyle, the great Scottish writer and philosopher, had a conversation, whilst on a visit to France, with Auguste Comte, a noted French thinker and scholar. Comte told Carlyle that he had decided to found a new religious sect which would sweep away Christianity, which he felt was outdated and had lost its appeal to the modern mind, outlook and belief. Carlyle, a man of find integrity and Christian faith, said in reply, "Splendid. All you need to do is to speak as no man ever spoke before, to live as no other man ever lived, to be crucified in bearing the sins of the world for its redemption, to rise again on the third day and convince the world that you are live for evermore. Then, perhaps, men and women will accept your new religion as a way of life." There's no record of Comte's reply, and no record of the establishment of his great new religious faith which was to supersede Christianity.
"Ye shall know them by their fruits!"

Face Value II

We lesser mortals have to exercise humility and tolerance in our criticism and judgement of others – reference the Sermon on the Mount – Matthew, Chapter 7 v 1–5. In his autobiography, Fred Lemon recalls that, in his youth, he drifted into a life of crime which continued over a long period and resulted in him serving a very long prison sentence. It was during this time that he became a Christian, which changed his whole attitude to life. After his release he became a popular speaker and one of the stories he tells is about a prison concert in Dartmoor which was attended by a titled lady of repute.

The Governor, as host, was pointing out to her the various prison members of the orchestra, dressed for the occasion in dinner jackets and bow ties – "That violinist, he's doing 5 years for robbery... the cellist is a noted forger..." etc. etc. The titled lady was very interested. "And the pianist, what did he do?" she asked. "He looks a real villain." The embarrassed governor replied – "Well, actually, he's our chaplain."

Retribution

He criticised her puddings and he didn't like her cake.
He wished she'd make the biscuits that his mother used to bake.
She didn't wash the dishes and she didn't make the stew and
She didn't mend his socks as his mother used to do:
Oh, well, she was not perfect, though she tried to do her best,
Until, at last, she thought it was time she had a rest.
So one day when he said the same old rigmarole all through,
She turned and boxed his ears – just as his mother used to do!

Wasted Words

A lady went to buy a drinking bowl for her dog. The shopkeeper asked her if she would like one with the inscription, "For the dog". "No," she replied genially. "It is hardly necessary. My husband never drinks water and the dog cannot read."

On the Ball

An ex-convict had to report periodically to the police. But that didn't worry him at all. On the contrary it enabled him to have "under police supervision" printed on the notepaper he used for inviting contributions to his "charity". This only goes to prove that necessity is still the mother of invention!

70. 1989

The Mind, Health and Healing

It was Goethe, the sage of Weimar, who wisely observed that he who is plenteously provided for from within, needs but little from without. If we really accept the idea that fundamental health comes from what is built up inside and not from what is so often sought outside, we will find it makes a tremendous difference to our day-to-day experience. The state of the mind and soul – not the body – is the measure of the wellbeing of each of us. Pains and numerous crippling disorders are presented to our doctors and, again and again, they find that it is a personality condition and rarely the condition of lungs, heart and digestive organs. Over nineteen centuries ago Plato said, "If the head and the body are to be well, you must begin by curing the soul." The Seer in the Old Testament observed that "a merry heart makes good healing, but a broken spirit drieth up the bones." Confucius also laid stress on the mind, as the reconciler between body and spirit, with healthy life as the result. Thus it is that when physical disorders appear, it is the soul that very often needs treatment. Caught up in the quagmire of life, with its stresses and strains, we flounder and struggle helplessly on, finally becoming the victim of physical disorders. We seek medical advice, and so often no organic problems are apparent. What is needed is a doctor of the soul, someone who can teach us to look life straight in the face and not to be dismayed.

To feel sorry for oneself is one of the most destroying things that can happen to us. Often in depression there is nothing organically wrong, but the mind and soul need to be stimulated to help us to respond to the challenge of life. It is the soul that breaks down and needs attention, so that it can rule the body effectively. It needs to be fed continually with food to make it strong and healthy. If, for its daily food, we feed it nothing beyond sensational news items and shallow amusements, frothy chatter and trivial interests, we starve it. Pettiness, trivialness, shallowness and self-pity are forever the soul's corrupter and destroyer. We have to find the motivation to face life's challenge and this requires effort, practice, concentration and perseverance. It would seem that every doctor of medicine needs also to be a doctor of the mind and soul, and every minister and priest needs to be a good psychologist as well as a good theologian!

Our religion and faith should give us the strength and courage to face life with capability. Unfortunately, for many it seems to be associated only as a connection with an organisation – a glorified club, unconcerned with the deeper needs of life and the inner life of the soul. They that know true religion loses the feeling of having to struggle alone. Dreads and fears are sublimated, confidence is restored and we lay hold and draw on a power greater than ourselves. The control which the soul can exercise over the body is paramount, provided that the soul itself is free from sickness. The treatment of sick bodies ever needs to be linked up, more and more, with attention to sickness of soul and the great physician of soul and body came so that we might have life and have it more abundantly.

Just Right

A postman reported to the postmaster that a dog had bitten him on the leg that morning.

"Did you put anything on it?" asked the postmaster.

"No," the postman replied, "he liked it just as it was."

Good Advice

Don't rest on your laurels – they make a poor mattress.

Better Advice

Face powder may catch a man – but it's baking powder that keeps him.

A live Church has parking problems;
a dying Church doesn't
A live Church has lots of noisy children around;
a dying Church enjoys peace and quiet.
A live Church invites people to risk involvement and tries new ideas;
a dying Church plays it safe and never risks anything.
A live Church worships;
a dying Church worries.
A live Church looks for challenges and opportunities;
a dying Church looks for problems and dangers.
A live Church evangelises;
a dying Church fossilizes.

71. 1989

Harvest Reflection

In that remarkable book Life on Earth, David Attenborough showed how each group of animals evolved, and in The Living Planet he observed the natural world from a different, but equally fascinating, angle. He explores every type of habitat that Earth has to offer, be it polar icecap or parched desert, and reveals how each natural region of the globe supports its own community of specially adapted plants and animals.

The Revd Dr Nathaniel Micklem, in his great book The Creed of a Christian with its splendid chapters on Intelligent Integrity, The Duty of Thought, Providence, Belief in God, etc. observes that nature proclaims her great original and declares by every sign that she did not conceive herself, but is the expression of another. No blade of grass but is God's handiwork, no human being but is, in some way, in His image, no being exists but by sharing in His being, no will, no power, no life, no joy, no beauty, but has its source, its end, its process by His word. All the visible things of the world show forth the glory and the wisdom and the power of their Creator.

Every child has asked the question, "Who made God?" For thousands of years people have wanted to know how everything began. How can we find out about the beginning of things? We know what happened last week, because we were there, or someone else was there who could tell us. But in the beginning, no one was there and therefore no one can tell us – except God. Can we think of a time when there was nothing anywhere at all but God? It was God who began to make all things and He has revealed part of the most wonderful story of all – the story of creation. Everyday He is telling us, through our developing intellect, a little more of that story one day all may be revealed. He tells us the story in many ways – in the Bible, and also in the Book of Nature and Life. Many say that we ought to rewrite the Genesis in the light of modern knowledge and tell the story in the language of today. But the Bible is not a scientific text book. Its purpose is not to answer the questions that science can answer but the questions that science cannot answer. It does not tell us when or how the world was made; but it tells us who made it. It does not tell us how we were created; it tells us who was our creator and why we were created. It passes through the doors of mystery to which science has no key. Galileo summed it up when he said, "The Bible was not given to teach us how the heavens go, but to teach us how to go to heaven." The subject of the first chapter of Genesis is not creation but the Creator. The God of the universe is a God of order and no advances of science out date the authority of the Bible which reveals that evolution is but the natural side of God's creation. "In the Beginning...God" (Genesis I v I).

Logic

There are two reasons for drinking; one is when you are thirsty to cure it. The other is when you are not thirsty to prevent it. Prevention is better than cure!

(Thomas Love Peacock)

The Butterfly and the Bee (Author unknown)

Once upon a time
A handsome honeybee
Fell in love with a butterfly
He met in a tulip tree
He said, "I love you madly
And want to share your life
Let's fly away together
Will you be my wife?"
She shook her head in sorrow,
"No, no, no," cried she.
"For I'm a monarch's daughter
and you're just a son of a bee."

The Gardeners prayer

O Lord, grant that in some way it may rain every day, say
from about midnight until three o'clock in the morning, but,
you see, it must be gentle and warm so that it can soak in;
grant that at the same time it would not rain on campion,
alyssum, helianthemum, lavender, and others which you in
your infinite wisdom know are drought-loving plants I will
write their names on a piece of paper if you wish – and grant
that the sun may shine the whole day long, but not everywhere
(not for instance on spirea, or on gentian, plantain lily and
rhododendron), and not too much; that there may be plenty of
dew and little wind, enough worms, no plant-lice and snails,
no mildew and that once a week thin liquid manure and guarno
may fall from heaven. Amen. Karel Capek

LAUGHTER LINES

An epistle is the wife of an apostle.
An evangelist is one who brings gossip
A horse divided against itself cannot stand.
Jesus healed ten leopards and the one that
lost his spots came back to thank Him.
(Schoolboy howlers)

1990–99

72. 1990

Tempus Fugit

As I write these notes, I realize that the Christian year will soon pass into Advent. "The time draws near the birth of Christ" and the face of the whole world (almost) is turned towards Christmas. One would like to feel that this change of direction, and spirit of expectancy, was no shallow observance of mere custom but a rich and deep appreciation of the difference that Christ makes to our civilization – of the bedrock of hope that He provides of our finally emerging from our struggle with selfishness into a social order worthy of Himself.

The threefold fact that He came, that in a real sense He abides, and the He grows, in spite of all opposition, constitutes a sharp challenge to all who are heedless of Him. Advent reminds us that this Christ is not a mere historical fact, but a present and powerful initiative. Christianity has been reported many times in history, to be upon its last legs and tottering to its grave, only to confound its mourners with a new sudden outburst of life. Christianity has a monopoly of hope and trust in God. Without that what is there to live for or look forward to? Byron writes of hope:

Be thou the rainbow to the storms of life!
The evening beam that smiles the clouds away
And tints tomorrow with prophetic ray.

The gateway to a fuller life is found in service to and with others. The worst calamity that could happen at Christmas would be to find oneself grown niggardly and mean. It is a time for 'living dangerously' rather than diminish by one iota the joy and goodwill of Christmas. St Paul thoughtfully preserves for us that other great beatitude that fell from the lips of the Master of Life, "It is happier to give than to receive."

No person is so sick as the one who is sick of themselves and to turn from ourselves to the Giver of Life, is to find a meaning and purpose in life which always eludes the self-centered. God is our Father, "Hope in God," says the psalmist, "for I will yet praise Him; who is the Health of my Countenance, and my God." The hardest arithmetic to master in life is that which enables us to count our blessings. As the New Year approaches we must look forward with keen anticipation – "the best is yet to be." And were the 'good olde days' as good as they were made out to be? Recollect that our forefathers did without sugar until the thirteenth century, without coal fires until the fourteenth, without buttered bread until the sixteenth, tea or soap until the seventeenth, without gas, matches or electricity until the nineteenth, without cars, canned or frozen foods until the twentieth century. So what are we grumbling about? Be of good cheer! A happy Christmas and a peaceful and healthy New Year to all.

Letter from small boy to Santa Claus – after Christmas

Dear Santa Claus – at Christmas I was given a sister instead of a bike. Maybe some other boy wanted a sister and received my bike. We have kept the sister but I'd still like a bike.

73. 1990

Unity not Uniformity

A traveller who arrived in a small town asked a local how many churches there were. The reply was, "Well, we used to have two, but last week we had a union, so now we have three." This apocryphal tale illustrates the sad tendency there has always been for division and separation within the fold of the Christian church. This doesn't mean that we should be 'ecumaniacs' – totally determined to hammer out one rigidly uniform system of belief and practice, and to ram it down everyone else's throat. A healthy diversity to accommodate individual needs is reflected even within the New Testament itself, nevertheless, the major denominations of the church should strive to extend the gracious acceptance of each others baptism to cover also the Lord's Supper and the wider Ministry of the Church.

A major argument of the 'ecumaniacs' has been that the Christian church loses face in comparison to the other world religions when it demonstrates disunitedness. But there are just as deep divisions between their various branches as there are within the Church and ghastly armed conflicts of a barbarity which makes the troubles of Northern Ireland, terrible though they are, seem slight in comparison. Islam has been torn apart between Shiites and Sunnis almost from birth.

What we need is not the kind of woolliness which says it doesn't matter what you believe or how you worship, because we are all travelling the same road anyway; but a combination of an informed confidence in the worthiness of our own tradition, and an equally informed respect for those who, while manifestly our brethren in Christ, belong to a different tradition, with perhaps only some aspects of which we can whole heartedly accept. We have to find the things which our consciences permit us to hold and to do in common, and share in them together wholeheartedly. In this we can attain a unity much more deep and lasting than any which could be found through the drably uniform life of a single 'Super Church' into which many would be dragged with grave reservations, while others would, for deep reasons of conscience, prefer to remain outside. It is apparent that the word 'informed' is the operative word. One of the tragedies of church life today is that so often we have little understanding ever of the beliefs and practices of our own tradition, and even less desire to do anything about it. We cannot face, with confidence, uncertainties of life if we are not prepared to share with, and learn from, one another – and the Bible and its study should be focus and goal of our togetherness and unity.

A Response

The poem "The Butterfly and the Bee" featured in the October/November Newsletter, has evoked a response as follows, from our poetess Elsie Parkinson entitled Beastly Bug.

> Oh, how I hate the greenfly bug
> It camps on all my flowers
> Nothing will dislodge it,
> Not even April showers!

When you and I the roses prune
Our hands get full of pricks
But the obnoxious little aphid
Just sticks and sticks and sticks!!

A parson, after parking his car in a prohibited place, put a note on the wind-screen... "Clergy in a hurry, seeking God. Forgive us our trespasses."

Upon returning he found a reply... "Traffic warden trying to do his duty, lead us not into temptation."

74. 1990

Lift Up Your Voice

The Friendship Service was an outstanding success – a packed church, good fellowship, super food and great singing! The latter invites comment and probing into memories' recess! The Brains Trust of blessed memory – Messrs Joad, Campbell and Huxley, were once asked a question. "Why is it that if you talk to yourself you are regarded as being not quite right in the head, yet no one thinks like that if you start singing to yourself?" Obviously there is, indeed, something funny about talking to oneself. If we meet a man talking to himself we cannot help thinking – "Poor fellow! He can't be all there!" Yet if we sing to ourselves at our work, or even in our bath, nobody sends for the doctor. The Brains Trust – all clever dicks – had some interesting comments, saying that speech is a means of communication between persons, and does, in itself, involve an "I" and "Thou" relationship. Where someone speaks aloud, it requires a listener. If you have anything to say to yourself, you don't need to say it aloud. Singing on the other hand, is a natural gift which gives release, satisfaction, and joy to you yourself, whether anybody else listens or not. Speech is a rational exercise, song is artistic, often a spontaneous outburst of spirit or feeling. The three wise men even suggested that singing to yourself was much better that whistling while you work!

The writer treasures many of the old Victorian songs of sentiment recorded on old 78 rpm records, by such artists as Peter Dawson, Clara Butt, and others, – many set to music by our old friend, Pinsuti. The words of one of them is as follows:

(A two-part song)

I sing because I love to sing
Because instinctive fancies move.
Because it hurts no earthly thing
Because it pleases some I love.
Because it cheats night's weary hours,
Because it cheers the brightest day,
Because, like prayer and light and flowers,
It helps me on my heavenly way!

For our human voices there are many kinds of songs to sing – some today beyond this writer's understanding or comprehension, but there is no doubt that the Bible is right when it says that God gives His children a new song, a song which never grows old, and which they cannot help singing to themselves and for others. He gives it to us today with the Easter message of Resurrection. You can put some of the meaning into words, but when you try to do it, it makes you feel how lame talk is, and you cannot help singing. Hence the oratorios of our great composers – and Isaac Watts – "When I Survey the Wondrous Cross".

The nursery rhyme tells of "Little Tommy Tucker who sang for his supper," and we can all agree that it is far better to sing for your supper that to cry for it. But by far the best way of singing is to sing because you love to sing. It does not mean that we shut out others, indeed it is just that kind of singing which also reaches other people's hearts and lives. Wherever we find Jesus Christ we also find singing – in pages of the New Testament, in Bunyan's Pilgrim's Progress (Who would true valour see) and in His church. It breaks forth because He brings joy, gladness and melody to our hearts and lives.

> Wonderful, wonderful, Jesus
> In the heart He implanteth a song
> A song of deliverance, of courage and strength
> In the heart He implanteth a song.

75. 1990

This Mad World

Every minute 2 million dollars are spent on armaments, yet half-a-billion people are undernourished worldwide – equal to the population of Europe. Almost every day in the world, trees covering an area as large as Wales, are cut down to make paper and supply building timber.

> I think that I shall never see
> Aught lovely as a pulpwood tree,
> A tree that grows through sunny noons
> To furnish sporting page cartoons.
> A tree designed by providence
> For classified advertisements.
> A tree whose shady arms give scope
> For reams of editorial dope.
> A tree widespreading t'ards the skies
> Will soon spread propaganda lies.
> A tree whose friends die hour by hour
> To give press barons wealth and power.

It always seems so strange to me
That only God can make a tree.
Yet, when it's into 'newsprint' made
The devil often plies his trade.

Hallelujah (Praise Ye, Jehovah)

I like the sentiment expressed in the following verse:–

If you've a song, try it.
If you've a tear, dry it.
If you've a cross, bear it.
It you've a joy, share it.

An oft repeated saying of Jesus was, "Be of good cheer (courage)" – the urge to rejoice in the Lord always. As one who is privileged to preach in many different churches, I find so often, that this is a virtue singularly lacking in church congregations! Sometimes, viewed from the pulpit, a congregation is a most depressing sight! It is on record that Neville Talbot (Toc H), an unconventional giant of the faith, suddenly stopped in the middle of his sermon and said, "Why are you so glum? Am I boring you? Why don't you laugh?" And when he did tell them something amusing and there was a respectable titter in response, two most orthodox people got up and walked out in protest! So often our religion does not include humour any more than it does joy – yet Jesus, in His teaching and parables, must sometimes have had his audience rolling on the floor convulsed with laughter.

The Revd Philip Doddridge (1702–51), whose hymns of joy and faith are well represented in Congregational Praise (55, 144, 319, 394, 437, 491–2–3, 669, etc.) commented thus!

Live while you live, the epicure would say,
And seize the pleasures of the present day,
Live while you live, the sacred preacher cries,
And give to God each moment as it flies.
Lord, in my view, let both united be.
I live in pleasure when I live in Thee.

76. 1990

Cases 417 and 418 – National Council for the Welfare of Prisoners Abroad

The two young teenaged British girls charged in Thailand with attempting to smuggle heroin, worth £4 million, Patricia Cahill (17) and Karyn Smith (18) makes tragic reading. The girls, both from the West Midlands, were arrested at Don Muang Airport, Bangkok, with a vast quantity of heroin found hidden in their baggage, and they claim that they were 'tricked into smuggling' and were innocent. This sorry affair recalls the case of Rita Nightingale, the young woman from Blackburn, Lancashire, who was 'framed' by her 'lover' on a drugs smuggling charge and sentenced to 20 years imprisonment in Bangkok. Until she found herself in prison, Rita's attitude to Christianity was non-committal. Her marriage at 17 was a failure. Possessed by a wanderlust she spent some years in Australia and Hong Kong, where she became a nightclub receptionist. On her way to England to visit her mother, she was arrested at Bangkok Airport with 3.3 kilos of heroin found in her luggage. Awaiting trial, she was visited by two women missionaries who impressed Rita by the perfectly natural way in which they talked of God and of the friendship of Jesus Christ. They left with her a booklet 'The way out – Christ!' Rita realised that, to date, her life had been a complete failure and she asked God to come into her life and change it, saying,"I want to give it to you." Shortly afterwards she received her 20 year prison sentence, but she now realised that she was not alone, Christ would always be with her.

Her plight attracted widespread attention in the media and prayer groups were praying for her. The happy ending was that after 2 years, the King of Thailand pardoned her. Rita returned to England to work for the Prison Christian Fellowship, visiting prisons and borstals all over the UK. Her story is told in Freed for Life, a Marshall paperback (£1.75).

Advice to Young Men

Charles Haddon Spurgeon was not only the 'Prince of Victorian Preachers', he was also a wise and witty adviser, whose knowledge and wide humanity enabled him to answer, with insight and understanding, every question which the young people of his day put to him. His advice to students going on vacation was as follows: Now you will have a brief holiday. If you are invited to address meetings, talk sense, and don't go courting – that is not good for students. Keep yourselves to yourselves. Come back with your hearts and manners uncracked. Walk in the fields, like Isaac, by all means and meditate on life – but don't lift up your eyes for Rebecca – she will come soon enough!

77. 1990

Sombre Reflections

John Ruskin, the great Victorian writer, critic and philosopher, has well expressed for all of us, the rule of life which brings contentment and happiness. "Let every dawn of morning be to you, as the beginning of life, and every setting sun as its close; then let every one of these short lives leave the sure record of some kindly thing, done for others, some goodly store of knowledge gained for ourselves."

The assurance of the Christian faith is that there is no death in the sense of extinction; no snuffing of the candle of life, no going out of the soul in blank nothingness. Physical death of the body is no accident, it is an inevitable incident upon the way of life, a station at which all travellers arrive, and through which they must pass. It has been so from the beginning, and will surely continue so to be –

Rest after toil, port after stormy seas;
Peace after strife; death after life;
Doth greatly please.
Hail and farewell, John and Frank, dear friends and comrades on life's way.
One day, in God's nearer presence, we will meet again.

I never preach to a congregation without wondering how, and when, death will come to us. For some it will be at home, for another at the wheel of a car, perhaps in a train or aeroplane or in a hospital room. Somewhere, sometime, the final testing of our lives awaits us. Do we have the spiritual resources to meet it triumphantly? Are our lives founded on a reality that is greater than death?

Two little girls were discussing their relatives, said one, "Your grandmother certainly spends a lot of time reading her Bible". "Yes," replied the other, "I think she is cramming for her finals." Cramming for finals, (as we learnt in school) is always foolish, it's the overall previous and consistent application and work that matters – and this applies when we come to face the great finale of death. We don't need to be afraid of death. In Jesus we have the spiritual resources to meet it, not as a dread enemy, but as a friend and deliverer. A life firmly established on the foundation of faith in Jesus Christ, has no fear of death – "because He lives, we will live also."

Give me a good digestion Lord,
And also something to digest;
Give me a healthy body Lord
With sense to keep it at its best.
Give me a healthy mind good Lord,
To keep the good and pure in sight,
Which seeing sin is not appalled,
But finds a way to set it right.

Give me a mind that is not bored,
That does not whimper, whine or sigh;
Don't let me worry over much
About the fussy thing called 'I'.
Give me a sense of humour Lord;
Give me the grace to see a joke;
To get some happiness from life
And pass it on to other folk.

Some think of God, like Guthrum
sat with a great beard curled:
I think of God like a Giant,
who labouring moves the World.
　　G.K. Chesterton
(author of St Francis of Assisi)

For sweeter things turn
sourest by their deeds:
Lilies that fester smell
are far worse than weeds.
　　(author unknown)

78. 1990

═══════════════════════════════════════

Minister's Letter – A Farewell

Marjorie died at 8:50 a.m. on Wednesday 31 October in Wythenshawe Hospital. The end was peaceful after much suffering, patiently and serenely borne, over a period of two months. The hospital staff, doctors and nurses were marvellous, in their skill, devotion and caring services; also the local doctors and nursing staff.

Sheila and Justine came by separate routes from America, arriving at the hospital on Monday morning 29 October, and Paul travelled overnight from Watford, arriving early the same day. Marjorie recognised them and it was a glad reunion. Early Tuesday morning she lapsed into unconsciousness and I was with her until the end.

I am thankful for 53 wonderful years together. It has been a great and enduring partnership, through good times and bad times, especially through the war years (1939–45). It has ever been a caring and sharing relationship. In helping others we enriched ourselves. At Providence Church, Middleton, Tatton St Hulme, Long Lane and Morley Green, Marjorie encouraged and supported me in every endeavour, necessitating great sacrifices to herself and the family. She has been a wonderful companion and help-mate, sharing with me all the love and friendship received from these and many other Fellowships over the years.

The Funeral Service at Morley, on Monday 5 November was a very humbling experience, with an attendance of 250–300, representing over 30 churches and clergy, including the Moderator. My friends in the Ministry, Revds David Westhead and Fred Noden conducted the service with great dignity, beauty and sincerity. It was a memorable occasion and I and the family are eternally appreciative for their support and testimony.

I have received hundreds of letters, messages of condolence and telephone calls, and donations received – for the Buy-a-Brick Cancer Care Appeal, Wythenshawe Hospital now stands at £610.00. Through the medium of this Newsletter may I, very sincerely and humbly, thank everybody for their support and sympathy. It is very much appreciated and valued.

Looking through Marjorie's diary, I found a quotation which is on a sundial in Alderney (Channel Island). It reads, "Do as the sundial does, count the bright hours only." It was Adelaide Anne Procter (1825–64), who wrote a fine hymn which thanks God for our bright hours – "My God I thank thee, who hast made the earth so bright, so full of splendour and of joy, beauty and light. So many glorious things are here, noble and right". Nevertheless, she was careful to correct any notion that life is made up solely of bright hours – going on to say – "I thank thee, too, that all our joy is touched with pain; That shadows fall on brightest hours' That thorns remain' So that earth's bliss may be our guide, and not our chain."

I suppose all sunshine can make a desert – and the same is true of life. Life is a mixture of sadness and gladness, heat and cold, rain and sunshine. It's good, in memory, to count the bright hours, they have a sustaining influence, but in life sunshine and shadow are combined for our counting, and together give us perspective on life, with gratitude to God and consideration for the pain and travail of others.

If I should die and leave you here awhile
Be not like others sore, who keep long vigils by the
Silent dust and weep.
For my sake turn again to live and smile.
Nerving thy heart and trembling hand to do,
Something to comfort other hearts than thine.
Complete these dear unfinished tasks of mine,
And I, perchance, may therein comfort you.

(Anon)

Make no long tarrying, O my God!
And as the sun sinks in the sea
Nor dim, nor pale, nor overcast,
By no sad change, nor slow degree,
Radiant and royal to the last;
So take the gift Thou gavest me.

Holy is the true light, and passing wonderful, lending radiance to them that endured in the heat of the conflict; from Christ they inherit a home of unfading splendour, wherein they rejoice with gladness evermore.

79. 1991

Change & Human Nature

It doesn't take a statistician to tell us that society is changing fast in all European countries. For example, the over 65s as a proportion of the population in the UK in 1950 was some 10 per cent, by the turn of the century it will be approaching 20 per cent. Church attendance, as a percentage of the population, in the UK is about 12% (Irish Republic 82%, Spain 41%, Italy 36%, Belgium 30%, Netherlands 27% and West Germany 21%). This indicates a steady decline over the past years. Nevertheless, we must keep things in perspective – those who attend come because they want to attend, there is no compulsion and no coming, as in Victorian times (and in the USA), as a 'status symbol', a one-upmanship over one's neighbour, depending on the 'quality and social standing' of the church attended. We remember Hogarth's fine picture and etching of 'The Sleeping Congregation'.

Further back in our history, the 'common people' were 'expected' by the 'gentry' to attend church and their livelihood, and that of their families, depended upon their 'obedience'. William Cowper (1731–1800), poet and hymn writer, a man of fine Christian character and sensibility, wrote an essay to his cousin, entitled 'Country Congregations', in which he commented on his visits to country churches, and the behaviour of the congregations. Some of his observations were as follows – "The ruinous conditions of some of these edifices gave me great offence; and I wish that the vicars, instead of indulging their genius for improvements by enclosing gooseberry bushes within a Chinese rail, and converting half an acre of glebeland into bowling greens for their own use, would apply part of their income to the more laudable purpose of sheltering parishioners from the weather, during their attendance in divine service." Again – "I could wish that the clergy would inform their congregations, that there is no occasion to scream themselves hoarse in making the responses; that the town crier is not the only person qualified to pray with due devotion; and that he who bawls the loudest may, nevertheless, be the wickedest fellow in the parish." Finally, "The Squire's lady and the gentry are stared at for their finery and the wives and daughters of wealthy merchants and tradesmen vie with each other every Sunday in the elegance of their apparel. The ladies, immediately on their entrance, breathe a pious ejaculation through their fansticks, and the beaux very gravely address themselves, in silence, to the haberdashers bills, glued upon the linings of their top hats. This pious duty performed, then the exercise of bowing and curtsying succeeds, followed by the locking and unlocking of the pew doors. The noise drowns the parson's voice at the beginning of the service, and the rustling of silks, added to the whispering and tittering of so much goodly company, renders the service totally unintelligible to the very end of it."

We must still give priority to search for God. He is still in His Universe. Our new technological and scientific developments can neither banish Him from the microscopic compass of the atom, nor from the vast, unfathomable ranges of interstellar space.

80. 1991

A Paradox of Joy and Suffering

Everyone desires happiness in life, but relatively few people find it. Social workers, clergymen, psychiatrists and psychologists fill their hours trying to help unhappy and neurotic people. Radio and television with 'canned' entertainment of all kinds, are available to multitudes at the switch of a dial and we while away precious hours with sporting events and all forms of entertainment. Yet no age has ever seen so much unhappiness! Nervous breakdowns, suicides, broken homes, drug addiction, alcoholism, boredom and unrest are the hallmarks of our time. Behind the façade of gaiety and the appearance of wellbeing, lies a deep and pervading sense of isolation, anxiety and uncertainty.

The answer must be found in our lack of faith, trust and belief in God. Augustine was surely right when he wrote in his Confessions – Thou madest us for Thyself, and we shall never find rest save as we rest in Thee." To escape from frustration, fear and a sense of failure, we must be right with God.

The Christian has problems! Life abounds in paradoxes. For example, Jesus says "If any man would come after me, let him deny himself, and take up his cross and follow me." (Matt. 16 v 5). He also says, "These things I say unto you that my joy may be in you, and that your joy may be full." (John 15 v 11).

It is a recurring practical question for the Christian as to whether he should be predominantly sober, or exuberantly happy? Should he be as jolly as the portly abbot, or as grave as many a parish priest? Quiet and unassertive as the Quaker or as eager and gay as a young Evangelical? Should he be carefree and happy with St Francis, 'God's gay troubadour' or solemn and dour like Cromwell's Puritans?

We must admit that most of us do not fall into any of these types. For the most part we simply register circumstances – 'the weather of life'. We are like barometers, we simply record the sun when it shines and the rain when it pours. We go up and down with circumstances like flotsam and jetsam on a rough sea. Probably, for this reason, the world at large doesn't take a great deal of notice of us! It hasn't much use for 'Christians' who, professing to know God, show no stability in their emotions and reaction to circumstances. We are too much like 'them' in this matter – having nothing but the weather – no chart or compass, no harbour or port.

Life for many is just a succession of good and bad, one thing after another, ups and downs, and humanity is lost and bewildered by ever-changing fortunes and circumstances. Have we no message for people in such a plight? Surely the answer is found in Jesus. The secret of His serenity was in His ability to weave joy and suffering so marvellously together. For Him neither joy nor suffering were really important, but only absolute trust in God. He ever fixed His gaze upon a goal that lies beyond the weather of life. He took sunshine and calm, wind and storm, the fair and the foul and used them in the furtherance of Life's Voyage, to each the desired haven, the harbour and port for which He was sailing. "Seek ye first" he declared "the kingdom of God." There is no other way of triumph over the weather and adversity of life.

Hubbard, my favourite philosopher, who in the prime of life, went down in the torpedoed *Lusitania*, wrote in his 'Note Book' some wise words concerning worry and stress.

> God always gives us strength to bear our troubles day by day; but He never calculated on our piling the troubles past, and those to come, one top of those of today.

81. 1991

"Showing the World"

> If you've a song, try it. If you've a tear, dry it.
> If you've a cross, bear it. If you've a joy, share it.
> When hope grows faint, brace it. When trouble comes, face it.
> When there's a wrong, right it. When life is grim, fight it.
> If you've a hand, give it. If you've a creed, live it.
> If you've a faith, show it – and let the world know it.

The two lines underscored are a challenge to our Christian faith and witness. A recent article in *Time* magazine asks the readers to try to imagine the pain and horror of Daniel Scott's last hours. The seven-month-old baby was found by police lying in a pool of blood next to his crib in a Bronx tenement. His mother – off on a six-day crack binge – had left him in the care of his father, who abandoned the child in his unlocked apartment, without as much as a bottle of water. Emaciated, filthy, desperate, the infant had apparently hoisted himself out of the crib and tumbled onto the wooden floor before finally dying of starvation and dehydration. Both parents were charged with man-slaughter. The mother was 28, the father 26. Many such parents start in their early teens or earlier, with alcohol and pot, then cocaine and crack, living in an environment where this is a way of life. Social service workers and law enforcement personnel find them-selves in a dilemma – should the kids be taken away or is the best way to save the child, to save the mother as well.

Some years ago, Sir Ronald Gould, in his presidential address to the World Confederation of the Teaching Profession, suggested (cynically) a new version of the Ten Commandments for our modern age. This included – 1. Thou shall have no other gods before thyself. 3. Thou shall not call on the name of the Lord except in vain. 5. Honour thy father and thy mother whilst thou art very young and has no alternative, but when thou has reached the teens, treat them as the old fogies they are. 6. Thou shall not try to settle thy quarrels by reason but by force. Thou shalt be quick on the draw, for if thou dost not get they man first, he will certainly get thee. 7. Thou shall not be faithful to one man or to one woman. 8. Thou shalt not steal carelessly or thou shalt be discovered. Rather shalt thou steal carefully, or fiddle or scrounge. 9. Thou shalt not refrain from bearing false witness against they neighbour, for every man must take care of himself. And the last one 10. Justifies any action which enables one to keep up with the Joneses!

In the US last year, the Report to the President entitled, "The Family, Preserving America's Future," gave certain statistics. Of 3.6 million children who began formal schooling (aged 6), 15% were children of unmarried parents and it was estimated that 40% would, within the next few years, live in a broken home. Nearly 30% were latch-key children – no one to greet them when they came home from school. In 1960, 393,000 were divorced, in 1985 1,187,000 (x3) and ever increasing. Births out of wedlock had increased by 45% in the last decades. The Report ended – "The Family as a unit is in deep trouble, and is desperate for Help and Hope." The book, 'Growing Wise in Family Life' (Swindoll) makes a point which is relevant to all of us, "If your family is still intact. If there is still love and affection. If partners are still communicating and supportive, still laughing and playing together – you're the exception rather than the rule. You should be deeply grateful for this. Our tired, tragic, unsure society needs such people for survival."

Not to know what happened before one was born is ever to remain a child.

(Cicero)

In the hustle of the market place there is much money to be made. But under the cherry tree there is rest.

(Japanese proverb)

Let him that has two loaves sell one,
and buy himself anemones, for
bread is the food of the body;
but flowers are the food of the soul.
                    The Koran

82. 1991

Life, Living and Leisure

We all love W.H. Davies' poem entitled 'Leisure', which starts, "What is this life if, full of care, we have no time to stand and stare? No time to stand beneath the boughs, and stare as long as sheep or cows"... ending "A poor life this, if, full of care, we have no time to stand and stare." Life is what we make it. It is measured not in length, but in breadth and depth. To be alive only to appetite, pleasure, pride, ambition, money-making and position; and not to goodness, and kindness, purity and love, poetry, music, flowers, stars, God and eternal hopes, is to be all but dead.

In the pre-war years, Canon Peter Green ministered, with love and devotion, to the people of Salford. He had all the attributes for 'success' in his calling: scholarship, ability, charm, a splendid preacher, writer and pastor. He could have become a bishop, but he chose to remain a parish priest and pastor to his people. That, to him, was his calling, that was where he felt he could best serve his maker.

It is on record that many years before this, another splendid, hardworking clergyman, brave, genial, talented and courageous, had a town parish also doing work he loved and doing it well. He was the friend of all the young people, he worked and organised many useful and necessary institutions. He was nothing of a preacher and a poor speaker, but generosity and happiness radiated from him. But 'They' had their eyes on him, and he was offered a bishopric. His friends persuaded him to accept, saying he could not refuse such a sphere of wider influence.

The result, he became a worried man. He had a big house and a big household, was a welcomed guest in country houses and vicarages, opened churches, presided at confirmation ceremonies, made endless poor speeches, and preached uninspiring sermons. His time was frittered away in directing the elaborate machinery of a diocese. He was not a clever man, not a sower of thoughts, but a simple pastor. His strength lay in his personal work as a neighbour, pastor and friend. Instead of being the stoker of the engine, he became simply a very distinguished passenger in a first-class carriage – but still a passenger.

Life is for living and we have to make the best use of it whilst it is day, as Jesus said, "The night cometh in which no man can work." In our service to and for others, we must be quite sure that it is a summons from God, and not a temptation from the world. We must ever assess our own strengths and weaknesses. God puts us into the world to live and serve, not necessarily to get influence over other people. The influence comes when we prove ourselves in the quality and service of our lives. We must always be ready to learn and not too desirous to teach. We are all children at school – as far as knowledge and understanding goes – "forever as children gathering pebbles on a boundless shore." Many of us (myself included) want to sit in the master's chair, and rap the desk and chastise the other children! (Father forgive us!) Enjoy the summer and make the most of your leisure hours.

83. 1991

Life and Happiness

It is surprising how many wise and clever men are pessimists! Disraeli for example – "Youth is a blunder, manhood is a struggle; old age a regret." Then the blessed St Bernard, "It is misery to be born, pain to live, grief to die." There is some consolation in the thought that there is this difference between happiness and wisdom; he that thinks himself the happiest man really is so; but he that thinks himself the wisest, is generally the greatest fool. Ingersol, the American, who made a vast fortune in manufacturing clocks and watches, in his old age at last found happiness in giving it away! His experience and advice stand the test of time and life:–

> Justice is the only worship, Love is the only priest.
> Ignorance is the only slavery, Happiness is the only good.
> The time to be happy is now, the place to be happy is here.
> The way to be happy is to make other people happy.

Christians should be known wherever they live, for their neighbourly kindness. They should be the people to whom anyone in trouble would automatically turn. Kindness is love in action, and Christians should be the natural channels of God's love. Unhappily, Christians are not always known for their neighbourly kindness. Some of us are too busy doing church work to be good neighbours. Some people may come to think of us as somewhat straight-laced, rigid, forbidding and far from friendly. Neighbourliness shows itself in simple day-to-day kindness. It is ready to do some shopping, or a bit of baby-sitting to give young parents the opportunity of having a night out. It is just as ready to visit and chat in the house of an elderly person who should never be left entirely alone and isolated. A good neighbour is there ready to be asked to help and always willing to offer as well. The relationship can be intimate but never intrusive. That is what neighbours are for. If Christians everywhere were known for their neighbourliness, what an impact it would have on our local environment and in the world at large.

What a Granny is

A seven-year-old girl wrote a school essay as follows – "A granny is a lady who has no children of her own, so she likes other people's little girls and boys. A grandpa is a man granny. He goes a walk with boys and they talk about fishing and tractors. Grannies don't have anything to do, but just to be there. They are old so they shouldn't play hard or run. They never say 'Hurry up!' Usually they are fat, but not too fat to tie children's shoes. They don't have to be clever, only answer questions like why dogs hate cats and why God isn't married. They don't talk baby-talk like visitors. When they read to us, they don't skip bits or mind if it is the same story over again."

Parable with a Moral (Stand up and be Counted)

There were four people everybody, somebody, anybody and nobody. There was an important job to be done and everybody was asked to do it. Everybody was sure that somebody would do it. Anybody could have done it, but in the end nobody did it. Somebody got very angry over this because it was really everybody's job. Everybody thought anybody would do it but nobody realised that everybody wouldn't do it. It ended up that everybody blamed somebody when actually nobody had asked anybody.

84. 1992

Seasonal Reflections

Christmas and Easter are inextricably bound together – the one signifies the Beginning, the other the End of the Beginning – which continues in perpetuity.

The Christian religion proclaims the sacredness of all life and above all, the infinite value of the human personality. Thus the sacredness of human life became an essential element in the structure of the Christian faith. At this time of the year, the 'season of goodwill', we are motivated to do something for the poor, the outcast and the neglected. Christianity believes in the power of love, from which springs all the Christian virtues of mercy, charity, peace – and above all, the capacity for sacrifice. Nietzsche's contempt for Christianity as the religion of women only, mirrored his contempt for women – which was the other side of his almost homosexual adoration for war and the warrior. Our religion has been, and is centred on the life-giving, life-continuing, life-sacrificing forces of our women. In this sense, every mother is a born Christian and even, the father knows that it is only by the capacity to surrender one's own private life for that other life one brings into the world, that the human race can survive. Parents come to realise that there is no creation without sacrifice. That same potential for love, that same capacity for sacrifice, is shown by the man who risks his life to save his fellows trapped in the mineshaft, and by the lineman who risks electrocution to pull a comrade away from a live wire. It is shown by the physician who enters into plague-stricken areas – and by honest, decent men and women everywhere.

Christianity does not depend upon going to church or observing the Sabbath; sometimes unfortunately, this becomes not Christianity, but churchanity. Both the Sabbath and the church were made for 'man' not 'man' for the Sabbath. It is by love and sacrifice that we daily recapture the spirit of Christ. This is the core of our Christian faith. Only those who act on this principle have a capacity for real freedom. If an individual's life is so dear that they will sacrifice anything – betray friends, renounce the truth, grovel in the dirt – in order to keep the heart pumping and the lungs breathing, then for all practical purposes, that is slavery, a denial of freedom and they are spiritually dead. Life, at its highest and most intense, has nothing to do with the mere maintenance of the physical body. At the moment of saying goodbye to that body, one may for the first time, truly live.

Our destiny is a great one because the essence of it is tragic. All that we build crumbles, all that we embody turns to dust, all that we love most, we must one day leave behind. That which alone endures, is our character and personality, the spirit in which we seek to understand and meet our destiny. This we pass on to our children and our comrades on life's way. Death comes to all, but death comes best to those who believe that it is but a transition to life everlasting. The words of Jesus are ultimate in their wisdom, "He that loseth his life shall find it."

Excelsior!

> Look backward with gratitude,
> Look onward with hope,
> Look upward with confidence and trust.

85. 1992

Query! "If you were on trial for being a Christian, would there be enough evidence to convict you?"

Dr Colin Morris reminds us that Christianity shares many truths with other great religions, but one truth is unique to it. Whilst other religions make great play of our dependence upon God, only Christianity dares to speak of God's dependence on us.

The word – Almighty Power – became frail human flesh, to symbolise the truth that God puts Himself at our mercy, entrust Himself into our hands.

Jesus needed a human womb from which to be born; a human breast at which to suck, a father to carry him to Egypt away from Herod's wrath; a group of friends to support – and sometimes betray him; and a conscript to carry his cross. He still needs human hands to wield the instruments through which He heals; a human voice to bring comfort to the distressed and to challenge the comfortable; human eyes to look in compassion on the lonely; a human presence to stand beside the outcast; human brain-power to help make deserts fertile again and feed the hungry; human political skills dedicated to the beneficent end of creating a more just and humane social order.

The word made flesh means ultimate power subordinated to mortal weakness; a reversal of conventional values, love melting stubborn will that iron bars could not break; the Cross a symbol of triumphant death; the empty tomb evidence of endless life. The word made flesh is a stupendous demonstration of faith. Not our faith in God – that flickers and fades, waxes and wanes – but God's faith in us, entrusting Himself and the fate of His Kingdom into our shaky and often unreliable hands.

The Challenge (Rabind Tanath Tagore)

> Leave this chanting and singing and telling of beads; who do you worship in
> this lonely dark corner of the temple with all the doors shut? Open your eyes

and see that God is not in front of you. He is there where the farmer is tilling the hard ground and where the labourer is breaking stones. He is with them in the sun and the rain and his garment is covered with dust. Put off your holy cloak and like Him come down on to the dusty road. Come out of your meditations and leave aside the flowers and the incense: What harm is there if your clothes become tattered and stained? Meet Him and stand by Him in toil and in the sweat of your brow".

Ever with me are the words and tune (Rutherford) which I remember as a boy from the old Bristol Tune Book. "The sands of time are sinking, the dawn of heaven breaks; The summer morn I've sighed for, the sweet morn awakes; Dark, dark hath been the midnight, but day-spring is at hand;

86. 1992

Reflections from a Convalescent

Schweitzer says, somewhere in the Quest of the Historical Jesus, that "faith which refuses to face facts is no faith!" During the past days in Stepping Hill Hospital and on returning home, I've realised the fact that a fortnight away from Morley and its good folks, is purgatory – not to be endured for a moment longer than necessary! So 'haste ye forward'. Sunday, 5 April (if I recollect correctly, a gee-gee named April Fifth was a previous Derby, or was it a Grand National, winner!).

Good friends plied me with literature to lighten the dark hours – Mavis supplied 'The Cheshire Village Book' (Cheshire Fed. of Women's Institutes) – a veritable mine of information which inspires me to do a pilgrimage of dozens of villages I'd never heard of! Geoff presented Jo Manton's lovely book 'The Story of Albert Schweitzer' – great reading! And Ethel, some American copies (large type) of the *Reader's Digest* which I found very entertaining and informative. From my own library I re-read 'Under the Eye of the Clock' – the life story of Christopher Nolan, author (when 15) of those marvellous poems in 'Dam-Burst of Dreams'. This latter book is the finest antidote to self-pity and depression imaginable! It is the strange and wonderful story of his childhood. He very nearly died at birth from asphyxiation, but survived with severe brain damage, cut off in his own silent world, restricted by a mute and paralysed body. He tells how he managed to break the barriers of that impossibly cocooned existence so that the reader can see into the thoughts and realities of a state nobody has ever known about.

What about my Bible readings? Well, it was the Old Testament which challenged me – a book I'm inclined to neglect! So I tackled Isaiah, and in Isaiah 40 v 28 read;

Life up your eyes and look at the heavens, who was it that made them? This Lord of ours who fashioned the remotest bounds of earth. He does not weaken or grow weary. He is wise beyond all our thinking.

These words of trust and triumph from Isaiah were first heard by people who were in the depths of despair. They had been – in their own words – abandoned by their God and had been conquered by their enemies! They were slaves in Babylon, and the oldest of them could look back fifty years to the frightful day when Nebuchadnezzar, conqueror of the world, had come down against Jerusalem and slowly strangled it, by seige. It had taken him a year-and-a-half to close the iron ring – causing famine, pestilence and terror, before the Jewish resistance finally cracked. The conquerors tore the place to pieces, burning everything that would burn and the stout walls that would not burn, they hammered to fragments. The Royal family were slaughtered, except the King, he was blinded, and with those of his people left alive who could walk, was dragged off into slavery. The Book of Lamentations recalls the fearful suffering of those days. They went 700 miles across the desert in chains, out of their homeland into exile from the hills of Judah, into the endless Babylonian plain. At last, by the rivers of Babylon they sat down and wept when they remembered Zion. They cursed Babylon and all her works, in words so terrible that although they still remain at the end of Psalm 137, they send a shiver up and down the spine to read them.

Isaiah said to them that God had neither abandoned nor forsaken them, reminding them that they still belonged to Him. He was still guiding them, He still had control of their destiny – "Life up your eyes..." – Great reading!

Jesus came in the fullness of time and revealed to us anew, not only God's immensity of power, but His infinity of love. We know that nothing in the universe can finally escape this love which is endless and enduring. "This, this is the God we adore. Our faithful, unchangeable, friend whose love is as great as His power and neither knows measure not end."

87. 1992

Survivors of the 1939–45 Dark Age (Age Concern)

We were born before the TV age, before the 'creation' of frozen food, plastics, nylon, contact lenses and the pill. Before refrigerators, dishwashers, tumble driers, electric blankets, central heating, air conditioners, credit cards, ballpoint pens and the like. The atom hadn't been split, no such things as laser beams and the man in the moon certainly didn't come from America.

We got married first and then lived together – how quaint could we be? We were before house-husbands, gay rights, computer dating, dual careers and computer marriages. Divorce was something that happened to film stars. We had never heard of Radio 1, tape decks, electric typewriters, artificial hearts, word-processors or yoghurt; time-sharing meant togetherness, not Spanish holidays, a chip meant a piece of wood, hardware meant a shop where you bought hammers and nails, and software wasn't even a word.

Everything at Woolworth's cost sixpence or less. For a penny, you could take a tram ride, and for sixpence go to the cinema and also treat yourself to an icecream. Grass was for mowing, coke was a cold drink and pot was something you cooked in. Rock music was a lullaby and AIDS was for those with hearing difficulties, while fax was something we looked up in an encyclopaedia. Nevertheless, we managed to survive and to live a full, useful and generally contented existence. Today, statistics inform us that four of every ten marriages will end in divorce and one-third of all marriages include people who have been divorced. One-parent families continue to increase and over 700,000 children in the UK never see, or enjoy the fellowship and support of their fathers. Our society is in a state of flux – in morals and in religious observance. In this era of monetarism, church loyalties are suffering. The Roman Catholic churches were down 14 per cent in adherents between 1979–1989, with the Methodists down 11 per cent and the Anglicans 9 per cent, and this also is a similar position in the URC. The appeal called 'A Decade of Evangelism', which started officially in January 1991, is a call for Christians to go forth and multiply. The Pentecostal and Afro-Caribbean churches are doing just that and the command in Matthew 28 v 19–20, is as relevant today as it was when Jesus lived in Galilee.

The Hidden Treasure

The owner of a vineyard who was on the point of death, called his children to him and said, "In our vineyard there is a treasure; dig for it carefully." "In what place?" they all cried out to their father. "Just dig for it and you will find it," said the father, and with that he died.

Scarce was the old man buried than they began to dig with all their might. With rake and hoe and spade, the vineyard was dug over again and again. There was no clump of earth left undisturbed. They even passed the earth through a sieve and drew the harrow hither and thither. But they found no trace of any treasure and each one thought himself deceived. But when next year the spring had scarcely arrived, each one saw to his amazement that the vines were bearing a threefold crop; and thus the sons learnt a lesson and year by year they dig out of the vineyard an ever increasing treasure.

88. 1992

God The Creator (Harvest Reflections)

W.H. Carruth wrote a splendid poem, the first two verses of which are as follows:

> A fire-mist and a planet, A crystal and a cell, A jellyfish and a saurian, and caves where the cavemen dwell; then a sense of law and beauty, And a face turned from the clod – some call it Evolution, and others call it God.

> A haze on the far horizon, and infinite tender sky, The ripe rich tints of the corn-field, And the wild geese sailing high; And all over upland and lowland, The charm of the golden rod – Some of us call it Autumn, And others call it God.

We did not create the beauty of the world. We found it. Artists like Turner may capture a fragment of a sunset and put it on canvas, but he did not create it, he copied it. We may cultivate some fine species of rose or rhododendron, but we cannot create the sun and the air and the fruitful powers of the earth. Who taught the dragonfly to climb from the slime to the sunshine and who painted the vivid green of a woodpecker's wing? All beauty is dreamed before it is fashioned. If you see a lovely piece of embroidery, or a beautiful vase, you know that it was fashioned first in mind and imagination. It is the expression of someone's thoughts. So when we look on the beauty of the world we know that it is an expression of the thoughts of God.

The world of nature is a world where all things are fitted for the work which they have to do and where each fulfilling its task, fulfils a greater purpose than it knows. Thus the bee's relationship with flowers! Because the winds blow, the apple trees are fruitful, because God comes down in the rain, the grass and corn grow tall. All these miracles of organisation did not just happen, any more than an Atlantic liner could build itself, or run itself without someone in control. There must be someone on the bridge who knows what is happening all over the ship and the course being steered. There must be someone in charge of the world, to give direction, guidance and motivation, and that someone is God, revealed to us in Jesus.

A Remembrance Day Thought

I am tired and sick of war. It is only those who have neither fired a shot nor heard the shrieks and groans of the wounded who cry aloud for blood, more vengeance and desolation. War is Hell.

General William Sherman

Facts of Life

When the great clock of life was wound up, all mammals received the same amount of heartbeats to use up during their life times – 800,000,000. The rate at which the beats are used roughly determines how long a certain mammal will live. The elephant's heart pulses 30 times a minute and at that rate, it takes the average elephant over 50 years to use its allotment, (whale 95 years, dolphin 35 years, tortoise 138 years). So if you think your meter is ticking too fast, relax! In fact, human beings don't conform to the rule, scientists now believe the size of the brain prevails over the rationing of heartbeats. For the pigmy shrew, life is short. It is one of the world's smallest mammals, weighing as little as 1/20 oz and measures between 1½ and 2 inches from its nose to the base of its 1 inch tail. It has very poor eyesight and its sense of smell is effective only at fairly short range. The pigmy shrew's heart is twice as large as other mammals in proportion to its body dimensions and it pumps at the rate of 900 to 1,400 beats per minute. The shrew has the highest metabolic rate of any mammal and its lifespan averages 1½ years. Simple to live at such a rapid pace, it must consume the equivalent of twice its body weight every day. Aren't you glad you weren't born a pigmy shrew!

89. 1993

A Parable for Today

A man owned a lake with five fishes which he lacked skill to catch. Being hungry, he said to a fisherman who was as hungry as he, "You can show your skill in my lake, doing what you will with the catch, if you pay me a rent of two fishes." The fisherman answered, "I would agree but I have no rod." So he went to a maker of rods who said, "I will sell you a rod for two fishes". The fisherman replied, "I cannot bargain thus, for there would be only one fish left for me and I require two." He went back and offered a rent of one fish, but the owner of the lake would not accept.

The rodmaker reflected, "Why would I have less than others? What use is it to own a lake or to fish with skill, if you have no rod? It is you," he said to the fisherman "who asks too much. What do you do but pull out of the water the fish which are not yours with a rod which you yourself could not make? You should be content with one fish." The fisherman replied saying, "You may own all the lakes in the world and you may make thousands of rods, but of what use will they be to you if you have no skill to fish! I will have a wage of two fishes or nothing at all." They argued thus as they sat by the lakeside – and argued very well for each could see that the others were fools – as in fact they were.

And while they argued, they starved.

"Tu Sonrisa De Cristal"

I'm an old (or young) sentimentalist. In these days of Hi-Fi and compact discs, I love to sit and listen to old shellac records of pre-war vintage revolving at 78 rpm. Of such is HMV DA 1117, sung by one of the all time 'greats', the glorious tenor voice of Tito Schipa. The song (in Spanish) – The Sunshine of Your Smile (Ray) a beautiful melody, great words and heart-warming sentiment. It is said that smile costs nothing, but gives much. It enriches those who receive, without making poorer those who give. It takes but a moment, but the memory of it sometimes lasts forever. None is so rich or mighty that he can get along without it, and none is so poor but that he can be made rich by it. A smile creates happiness in the home, fosters goodwill in business, and it is the counter-sign of friendships. It brings rest to the weary, cheer to the discouraged, sunshine to the sad, and it is nature's best antidote for trouble. Yet it cannot be bought, begged, borrowed or stolen, for it is something that is of no value to anyone until it is given away. Perhaps some people are too tired to give you a smile! Give then one of yours, as none needs a smile so much as he who has no more to give.

For the New Year

Face life with a smile, take the changes and chances of this mortal life with courage and faith, facing rough and smooth alike as it comes.

(Charles Kingsley)

90. 1993

Words! – Fragile Fabrics of Forensic Fancy!

The power to use everyday words effectively is worth whatever it costs. Fowler, in his excellent book, English Usage, makes a useful distinction between working words and stylish words such as help (assist), oppose (antagonise), begin (commence), obscure (cryptic), champion (protagonist). The Authorised Version of the Bible in the story of the Prodigal Son, says so clearly, "And he would fain have filled his belly with the husks that the swine did eat, and no man gave unto him." This might have been put, "Now this impoverished deserter of the paternal roof sought to satisfy the imperious demands of physical nature with a small portion of that part of cereals which is least nutritious, the husk, but none was found sufficiently philanthropic to present him with so much as a morsel." Shakespeare, according to John Ruskin, was the greatest of all Englishmen. He wrote English – good English, the best English. He was the foster-parent of our language. He took it in and mothered it, teaching it to march, like the British Grenadiers and smile like the lass with the delicate air. He taught it to sigh like the foggy south and challenge like a herald's trumpet.

John Buchan (Lord Tweedsmuir) who wrote the best English in all his books and stories, offered a comparison of past (Shakespeare) and present (American style), "O mistress mine, where are you roaming? O stay and hear; your true love's coming, that you can sing both high and low: trip no farther, pretty sweeting; Journey's end in lover's meeting, Every wise man's son doth know"...

> Huh, sweetie, where you getting' to? Your big boy's here and pettin' you; And he's the guy that rings the bell. Say, kid, quit hikin' and sit nice, for shakin' feet cut no ice. The goopiest mut can tell.

Wrong words or phrases create false impressions. Literal sentences taken from actual letters received by public welfare departments show this very clearly, eg. "I am very glad to report that my husband who was reported missing is dead." "I am very much annoyed to find that you have branded my boy illiterate, as this is a dirty lie, I was married a week before he was born." And again, "Mrs Jones has not had any clothes for a year and has been visited by the clergy regularly." (I'm not guilty!)

J.B. Phillips (the Gospels in Modern English) says, "...if words are to enter our hearts and bear fruit they must be the right words, shaped carefully, to pass our defences and explode silently and effectively within our minds". Bacon, at his best, said "Reading maketh a full man; speaking, a ready man; writing an exact man". When communicating about Christ, a mist in the pulpit creates a fog in the pew. Paul (2 Timothy 3 v 16–17) was so correct when he said, "Every inspired scripture has its use for teaching the truth and refuting error, or for reformation of manners and discipline in right living, so that they who belong to God may be efficient and equipped for good work of every kind."

91. 1993

The Golden Rule (Matthew 7 v 12)

We are hearing calls, both from church and parliament, for schools to teach children the difference between right and wrong. According to numerous social commentators Britain is sinking into a cesspool of moral decay. Morals are concerned with how to behave; and to develop moral reasoning is closely linked to understanding relations between people, and to understand the function of social habits and behaviour. For some children the route to mature morality is through an increasing appreciation of codes of conduct, rights and fairness in relationships. For others, it is through an increasing appreciation of responsibility for other and the importance of building caring inter-personal relationships. These are so often nullified by home environment and conditions, and social pressures and expectations. Bible teaching is neglected in schools; the Ten Commandments are a mystery, the Sermon on the Mount unknown.

The eleven religions of the world, although dressed in different garments, preach the same simple message of tolerance, brotherhood, charity and love, when they are unadorned by ritualistic observances, forms and ceremonies, and shorn of mysticism and painful asceticism's with which they have gradually become encrusted. A Russian proverb says, "The road to the other world is the same from everywhere." The Talmud says, "The pious of all nations shall have a share in the life to come." The Bible says, "Of a truth I perceive that God is no respecter of persons, but in every nation he that feareth Him and worketh righteousness is accepted with Him." In Islam it is written, "The foundation of all religion is one, and God's is the East and the West, and wherever you turn there is God's face." A beautiful Hindu rendering tells the same story, "Kine (cows) are of diverse colours, but all milk is alike; the kinds of approach vary, yet all worship is one, systems of faith are different, but the Deity is one." Buddhism, the most tolerant of all creeds, says, "Never think, or say, that you own religion is the best, never denounce the religion of others." It also asks the question "Wherein does religion consist?" – and answers, "It consists in doing as little harm as possible, in doing good in abundance, in the practice of love, of compassion, of truthfulness and purity, in all the walks of life."

The Golden Rule for children and adults of all colours and creeds is universal and differentiates between right and wrong. Buddhism: Hurt not others with that which pains yourself. Christianity: All things whatsoever ye would that man should do to you, do ye even so to them; for this is the law and the prophets. Confucianism Is there any one maxim which ought to be acted upon throughout one's whole life? Surely the maxim of loving-kindness is such – Do not unto others what you would not they should do unto you. Hebraism: What is hurtful to yourself do not to your fellow man. This is the whole of the Torah and the remainder is but commentary. Go learn it (Talmud). Hinduism: This is the sum of duty, do naught to others which if done to thee, would cause thee pain. Islam: No one of you is a believer until he loves for his brother what he loves for himself. Jainism: In happiness and suffering, in joy and grief, we would regard all creatures as we regard ourselves, and should, therefore, refrain from inflicting upon others such injury as would appear undesirable to us if inflicted upon ourselves.

92. 1993

===

A Polyglot (Many Languages) Subcontinent (After a Personal Visit)

India: a federal republic, has a population of some 900 million and Pakistan, also a federal republic and member of the Commonwealth, a population of 130 million – in both instances – people, people everywhere! They are lands of startling contrasts – unity in diversity, centuries of invasion and migrations and the consequent mingling of peoples have resulted in a great variety of physical types. The palette of skin tones range from pale to swarthy, while facial features display tremendous diversity. The people speak one or more of fifteen different languages and over 200 dialects. They may be Hindus, Muslims, Sikhs, Buddhists, Christians, Zoroastrians, or Jews and with few exceptions, they all seem to tolerate each other. The rhythm of the seasons, with its impact on life and work, with local cults and beliefs, binds rural life into a common thread and pattern. In the cities the compulsions of industry and urban life, and the need for survival, seems to have created an impetus that holds the many diverse groups together as a community. Over most of the land the monsoons (starting sometime in late June) regulate the rhythm of life – the crops and the harvests and consequently, the seasons of labour and days of festivity.

Viewed very broadly, the evolution of Indian society goes back at least 3,500 years when the Aryans took over the northern parts, coming from Afghanistan and Iran, via the steppes of Central Asia. The grandeur and oriental opulence of the sub-continent is synonymous with the Mogul dynasty (the Mughal Age) which lasted for three centuries, 1526–1750. Their great leaders Barbar, Akbar, Jaha, Jahangir, and others, built mosques, forts and palaces, including the Red Fort, in New Delhi, and the Noble Jama Masjid Mosque, the largest in India, also the famous Red Fort on the River Jamuna, at Agra. The most famous of all Mughal monuments is the Taj Mahal, in Agra. It was built by Shah Jahan in memory of his beloved queen, Mumtaz Mahal, and is the culmination of the best in the Mughal traditions of architecture. It is one of the wonders of the world, 20,000 men were occupied for 20 years in its building and decoration. Its beauty and floral decorations incised into the pure white marble in marvellous patterns and filled in with colours brought from China, Italy and worldwide, have retained their colour and character. One expected something marvellous, but it exceeded all expectations in its magnificence.

British Rule was established in India in 1857, the capital of British India was removed from Calcutta to Delhi and in New Delhi, Sir Edward Lutyens and Sir Herbert Baker created magnificent government buildings in splendid settings between 1912–31. With Old Delhi, it's a fascinating city including the walls with seven gates, the Red Fort (formerly the Imperial Palace) and the Great Mosque, both seventeenth century.

Lahore in Pakistan has a population of 3 million. The old walled city, fort palaces and mosques associated with the Mogul rulers. Adbar, Jahangir and Aurangzeb are fascinating and beautiful, also the Pubjab University and the Lahore Museum of Fine Arts – a British India contribution which rivals the British Museum, in London, in splendour and contents.

From Dehra Dun (India) I travelled 12,000 ft into the Himalayas, near the Chinese border, to bathe in the sacred, cool, clear waters of the Ganges – which flows from its source in the mountains through the valleys and plains of India, past the holy city of Benares, into the Bay of Bengal beyond Calcutta. Dehra Dun – an 'outpost of Empire' means 'dwelling place of the saints' dehra (dwelling place) dun or doon (saint). Doon School, with 500 pupils (boys), mostly European and British – equates with Eton or Harrow and is very expensive.

Religion, in this sub-continent, is a way of life, and amongst the educated Rabindranath Tagore is highly respected as prophet and seer. In his lecture (The Religion of Man) delivered at Oxford in May 1930, at the age of 69, Tagore, a Nobel Prize Winner, said, "Our union with a Being whose activity is worldwide and who dwells in the heart of humanity cannot be a passive one. In order to be united with Him we have to divest our work of selfishness and become worldworkers, we must work for the good of all."

93. 1993

To Give, or When to Give – That is the Question

Material organisation is no substitute for moral order. The final test of any economic system is not the material wealth – oil, gold, textiles, etc. produced, but the ultimate product – the quality of men and women it nurtures, and the order, beauty and sanity for their communities and loves. The Christian believes in the power of love – the opposite to the worldly love of power. From love spring all the special Christian virtues – mercy, charity, peace and above all, the capacity for sacrifice. Nietzsche's contempt for Christianity as the religion of women only mirrored his contempt for women – which was the other side of his almost homosexual adoration for the domineering aggressive characteristics he admired in man. There is no creation without effort and sacrifice. In a time of unbridled worldliness and corruption, sometimes apparent within the church itself, we have to remember Christ's teaching that those who seek only their life shall lose it. It is by love, sacrifice and service that we daily recapture the spirit of Christ.

Having said this, we face a dilemma! I get many 'visitors' to my door asking for help. I usually give to ease my conscience. Begging says more about the giver than the taker. It says we are prepared to tolerate a system in which an increasing section of our society comes to depend on the lottery of our chaotic *ad hoc* payments. We give because we feel guilty, without questioning whether the person is genuinely unemployed, or is a layabout requiring money for drugs or drink. Our duty is to help rebuild a life, not hand the person the means to destroy himself. If we don't encourage them to help themselves, we create a dependency culture – a no desire to work complex.

The Revd Ken Hewitt, from St Augustine's Church, in London, has ministered to the poor, sick and needy for 26 years. Sadly his experience tells him that however much you give to beggars, it does absolutely no good. They grow older and poorer, reduced to a life on the streets becoming nothing more than inarticulate animals. Today we also have the 'professional beggars' using children with faked handicaps to stimulate sympathy and generosity, earning for their 'employers', according to Revd Hewitt £50 to £100 per day. Others claim to be refugees from Bosnia, Romania and Eastern Europe – how many are genuine? This is the dilemma – the crucial distinction between the increasing number of 'bogus beggars' and the genuinely desperate. We must continue to give and to give generously through organisations and agencies whose experience far outweighs our own spasmodic and often self-congratulatory efforts.

94. 1993

Harvest Reflections

Many wise sayings and proverbs come from China – for example, "Each interprets in his own way the music of heaven." "Ye are all the fruits of one tree and the leaves of one branch; walk then, with perfect charity, concord, affection and agreement." God gave us brains to use and eyes with which to see. In consequence when Hutton and Lyell demonstrated in the last century that the universe could not have been created by God in seven days at or around 4,004 BC, thinking Christians had to agree that the earth was very much older. At bottom there is no argument between science and religion. Science is about what can or maybe known and demonstrated. God, being defined as all-knowing; infinite and eternal, cannot be comprehended by the imperfect and the temporal. That is why belief requires Grace, or an Act of Faith. We did not create the beauty of the world. We found it. Artists, like Turner, may capture a fragment of a sunset and put it on canvas, but he did not create it, he copied it. We may cultivate some fine species of rose or rhododendron, but we cannot create the sun and the air and the fruitful powers of the earth. Who taught the dragonfly to climb from the slime to the sunshine and who painted the vivid green of a woodpecker's wing? All beauty is dreamed before it is fashioned. If you see a lovely piece of embroidery, or a beautiful vase, you know that it was fashioned first in mind and imagination. It is the expression of someone's thoughts. So when we look on the beauty of the world we know that it is an expression of the thoughts of God.

The world of nature is a world where all things are fitted for the work which they have to do and where each fulfilling its task, fulfils a greater purpose than it knows. Thus the bee's relationship with flowers! Because the winds blow, the apple trees are fruitful, because God comes down in the rain, the grass and corn grow tall. All these miracles or organisation did not just happen, any more than an Atlantic liner could build itself, or run itself without someone in control. There must be someone on the bridge who knows what is happening all over the ship and the course being steered. There must be someone in charge of the world, to give direction, guidance and motivation, and that someone is God, revealed to us in Jesus.

Maxims

Worry is like a rocking-horse, it gets you nowhere.

A smile is a thing you can always wear and still be in fashion.

Bad habits are like bad eggs, you never know how bad they are until you break them.

From the Wisdom of Shakespeare

For sweeter things turn sourest by their deeds; lilies that fester smell are far worse than weeds.

95. 1994

"Facts are Sacred! Comment is Free!"

This often quoted saying by 'Scott, of the *Guardian*', comes to mind after receiving a communication from a friend in Styal – a retired journalist. He recalls the old days of the then *Manchester Guardian*, when C.P. Scott was the Editor-in-Chief. Scott cycled daily from Didsbury to Cross Street, held meetings with his staff to arrange and plan the following day's paper, digested all the news to hand, wrote his Editorial, and rode home in the dark hours of the early morning. One morning he dozed off and fell off his cycle, coming to with his head in the lap of a young man who said, "Don't worry now, you will soon be all right again, my name is Paul". Scott, dazed, murmured through his mists, "Paul! There's something I've always wanted to ask you. Did you ever get any reply to that letter you wrote to the Ephesians?"

It is a fact of history that from March AD 60 to March AD 62, Paul was a prisoner in Rome, waiting, till it pleased that lawless tyrant the Emperor, Nero, to hear his appeal from the judgement of the Procurator Festus (Acts 25 v 9–12). During these two, weary, years, he wrote four letters – Ephesians, Philippians, Colossians and Philemon, commonly known as 'the Prison Epistles'. They were all conveyed to their destinations by the same messenger, the faithful Tychicus. Ephesus was the brilliant capital of the Province of Asia, Paul spent 2¼ years as minister there, far longer than anywhere else (Corinth 1½ years). His wish was to return there again, but it wasn't to be. After his second trial in Rome, he was condemned to death, accused of being the Christian leader. He was beheaded – probably it was only his Roman citizenship that saved him from torture and a more cruel fate (AD 67 Rome).

Goodbye or au revoir, means 'until me meet again' and this is the Christian Hope.

This thing we call 'death' is really like a big railway terminus where we say, 'Goodbye' for a little while to our friends who are going off to a fascinating new life in a far lovelier place than anything we know here. For us, left standing on the platform, it is a sad time, but not for them. For them it's not the end, but a new beginning. We are sorry for ourselves, we will miss their friendship and society, which is natural when we part from those we love, but we ought never to feel bitter. Death is not the final end, but the end of the beginning. Our life here is only a tiny part of a much greater life, only the first stage of the journey, and death is only like a station where we change from one train onto another, on a station platform, to continue and complete our journey. Thus our prayer, on our journey and pilgrimage as we travel, is – "Receive into Thy sure keeping, O God, ourselves and all those we love, and teach us, in life and in death, to put our trust in Thee.

96. 1994

The New Year – Hasten Slowly

As Christians, our philosophy of life should be, "the best is yet to be," always anticipating in hope. We should make the best of circumstances – why moan about the weather – it's true to type, as the poet said – "no sun, no flowers, no birds – No-vember!" Oliver Goldsmith, blessed be his memory, wrote, "Hope, like the glimmering tapers light, Adorns and cheers the way, And still, as darker grows the night, Emits a brighter day." Byron, in one of his saner moments, said of hope, "Be thou the rainbow in the storms of life! The evening beam that smiles the clouds away, And tints tomorrow with prophetic ray."

December 21 is the shortest day – so look forward to spring! The dull brown earth will soon stage a resurrection. Anna de Bary, a true poet, in days of sickness and prolonged illness could just see through her sickroom window a single snowdrop in flower, she wrote:

Close to the sod, There can be seen.
A thought of God, In white and green.

In the Daily Readings, of W.E. Sangster, we read words which could help us to face 1994 with faith and serenity:

Slow me down, Lord! Ease the pounding of my heart by the quieting of my mind. Steady my hurried pace with a vision of the eternal reach of time; Give me, amidst the confusion of my day, the calmness of the everlasting hills. Break the tensions of my nerves and muscles with the soothing music of the singing streams that live in my memory. Help me to know the magical restoring power of sleep. Teach me the art of taking minute vacations – of slowing down to look at a flower; to chat with a friend, to pat a dog, to read a few lines from a good book. Remind me, each day, of the fable of the hare and the tortoise – that I may know that the race is not always to the swift, that there is more in life than measuring its speed. Let me look upward in the branches of the towering oak, and know that it grew great and strong because it grew slowly and well. Slow me down, Lord, and inspire me to send my roots deep into the soil of life's enduring values, that I may grow toward the stars of my enduring.

In Pilgrim's Progress, Interpreter led Christian to a place where a fire was burning against a wall. One standing by cast much water on it – "yet did the fire burn higher and hotter." Christian understood why, when he was taken to the other side of the wall, and there saw a man with a vessel of oil constantly, but secretly, feeding the fire.

This is a parable of the church. She lives in a world where influences are at work to damp down the flame of her faith and the zeal of her members. Only by the power that God gives will she resist this and succeed. Such power is bestowed, and the flame of faith is fed in the secret places of prayer and by the gathering of the church in worship.

97. 1994

Intellect and the Human Brain

Albert Schweitzer once asked an African to perform a menial task, he refused to do it on the grounds that he was an intellectual. The good doctor did the job himself, remarking that he, too, had once thought of being an intellectual but found it too difficult! John Milton in Paradise Lost, says, "What in me is dark illumine, what is low raise and support: That, to the height of this great argument, I may assert Eternal Providence, and justify the ways of God to men."

In Oliver Goldsmith's epic poem, The Deserted Village, (the village parson was 'passing rich' with a salary of £40 per year) we read; "In arguing too, the parson own'd his skill, For e'en though vanquish'd he could argue still; While words of learned length and thund'ing sound. Amazed the gazing rustics rang'd around, And still they gaz'd, and still the wonder grew, That one small head could carry all he knew."

During these long summer evenings (and nights) I've been rereading Bryan Magee's book The Great Philosophers – from Plato, Aristotle, through Descartes, Spinoza, Leibniz, Kant to Wittgenstein. A sense of wonder is the mark of the philosopher and I marvel at the capacity of the human brain. For thousands of years people have tried to understand the brain. It has been compared to a switchboard, a computer, and a hologram, yet none of these analogies is adequate. The brain is uniquely complicated and mysterious, unlike anything man has ever made – to carry the workload of its 20 million cells would require a computer the size of Texas – America's largest state! Yet a tiny nick in the cortex can destroy speech or particular parts of the memory, and a tumour the size of a pea can change the mildest of men into a rapist or a murderer. The brain regulates all bodily functions; it controls our most primitive behaviour – eating, sleeping, keeping warm and is responsible for our most sophisticated activities. The creation of civilisation, music, art, science, language, stem from the brain. Our hopes, thoughts, emotions and personality are all lodged somewhere inside it. May we, like Milton, continue to justify the ways of God to humanity.

Ancient Wisdom

The tree of deepest root is found
Least willing still to quit the ground
T'was, therefore, said by ancient sage
That love of life increased with age

98. 1994

Blessed is Simplicity

Matthew Arnold commented that one English book and one only combined perfect plainness of speech – allied with perfect nobleness, and that book is the Bible. Macaulay, the great historian, remarked that the English Bible is a book which, if everything else in our language should perish, would alone suffice to show the whole extent of its beauty and power. They referred, of course, to The James Bible of AD 1611. Take, for example, the sentence, "And he would fain have filled his belly with the husks that the swine did eat: and no man gave unto him". This might have been put, "Now this impoverished deserter of the paternal roof sought to satisfy the imperious demands of physical nature with a small portion of that part of cereals which his least nutritious, the husk, but none was found sufficiently philanthropic to present him with so much as a morsel." Simplicity and sincerity have much in common. The words of our mouth should express the thoughts of our heart. Words should never mask a semblance of truth. If so, we become hypocrites whose business in life is to deceive. The tongue of sincerity should be rooted in the heart, so that hypocrisy and deceit have no place in our words.

The book, translated into more languages than any other book save the Bible, appeared in Latin in the year 1470, with its first English translation in 1677. It is 'of the Imitation of Christ' by Thomas à Kempis (1380–1471). His father was a hard working peasant, living in the town of Kempen, near Dusseldorf, the family name was Haemmerlein (Hammerken). Thomas entered the convent of Mount St Agnes, at Deventer, when barely 12 years old and received priests' orders at the new convent, in Zwolle, in 1425. After the fashion of the time he was called Thomas of Kempen, thus the name known to the whole Christian world. He gave us the beatitude 'Blessed is simplicity' plus many soul-searching sayings in his great book, for example;

Jesus hath now many lovers in His Heavenly kingdom, but few bearers of His Cross. He hath many desirous of consolation; but few of tribulation. He findeth many companions of His table, but few of His abstinence. Many follow Jesus unto the break-ing of bread; but few to the drinking of the cup of His Passion. Many love Jesus as long as no adversities befall them. But if Jesus hides Himself, and leaves them but a little while, they fall either into complaining or into too much dejection of mind. But they who love Jesus, for the sake of Jesus, and not for some special comfort of their own, bless Him, in all tribulation and anguish of heart, as well as in the state of highest comfort."

99. 1995

"Fame is the spur that the clear spirit doth raise (the last infirmity of noble minds) to scorn delights, and live laborious days."

Thus wrote John Milton (1608–74) in Lycidas, one of the great poems of the English language – which should be read, in this age of sleaze and double standards, by politicians and church leaders. I'm young enough to remember during the 1939-45 era, the devastation wrought among American womanhood by an Army Board that had callously passed a well-known 'swoon crooner' as medically fit for military service. Military police had to be mobilised to 'rescue' him from hundreds of swooning girls. Many of the girls had been waiting for hours in the ice and snow to meet him. When news came that Sinatra was passed for service duties, girls began demonstrating and screaming – "Frankie, I don't want to live." Some dived head first into snow banks. Many others went to church and prayed.

Thus the real stuff of human nature, recalling the golden days of Edwardian and Victorian times when enthusiasts used to take the horses out of a prima donna's carriage and draw her in triumph to her hotel. The time when gilded youth, seeking the divine ultimate of intoxication, would quaff champagne out of an actress's shoe. The time when Bacchantes broke into Liszt's hotel, the morning after a recital by the handsome, fascinating, young Don Giovanni of the piano, to carry off in bottles, the contents of his washbowl. When a woman (American) cut out the cover of a chair cushion on which the godlike body had rested and had it framed. When the secret of the puzzling odour emitted for a quarter of a century by a noticeably clean, old, German lady was one day revealed – she had carried in her corsage all that time, the remains of a cigar that Liszt had once smoked! Fame is the spur?

Let us remember, this Christmastide, the coming of ONE who came that all of us might have life and have it more abundantly. He was, and is, the great self-effacing genius of mankind, the WAY He followed was one of service, not self. Albert Schweitzer, in the last words of The Quest of the Historical Jesus, is profound in his simplicity –

> He comes to us as ONE unknown, without a name, as of old, by the lakeside,
> He came to those men who knew Him not. He speaks to us the same word:
> "Follow thou me!" and sets us to the tasks which He has to fulfil for our time.
> He commands; And to those who obey Him, whether they be wise or simple,
> He will reveal Himself in the toils, the conflicts, the sufferings, which they shall
> pass through in His fellowship; and, as an ineffable mystery, they shall learn in
> their own experience who He is.

100. 1995

Whence, Where, Whither!

The Venerable St Bede (AD 673-735) is recorded in the Ecclesiastical History of the English People, as having had a conversation with the pagan King of Northumbria as follows:

> The present life of men on earth, O King, as compared with the whole length
> of time which is unknowable to us, seems to me to be like this; as if, when you
> are sitting at meat with your chieftains and ministers in wintertime – one of the
> sparrows from outside flew very quickly through the hall, as if it came in at one

door and soon flew through and out at the far door. In the actual time it is indoors it is not touched by the winter's storm; but yet the tiny period of calm and warmth is over in a few moments, and having come out of the winter it soon returns to the winter and slips again out of sight. Man's life appears to be more or less like this; and of what may follow this earthly life, or what preceded it, we are absolutely ignorant, it is a mystery.

Tagore, the great Indian philosopher, poet and mystic, tells us a parable of life:

"Imagine," he says, a family of mice who lived all their days in a large piano, just as we live our lives in our fragment of the universe. And to them in their piano world, came the music of the instrument, filling all the dark places with sound and harmony. At first the mice were very much impressed by it. They drew comfort and wonder from the thought that there was someone else who made the music – though invisible to them – above, yet close to them. And they loved to think of the great player whom they could not see.

Then one day a daring mouse climbed up part of the piano and returned very thoughtful. He had found out how the music was made. Wires were the secret, tightly stretched wires of graduated lengths which trembled and vibrated. They must revise all their old beliefs, none but the most conservative could any longer believe in the unseen player! Some time later, another intrepid explorer carried the explanation further. Hammers were now the secret, numbers of hammers dancing and leaping on the wires! This was a more complicated theory, but it all went to show that they lived in a purely mechanical and mathematical world. The unseen player came to be thought of as a myth, but the pianist continued to play the piano!

The eternal question of the Riddle of Life was propounded to Oedipus long ago by the Sphinx of Thebes. One of our modern Oedipus, the French anatomist (Marie Bichat) is equally nebulous in answering this eternal question – "life is the sum of the forces that resist death."

Up from Earth's Centre through the Seventh Gate
I rose, and on the throne of Saturn sate
And many a knot unravel'd by the Road;
But not the master-knot of Human Fate.

Miracles

A Japanese magnolia, grown from a 2,000-year-old seed, has recently flowered – waxen, white and beautiful. The first snowdrops are beginning to appear – as a small child (a long time ago!), I was made to stand on a table and repeat my party piece – "Where are the snowdrops," said the sun. "Dead," said the frost. "Buried and lost." "A foolish answer," said the sun. "They do not die, asleep they lie, and I will wake them I, the sun into the light, clad in white, everyone."

Anna de Bary, a true poet who suffered long from illness and pain, could just see a single snowdrop in flower from her bedroom window. She wrote:

Close to the sod There can be seen
A thought of God In white and green.

101. 1995

e.g. (Exampli Gratia) – For Instance

Seldom does one feel more of an ignoramus than when one looks up a word in a dictionary and then gets immersed in words adjacent to it! I recently came across the word paraemiologist and 'looked it up', and found that it referred to a person who was an expert on proverbs (short familiar sentences expressing a supposed truth or moral lesson). I was confronted by pages of words that were as strange to me as Hebrew. Paraffle: (an ostentatious display), Parafront: (a hanging for an altar), Paragaster (the central or gastric cavity of a simple sponge), Paraglobulin, paragonite, paranatellion, etc. etc. If you're inclined to be a big-head (like me) read a dictionary! There is no better antidote to the vanity of knowledge. It's a humbling experience, as John Ruskin observed, as far as knowledge is concerned, "We are forever as children gathering pebbles on a boundless shore."

Whilst so engaged, I checked on the word parable and found it was described as a short allegorical story designed to convey some truth, religious principle or moral lesson. A statement or comment that conveys a meaning indirectly by the use of comparison; analogy or the like (*LL* parabolia – comparison). Jesus was the master of the parable, and He found His inspiration in the Torah and the Talmud. They express the relationship of God with humanity; which Victor Gollancz, of blessed memory recorded so beautifully in his anthologies. Eastern stories and legends abound in examples, as for instance:

As Abraham sat at his tent door at Beersheba, watching the sun sinking in the west, he saw a traveller wearily approaching; a man of about fifty years, worn and travel-stained, leaning on his staff. When the traveller reached Abraham he humbly asked for water, "Enter," said Abraham, "rest and we will kill a kid and eat." The stranger entered the tent and the supper was soon on the board. Abraham rose and lifting his hand said, "Let us praise the Lord." The stranger did not move, "Why do you not join in my praise?" asked Abraham. "Because I do not worship, or believe, in your God," was the reply. Abraham was very angry, "If you will not worship my God, you shall not stay under my tent. Go!" – and the stranger went.

Then Abraham heard the "still small voice" speaking to him, and he fell prostrate on the ground. "Abraham," said the voice, "where is the stranger who asked hospitality of thee?" "Lord," replied Abraham, "he does not believe in Thee or worship Thee, therefore I have driven him forth". "What age was he?" asked the voice. "About fifty years, Lord!" The voice said sorrowfully, "I have borne with him for fifty years and you cannot bear with him for one night!" Silently Abraham rose, followed his guest into the desert and found him cast down on the earth in despair. Abraham led him back, with kindly words, to his tent, gave him food and shelter and then told the astonished stranger what had changed his thinking. The stranger bent his head and said, "Your God must be the true 'one'.

Our self-righteousness must often trouble God, who is the Father of all. Sometimes, even in our inter-church relationships, creeds, dogma and ritual cloud our vision, causing us to un-church others who approach God in differing ways. Yet we seek the same city by our different paths, and tolerance, compassion and understanding are necessary in our Christian life and witness. The writer of Hebrews (Chapter 13) expressed it well. "Never cease to love your fellow Christians. Remember and show hospitality, there are some who, by so doing, have entertained angels without knowing it."

102. 1995

Christian Stewardship

A bishop of the Church of England recently commented that the cost of discipleship is going up by leaps and bounds, which is as it should be in this day and age! He observed that it's time we stopped tipping God! – we've had religion on the cheap for far too many years in the UK, "come to church when you feel like it, drop a coin on the plate and the vicar will be grateful to you (and so will God)." He added, "There is no financial problem in the Church of England, the problem is a spiritual one, not a financial one. A family earning an average wage with average outgoings should not be covenanting less than £12 per week to the church. And even this is less than a decent seat at the theatre and is less than many spend on so-called luxuries." Strong words indeed!

A recent newspaper report (in the *Guardian*) stated how a rural vicar had outclassed the wiles of the City investment managers by following Biblical advice on how to make money work. Taking his cue from the parable of the talents, he gave to members of his congregation £5 plus instructions to go forth and multiply it – the result a six-fold increase in church funds. He handed out £95 in fivers, which netted almost £700. This included £25 from a successful £5 bet on the Grand National! The profits of a cheap wagonload of manure sold at a handsome profit. The church treasurer appeared to have got the wrong message by burying his £5 in the ground like the dim steward in the gospel story – but he then organized a treasure hunt at £1 per head, and handed in several tenners! An elderly lady parishioner invested her fiver in the traditional mainstay of jam-making, this brought in a profit of £50.

It is important that we support the church, but it is vital that we remember that the churches' function is to serve and save the world. "The Son of Man came to serve..." Any church that is not a serving church is not a church of Christ. His life taught us that true greatness does not consist in the abundance of our possessions. If, as congregations, we are intent on building ourselves up rather than on spending ourselves for others, we fail in our discipleship. Big buildings, big memberships, big statistics, impress us as a mark of success, but this is a worldly standard. I recollect hearing of a church in a large American city, not a very large membership, but very wealthy. They built a new church covering a huge area with a 2 million dollar sanctuary, plus a motion picture theatre, swimming pool, tennis courts and a full gymnasium. Within three miles of that new complex, in the coloured district, were families of six and eight living together in small cramped rooms! "The Son of Man came to serve..." Of such a church the following dog-gerel could possibly have been written – "Our new church will have padded pews; Aren't we the lucky ones? There's air-conditioning planned for, too; Aren't we the lucky ones? The chancel cross is made of gold; Aren't we the lucky ones? And the stained glass windows are a sight to behold; Aren't we the lucky ones? With its five thousand pipes, our organ is grand; Aren't we the lucky ones? In fact our building can't be bettered else-where: Aren't we the lucky ones?

And the Cross that lifted Our Saviour to the sky, was made of two rough planks; Aren't we the lucky ones?" There is nothing wrong with beautiful sanctuaries or comfortable churches, if these help us to become more effective servants in the world, so be it, but we must never turn our religion into a form of self-glorification. The greatness of our churches does not depend upon the size of the buildings or even the number of the members, we are called to serve and our only wealth, or glory, is our willingness to lay down our lives in service for others. What is a church for? What are Christians for? Jesus said, "I came to seek, to save, to serve: as the Father sent Me, even so I send you".

103A. 1995

VE Day (1939-45) Anniversary 8 May 1995

Sunday, 7 May 1995 is a day for thanksgiving and remembrance. The final six years of the Second World War cost 53 million lives, 38 million of whom were civilians, includ-ing many women and children. During those years there were many horrific examples of brutality and mass killing, including the Holocaust with its systematic planning, which massacred 6 million Jews. This was formulated by politicians, but was only possible because of the apathy of an entire people towards the fate of their former friends and neighbours.

Today we are still the silent witnesses of man's inhumanity to man. An estimated 90 million people have died since 1945 as a result of wars in the last 50 years; and the tragedy and slaughter of the innocent still continues. We ask ourselves what lessons we have learned as we commemorate from D-day to VE Day? Martin Niemöller, the German Lutheran pastor, was arrested in 1937 for his anti-Nazi activities and spent seven years in concentration camps. He regretted that prior to this he was silent on the persecution of the Jews. On reflection, he comments:

First they came for the Jews and I did not speak out – because I was not a Jew.
Then they came for the communists and I did not speak out – because I was

not a communist. Then they came for the trade unionists and I did not speak out – because I was not a trade unionist. Then they came for me – and there was no-one left to speak for me!

I love those words we speak at Remembrance services, "When you go home, tell them of us and say – For your tomorrow we gave our today." They are not original words, J.M. Edwards in 1916, asked to compile a series of epitaphs for those who had made the supreme sacrifice, found inspiration in the commemoration by Simonides of Ceos of the Spartan dead at the battle of Thermopylae (480 BC). The battle was lost, but in defeat the bravery of all who died inspired other Greek nations to unite to repel the Persian hordes and save civilisation from barbarism.

We live in a scientific and technological age and its benefits must be used for all human happiness and progress. Knowledge must be shared and used in mutual confidence and sincerity for the good of all. Ethical standards must be restored and observed so that the misuse of scientific knowledge and discovery, either for selfish exploitation or for mass destruction, should be regarded – like cowardice in a professional soldier, or dishonesty and sleaze in a banker or politician – as the unforgivable sin. Principle is more relevant to envy, anger, pride, sloth, lust and covetousness (greed) – six of the seven deadly sins! We must ever learn from past mistakes and shortcomings. The philosopher Santayana's words can be seen today on a tablet in the main Auschwitz camp – "Those who cannot remember the past are condemned to repeat it."

103. 1995

Last Post

The 1939–45 war ended 15 August 1945, with the surrender of Japan. The Second World War cost 53 million lives, 38 million of whom were civilians, including women and children. Today we are still the silent witnesses, in Bosnia and elsewhere, of man's inhumanity to man. An estimated 90 million people have died since 1945 as a result of wars in the last 50 years. As G.S. Studdert Kennedy said of the First World War – "Men do but reap the harvest of their sowing; Sadly the songs of human reapers sound." There are people who use modern exploitative technology to extract a maximum profit regardless of the cost to other human beings, or the earth itself. The gallery of despoilers includes first and foremost the merchants of death, who control and promote the armaments industry. Without the supply of armaments there would have been no Gulf War and the tragedy of Bosnia today would have been avoided.

On 15 and 20 August the haunting notes of the Last Post will be heard throughout the land. In past days in the army barrack-room jesters would send a raw recruit to the quartermaster-sergeant for a bucket of whitewash 'to whitewash the last post'. The joke died a natural death when the Last Post became as familiar to everybody at the National Anthem. It needs no whitewash. The one signal call that persists in haunting the memory, when the rest are forgotten is 'Last Post'. It is a ceremonial call, sounded by long tradition at the close of the day. On the stroke of ten, after the drum beat Tattoo, when all are safely gathered in, the majestic notes of Last Post calls 'finis' to the day's labours. By a simple association of ideas, the custom arose of sounding Last Post at every military funeral as a requiem over the open grave. Death was very like the end of a day. That is why it was remained the only bugle-call in the army that has never had ribald words fitted to it, and why the noise in the roughest barrack-room will sink to a murmur when the call is sounded. It is no longer the monopoly of the barrack-room, it touches the hearts of all of us. The army bugle has a range of only five notes. Last Post's unknown composer was a genius, he took these five notes and created from them one of the most eloquent fragments of music in the world. C.E. Montague described it as "that most lovely and melancholy of calls, the noble death of each day's life, reminding us of the brevity of our earthly life." Who can fail to be moved by it, especially by the last note of all, that magnificent, unexpected prolonged E, which remains in the ear like a benediction, to assure us that 'All's well'? May it's notes augur well for peace and brotherhood in the world in the coming days.

Question

Why is it that opportunity always knocks but temptation feels free to walk right in?

Still the Boss!

George Bush commented on how his wife had not changed since he was knighted by Queen Elizabeth. He asked her how she liked being married to a knight – reply, "Sir George, get moving and make the coffee."

104. 1995

"Do not squander time, for that's the stuff life is made of." (Benjamin Franklin)

The word bible, which in English, as in medieval Latin, is treated as a singular noun, is in its original Greek form a plural, meaning 'the sacred books'. This correctly expressing the fact that the sacred writings of Christendom are made up of a number of independent records, which set before us the gradual development of the religion of Revelation. In the Bible there are 66 Books – 39 in the Old Testament and 27 in the New Testament. It is a good thing in the midst of the rush and bustle of life, to be able to withdraw for a while, and either alone or in the fellowship of kindred minds, to study a book – especially when that book reflects the collected experience and wisdom of humanity before and after the ministry of Jesus. In this modern world, we are the objects of a ceaseless assault upon our privacy. So often we are the slaves of circumstance and not the masters. The radio, video and television dominate and occupy so much of our leisure time, giving us little time or inclination for reading. Books are quiet things; they serve our bidding; they fall into our speed. We can lay them down or we can put them aside. A wise man once said that the best books are those which are open in your lap while you think over what they have told you. They are still the best nourishment for the mind.

Something like 300 books are published every week in the UK alone. Most of us will never know the names of a fraction of them and they are books on every subject under the sun. To discuss a serious book from time to time, with a group of friends in church or elsewhere, can be a revelation about the deepest problems of life. To know how people of the past lived and thought and suffered, can be an inspiration to our own living. Those who wish to take their Christian faith seriously should consider whether they are sufficiently acquainted with the literature of their faith. Many of us read the technical, trade and home journals which concern us in our daily work and life, but should we not pay at least the same attention to the material which awaits us in the greatest of all things, the study how to live in Christian faith? We are called to fight the good fight of faith, and good living is helped by good thinking, and good thinking by good reading – and the greatest of all books is one – the Bible. Every day is a day which God has given; and we ought to be able to say of every day, "This is the day which the Lord has made, let us be glad and rejoice in it." God wants us to count the day with eager, happy anticipation – not just special days, but every day, for each day is a new beginning. We are now in autumn – the time of mellow fruitfulness and harvest, and in no time we will be celebrating Christmas and greeting the New Year! We must learn to 'number our days' using them eagerly as they come, looking forward to all their opportunity and challenge. The days that were, the days that are, they all are days with God.

New every morning is the love
Our wakening and uprising prove;
Through sleep and darkness safely brought,
Restore to life and power and thought.

And (with John Keble 1792–1866) help us, this and every day, to live more nearly as we pray.

NB. After thoughts – Both Relevant!

A good book is the precious life-blood of a master spirit, embalmed and treasured up on purpose to a life beyond life.

(John Milton 1608-74)

Beware you be not swallowed up in books! An ounce of love is worth a pound of knowledge.

(John Wesley 1703-91)

Too True

The secret of being miserable is to have leisure to bother about whether you are happy or not.

(George Bernard Shaw)

The Tower of Bable was the place where Solomon kept all his wives.

(schoolboy)

105. 1996

Exuberant Verbosity!
In the beginning was the Word, and the Word was with God, and the Word was God (St John 1 v1)

Speech and language are part of the great and sobering mysteries of life. Whenever I feel 'cocky' and need to 'take myself down a peg; I peruse the Random House Dictionary of the English Language (2,060 pages) and in humility agree with John Ruskin in that as far as knowledge is concerned – "we are forever as children gathering pebbles on a boundless shore." Language is an indispensable instrument of human society. It is the means by which individuals understand each other, and are enabled to function together as a community. Indeed it is unlikely that any human organisation could either be formed or long maintained without language. Certainly, in the absence of communication, the complex structure of modern society would be utterly impossible. We have not the faintest idea whether the first words spoken were uttered 20,000 or 200,000 years ago! What is certain is that mankind did little except procreate and survive for some 100,000 generations (less than 100 generations separate us from the birth of Christ). One of the great mysteries of prehistory is how people in widely separated places suddenly and spontaneously developed the capacity for language at roughly the same time. It was as if a genetic alarm clock in the brain suddenly went off all around the world and led different groups in widely scattered places on every continent to create language. The English speaking world has the finest dictionaries available and new words are being increasingly added – at the turn of the century about 1,000 a year, now over 15,000 yearly (including sleaze). Words change in their meanings; often now the opposite to their original intention. Once brave implied cowardice (bravado); crafty was good work and skill; garble meant to sort out, not to mix-up; a harlot was a nice little boy; counterfeit meant a perfect legitimate copy; politician was once a sinister word – perhaps one word which hasn't altered it's meaning! The first comprehensive dictionary in England, by Nathaniel Bailey, was published in 1721, 34 years before Samuel Johnson's classic volume. They contained words and meanings as quoted above. The Greeks, in classical times, interpreted words which differ from our modern understanding of them. For example, Socrates' apology at his trial was not an expression of regret or shame, but a defence of his philosophy and way of life, as well as bitingly sarcastic attack on his judges. At the end of his speech, the jury of 501 Athenian citizens voted, found him guilty, and condemned his to death by poison. The Apology found among Plato's Dialogues is itself a monologue, or speech, given at length by Socrates in which he inter-prets the letter and meaning of the law. In his speech he refuses to compromise his loyalty to the pursuit of truth even at the cost of his life. Like Jesus, he felt that his beliefs and principles were worth dying for. Actions speak louder than words. Samuel Johnson, the great early British lexicographer, observed that knowledge, without integrity, is dangerous and dreadful.

In the New Year (1996 and beyond) may we resolve to practice what we preach – to be not only readers and hearers of the Word but to be doers thereof!

Wisdom from the East

Marry a frugal and thrifty woman, even if you have to wear out a pair of shoes looking for her.

(Japan)

Those who close their windows to the sun, open their doors to the doctor. Those who fail to support good causes can never know real happiness and contentment.

(China)

Every culture enriches our lives with its own unique beauty and wisdom, yet we all share the same hopes and dreams, the same need for love and home and kinship, these are the common threads that bind us together as one family in one world.

A birthday is not a measure of how old we've become, but a celebration of where we are in the magical circle of life.

106. 1996

Paradise or Purgatory by way of Morley Green

In Christian doctrine (and Islam) Hell is a place to which unrepentant sinners suffer the eternal torments of the damned. Fortunately modern theologians regard it as a state of mind rather than a place. My dictionary defines it as the place, or state, of punishment of the wicked after death – the abode of evil and condemned spirits – Gehenna or Thartarus. Dr E.W. Barnes in 'The Rise of Christianity' recalls the hopes and dreams which arose within Judaism for the coming of a 'Son of Man' who was to be God's agent at the end of the age.

Simultaneously a debased form of Zoroastrianism, from Persia, gives to the Jews a belief in evil spirits, and in Satan and Beelzebub 'the prince of the devils' with such development there came a growing belief in magic, which Pharisees and Christians alike seem to have allowed to be real, though morally wrong. Jewish and Samaritan magicians had a considerable vogue in the ancient world. Their profession was not reputable, but, doubtless there was money to be made in it!

Now, in 1996, the flames of Hell have been extinguished by a Church of England Report! Think of hell, senior churchmen tell us, not as some sadistic place of fire, brimstone and perpetual torment, but as being so opposed to God that you are cast into an outer darkness of non-being, thus it would seem that the gates of hell are shut forever and heaven is our eternal home – provided that we respond to the love and compassion of God as revealed in Jesus. But is this accepted by orthodox teaching? Pope Paul VI 'Solemni hac liturgia' 1968 states "that those who have refused to respond to God's laws will, in the end, be consigned to the fire that is never extinguished."

Words can have many meanings and interpretations – fragile fabrics of forensic fancy – which takes me back to Dante's The Divine Comedy, written between 1308 and 1321 in which he tells of an imaginary journey through Hell, Purgatory and Paradise. The journey is symbolic of the spiritual quest for salvation. It involves recognising sin (the journey through Hell or the inferno), rejecting sin and awaiting redemption (the time in Purgatory) and finally achieving salvation through faith in divine revelation (seeing the light of God in Paradise). Dante believed that faith was the most important value in life. Next to faith, however, he saw reason as the highest human value. Dante Alighieri was born in Florence of an old distinguished family. Little is known of his early life, but one event from his youth stands out. At the age of nine he attended a May Day party at the home of a gentleman named Folco Portinari. There he met and fell in love with Portinaris daughter, Beatrice who was eight years old. He met Beatrice again nine years later and it was at this meeting that she first spoke to him. A misunderstanding developed between them, and before it could be mended Beatrice died. Dante was heartbroken. Although he eventually married and had children, Beatrice's spirit dominated his emotional and religious life, as well as his literary work, for as long as he lived. He died in exile in Ravenna in 1321 away from his wife and children, in his beloved Florence, aged 58.

Eureka!

According to the space scientists there is a Hell! – a crater in the third quadrant of the face of the moon about 20 miles in diameter. Perhaps, one day I'll visit it!

107. 1996

In Praise of Entomology

"All creatures great and small – the Lord God made them All." I'm a reluctant gardener – one of necessity not choice! I take up the spade in springtime without any feeling of exhilaration or enthusiasm – I like to see things natural and undisturbed. The enigma of life and of natural phenomena is ever a mystery – is life the sum of the forces that resist death?

Consider for instance the snail – the common one, not the special small species interesting conservationists concerned with the Newbury bypass – the Desmoulin's whorl snail. When its ancestors first went ashore in the dim and distant past, food awaited them in plenty. There was everything that the heart of an amphibian could desire. Then, ages later, along came man. First of all, by industrious weeding, he takes away their natural food supply, and grows a more succulent alternative. It may be annoying when a row of precious seedlings disappear overnight – but can it be wondered that these little creatures came along from all directions to breed and multiply in a land of plenty? Chronologically speaking it is we who are the thieves and intruders not the snails – who are a pest only because we have made them thus!

In many respects it is our superior – we envy the snails ability to see round corners? With its periscope eyes, sprung in such a way that the slightest touch sends them travelling down to safety inside the hollow tentacles, it can see without being seen, and if, by some mischance an eye is damaged or lost, at little or no inconvenience, another is grown. It can head for a row of cabbages without lifting a foot. The technique is to glue itself to the ground and glide forward by means of a series of muscular contractions that ripple across the underside of its single foot. A pedal gland at the front end of the foot, just below the mouth, is the organ by which a smooth mucous carpet is laid on which to tread. The mouth of the snail is a mowing machine of the highest efficiency, consisting of a horny jaw and a tongue with some 15-20,000 teeth. Unlike our machines, the cutters are always sharp with the teeth renewed as fast as they wear away.

Common garden snails are protandric hermaphroditus in which the male elements ripen before the female. The individual functions first as a male and then goes off and fulfils the role of a female, each laying the eggs that the other has rendered fertile. Prior to the union, each individual unsheathes a small calcareous dart or arrow and with a slight screwing motion fires it firmly into the body of its partner. Before it is fired, the cupid's love dart lies in a muscular sac on the right side of the head. Once the bolt has been shot, the sac is empty and it takes about a week for another dart to form – thus the shaft of love must be aimed strong and true! Expectation of life is approximately eight years – barring man's inhumanity to this lesser breed which with him forms part of the fine flowers of the tree of life. During this period the snail travels a sum total of some three score miles! Perhaps, next time, when with murder in our heart we raise the spade to strike – we may spare a thought to ponder on the mystery and incomprehensibles of this our earthly life, and when the blow falls, as needs it must, think and act on the words spoken by the Lord of Life in compassion and sorrow to Judas Iscariot, the prince of evil-doers – "That thou doest, do quickly!"

Quote

Many a man thinks it is his goodness that keeps him from crime, when it is only his stomach. On half allowance or less, he would be as ugly and knavish as anybody.

(Thomas Carlyle, the Sage of Chelsea,
born 4 December 1795, at Ecclefechan,
died 1881).

108. 1996

The Enemy Within

A recent newspaper article revealed that a major city bank had hired a management consultant to introduce Japanese religious techniques. We don't usually imagine banking and Zen Buddhism having much in common. But, apparently, major corporations are queuing for this service to 'uplift business performance and the human spirit'. We are told that there is a balance between intellectualism and intuitiveness, in which the latter learns by experience which generates wisdom – a feature of the Japanese religious faith. All my friends at Morley Green who have visited 'Boscobel' realise that I have a great affection for Gotama Buddha who died some 544 BC. His wisdom was profound – hence his statue in a place of honour in the lounge. What did he say and teach? For example:- "People are in bondage, because they have not yet removed the idea of 'I' as the centre of their lives." "Faith without knowledge leads to the conceit of ignorance; and knowledge without faith begets a stony heart. Therefore only as those two are well-blended do they become the basis of good deeds." "To see another's fault is easy; to see one's own is hard. Men winnow the faults of others like chaff; their own they hide as a crafty gambler hides a losing throw."

One greater than Buddha reminds us of "the beam in our own eye." Most of us have this defect, which causes us to squint. Since God loves all his children He must often find us very peculiar – some of us are so skilful that we deceive ourselves! Somebody, the name escapes me, has well said, "People who have to stand on their dignity, are usually of small moral stature." We stand on our dignity when it is not there. We battle strenuously for Truth, without knowing exactly what it is. We air our wisdom eloquently whilst we are in fact babes in understanding. How quaint and childlike we must seem to God! All of us claim to be rational beings. If we have some enthusiasms we seek to hide them. If we are deeply moved – unless it is something tremendously important – like body-line bowling or supporting Manchester United – we control ourselves. Other folks may get sentimental, but our conduct is always the result of calm reasoning and sober judgements! It is a pity we cannot laugh at ourselves sometimes. If you and I get to Heaven, we shall have lots of fun when, in reflection, we remember our past life on earth.

Of course the fact is our conduct is almost completely directed by our emotions. In women this is regarded as a virtue. We call it their sublime gift of intuition. Men, supposedly feel, then act, and later produce (very cleverly) reasons for their actions. Often they seem very good reasons, even then women usually see through them! Again our feelings often harden into opinions with the result that we are prejudiced about almost everything and everybody. The last stage of this insidious disease comes when we begin to call our prejudices principles. Mention words like Capitalist, Bolshevist, Catholic, Socialist, Conservative and the blood pressure of many of us is affected. Yet all the time we keep up our pose of rationality. We surround our pet fallacies with logic-tight barriers and refuse to face facts. Sooner or later we have to face them. Why not now? Prejudices poison life. We never have the whole truth on our side; almost always we have prejudged the issue. If we could curb our tongues and keep an open mind, the world would be a better place (who said – speech is silver, but silence is golden)?

Most of us, unfortunately, look at others and at life with a squint, thus we see things rather twisted. Glasses are available to correct this – but we don't need them we are sure we don't squint. It is a good job God can see straight. We know He can, for we have seen Jesus moving among us. If we were more like Him we should find that the world is peopled with interesting and loveable folk, of all colours and creeds – few of whom agree with us! It might be a good thing to include in our prayers the simple prayer – 'O God remove our squint. Give us clear, straight, vision, that we may see Thy beauty in all whom we meet.' Amen.

Sermons in Sentences

Seven days without prayer makes one weak. Think of self and trouble grows. Think of God and trouble goes.

109. 1996

After Many Years

I came across a quotation by Miguel Cervantes (1547–1616) the other day, which read "God bless the inventor of sleep, the cloak that covers all men's thoughts, the food that cures all hunger – the balancing weight that levels the shepherd with the King and the simple with the wise." During this warm spell of weather I find 'dropping off to sleep' very difficult. Normally, I'm a poor sleeper, probably due to a bad conscience, but in hot weather the problem proliferates. The quotation from Cervantes was on my mind and I recollected that many years ago I received, in my youth, a Sunday School prize. It was his masterpiece Don Quixote. I tried to read it, but its theme was beyond my comprehension and it has gathered dust over the years on my bookshelves. I decided to 'give it a go again' as bedtime reading and have found it very rewarding! Miguel de Cervantes, the son of a wandering apothecary or druggist, was born near Madrid, Spain, in 1547. In 1569 seeing no prospects at home, he enlisted in the army, was wounded at the Battle of Lepanto in 1571 leaving his left hand crippled. He was later captured by Barbary pirates and held as a slave for 5 years in Algeria. He returned to Spain in 1580, jobless, in debt, and without any hope of regaining his army career. Over the years he worked as a playwright, bureaucrat and tax collector, before finally landing in jail for failure to pay his debts, many of which had accrued as a result of his family scraping together the ransom money to buy his freedom from the pirates.

According to legend, it was while he was in jail that the idea for Don Quixote came to him. His hero, Don Quixote, is a poor, ageing landowner who reads nothing but romantic tales of chivalry. As he teeters on the edge of insanity, the old man becomes convinced that he is a knight-errant, even though the age of knights is long past. At the age of 58, Cervantes now became a famous author, but was still poor. The publishers retained the copyright of his book and reaped the lion's share of its profits. Spain's greatest writer died in poverty on 22 April, 1616. To his family, Cervantes left only a little money and many debts. To the world he left a comic masterpiece that earned him the title of 'father of the modern novel'.

Don Quixote is a satire, which, like all satires, seeks to ridicule human weakness, vice or folly. Cervantes satirised the romántic tales of chivalry that were still popular and portrayed a world that no longer existed, and indeed had never really existed. He included the institutions of his day using an exaggeration of verbal irony, saying one thing and meaning another. Quixote tries to set himself up like the knights of old, but his armour is rusty, his horse an old nag, and his noble squire a chubby peasant who does not particularly respect his master, much less feel like laying down his life for him. As observed, Cervantes' voice is often ironic – saying one thing and meaning another, e.g. the village curate is described as a 'learned man' a graduate of Siguenza, which was in fact, a minor institution with a poor reputation! The comment pokes fun at people who show off their learning and academic prowess. He differentiates between the romantic and the real, the false and the genuine. Probably there is something of Don Quixote in all of us, who wished to live before his time and like Cervantes himself who aspired to be a great military hero and was thus denied by circumstances. We, all of us, have dreams that cannot come true, but we cannot relinquish these dreams without giving up an importance part of ourselves.

> If there were dreams to sell, what would you buy?
> Some cost a passing bell; some a light sigh,
> That shakes from Life's fresh crown. Only a roseleaf down.
> If there were dreams to sell, merry and sad to tell,
> And the crier rang the bell, what would you buy?
>
> (Thomas Lovell Beddoes, 1803-1849)

A Northamptonshire Women's Institute ran a competition, some time ago, to find out 'the most useless gadget in your kitchen'. It was won by the member who submitted a photograph of her husband!

110. 1996

The Real Enemy

> Monday's child is fair of face, Tuesday's child is full of grace; Wednesday's child is full of woe; Thursday's child has far to go; Friday's child is loving and giving; Saturday's child works hard for a living, and the child that is born on the Sabbath day is fair and wise and good and gay.

Thus the old proverb – how wrong can it be! We are not born to failure or achievement in life – we make, or mar, our own destiny – integrity of character and the will to persevere and endure, are characteristics endemic to human nature – to rise on stepping stones of our dead selves to higher things. Goethe reminds us that talent develops in quiet places and character is the full current of human life. Helen Keller, blind and deaf, has stated that we could never learn to be brave and patient if there were only joy in the world; and William Penn (no cross, no crown) out of his own experiences of life said, "No pain – no palm; no thorns – no throne; no gall – no glory; no cross – no crown."

During the 1950s and 1960s when I was engaged in Further and Higher Education, I was invited to visit East Germany – (then the German Democratic Republic) several times, staying sometimes in the environs of Weimar and becoming acquainted with its two famous sons – Goethe and Schiller – lovers of freedom and humanity. Ironically nearby was the Buchenwald concentration camp – now a memorial to the dead, the grimmest possible reminder of man's inhumanity to man. Here are isolation cells with photographs of some of the many thousands tortured to death in them, plus many other relics of Hitler's Third Reich and the dreaded SS.

Pierre d'Harcourt, a member of a distinguished French family, enlisted in the French resistance movement and was betrayed and spent the last two years of the war in Buchenwald. His book 'The Real Enemy' tells of his experiences there. The degradation and inhumanity of the camp, starvation diet, torture and intense cold in winter, made beasts of some men and saints of others. It was hard to predict who would be the saint and who the beast when the time of trial came, men famous and honoured as soldiers and natural leaders, often showed neither spirit, or authority, in the camp. Other men, of seemingly mediocre brains, ability and character, who would never have been noticed in ordinary times, shone out like beams as the true leaders. Under the stresses and strains imposed by life in the camp, only one thing prevailed – strength of character. Cleverness, creativeness, learning, all went down, only real goodness survived. Sooner or later weakness of fibres were revealed in a man, and sooner or later it destroyed him, and he gave up the struggle for survival, self-discipline was essential and this is the basis of character. To d'Harcourt, those men displayed most character, who had the capacity for living, whatever the circumstances, and these men possessed something which is easiest described as religion, faith and devotion. He saw it exercised mainly by those with a Christian belief – who still had some inner core which gave them a belief in life, when the rest were lost. Buchenwald showed him that a man's real enemies are not always ranged against him along the borders of a hostile country; they are often among his own people, indeed within his own mind. He realised that the worst enemies we have to face in life are hatred, greed and cruelty. The real enemy is within ourselves.

The Reason

We all wondered why the Ladies Circle meeting was packed, until someone pointed out an item in the church magazine had announced that Miss Roberts would give a talk on glove-making, but had missed out the 'g'.

Too True

Free cheese is only found in mousetraps.
(Russian proverb)

111. 1997

Yesteryears and this New Year

I somehow recollect that it has been observed that memory and hope are intertwined, one looks backward, the other forward. The one is of today and the other is the tomorrow that we anticipate. Many years ago when I was engaged in serving Tatton St Hulme as minister, on occasions I attended Cavendish Congregational Church, All Saints, Manchester – long passed into oblivion – but in its day one of the university attended churches by students and staff in Manchester. In the pre-1914 days, a full-time sister was appointed – something of an innovation. A list of regulations was drawn up and she was required always to carry a Bible and pledge cards with her and, if possible, to read a portion and offer a short prayer in each home visited. She had to carry out the instructions of the minister under whose direction all her work must be done. She must spend twenty-five hours a week in house-to-house visitation and, unless engaged in sick nursing, she must make not less than one hundred visits a week! Saturday was a free day! She agreed to give or accept one month's notice from any date, and received £52 per annum, paid monthly, and an allowance of £2 per annum toward the costs of boots and uniform, no mention was made of any annual holiday, that was to be negotiated.

These were 'The Good Old Days'

Reading the report 'Households Below Average Income' (The Stationery Office) makes one realise that, in these days of 'progress', (due to modern science and technology), the gap between rich and poor should cause us some grave concern, nearly one household in six in Britain is living below the poverty line. One in three children are growing up in a family without anybody in a full-time job. The unofficial poverty line – half average income, almost tripled from 5 million in 1979, to 14 million in the 1990s. We accuse our juveniles of 'primitivism' but they have grown up in a society where the urge to work and provide for themselves and others, to win respect from the community, to father and rear children in a loving family, has been undermined by mass unemployment and poverty; giving them no future to strive for. The very few contemporary role models that exist for youth, reflect this inarticulate hedonistic resignation – certain 'football stars', entertainers and programmes on radio and television! One of the characteristics of the evangelizing church of the early years of Christianity which attracted the pagan world was the reality of its fellowship. The converts took upon themselves new responsibilities, becoming members of a community which, with all its limitations, was different in kind from any other, and in this community they found support, fellowship and joy. The church, in 1997 and beyond, will never get very far in its mission of evangelisation, unless it can offer the same attraction and witness as the family of God, breaking down those divisions and barriers which set people apart from one another, giving them a sense of unity and purpose and togetherness in life. May the spirit move us in the new year and equip us for the new age of fellowship, freedom and opportunity for all.

Quote

Use your talents some lives to brighten
As through life they weary plod;
Place your bank account in Heaven
And grow rich towards your God.

True love is drowned by no billows of mischance.
True love fears no thunderbolts of fate.
True love abides immortal, firm, unchangeable,
To have loved once, is to have loved for aye.

(Wisharts's – Deeds of Montrose)

112. 1997

Biotypes (The Link between Personality and Health)

Looking back over a long and eventful life, I'm conscious of the fact that I've been privileged to visit many countries including hundreds of cities and places of interest and beauty. Now the motivation for travel and adventure has departed and memories of yesteryears remain a sustaining influence. Two places I regret not having visited, the Caucasus mountains of the old Soviet Union and the Andes mountains in South America. Tradition says that in the former, the Golden Fleece, of Greek mythology, was supposed to have been sheared there, whilst the latter, the Inca Indian legend is that one of the valleys was the true Paradise from which Adam and Eve were expelled! The really interesting fact is that in these two areas there are well above the average number of people who enjoy long, healthy lives and who die, aged over ninety and one hundred years, not from disease, but from old age, with their faculties intact. Thus whereas humans' immune systems deteriorate with chronological ageing, opening them more to disease than when they were young, here people managed to live long, disease-free lives. Moreover the key to their exceptional lifespans appear to lie more in their personalities and lifestyles than in their genes or environment. We're all now familiar with the concept of psychosomatic treatment – the word derived from two Greek words – psyche (soul) and some (body) indicating the influence of mind and body and the physical health. We have become familiar with the concept of stress, the toll that it can take on a person's wellbeing, and the fact that we can modify our reactions to it. Yet ill health still threatens many of us in spite of this knowledge, and in spite of such wonders of modern medicine as vaccines, antibiotics, brain and heart scans and microsurgery. Psychosomatic treatment, as used by Jesus, goes back a long way. In AD 200 the Greek philosopher and physician Galen, estimated that some 60 per cent of his patients suffered symptoms derived from emotional rather than organic origin. Sydenham and Harvey in the seventeenth century stated that hysteria symptoms may simulate all forms of organic diseases.

People who have worked with centenarians often find a psychosomatic component – they are people who have aged without illness, because they have never let 'things' grind them down! Thus, in life, there may be such a thing as a disease free personality? Investigations in the Caucasus and the Andes into the lives of their many centenarians suggest that a major key to their health and longevity was their profound involvement with life from an early age up to the time of death. Helpless, hopeless, disease-prone persons they were not. They worked hard and they played hard all their lives. Life was always full of interest and purpose. Perhaps that was the secret of the longevity of Leopold Stokowski (95), Arturo Toscanini (90), Bruno Walter (85) and Bertrand Russell (97), Pablo Picasso (91) and Grandma Moses (102) was still busy painting right up to her death. All were able to confront stresses rather than to react helplessly to them. Caucasian children learn at an early age that excuses are not acceptable, problems are meant to be overcome and they must look for solutions and when something is broken, it must be mended, whether a vase or a friendship. Voltaire reminds us that work and interest in life banishes those three great evils, boredom, vice and poverty. When work is a pleasure, life is a joy! When work is a duty, life is slavery). (Maxim Gorky).

Ecclesiastes (9 v 10) states, "Whatsoever thy hand findeth to do, do it with thy might, for there is no work, nor device, nor knowledge, nor wisdom in the grave." Let us then be up and doing!

Let us then be up and doing!

A Sting in the 'Tale'

A policeman on night duty saw a stationary car outside a factory and being suspicious, waited beside it. A man came out shortly afterwards from the main gates and hurried into the car. The officer questioned him and asked him for his name and address. The man gave his name as Cuddlebrake. The officer, not satisfied, decided to check the man's identity. He went to the gatekeeper and asked, "Have you got a Cuddlebrake here?" The gateman replied, "I don't know about that, it has taken us 10 years to get a tea break."

That Essential Hyphen

A man-eating fish is likely to terrify swimmers, whereas a man eating fish is probably putting salt on his chips!

113. 1997

Relativity ($E = mc^2$)

The theory of relativity was formulated by Albert Einstein in 1905, recognising the impossibility of determining absolute motion and leading to the concept of a four-dimensional space-time continuum. It was devised to simplify the theory of electromagnetism. The Special theory (1905) was followed in 1915 by the General theory which involved a new twist in the concept of space-time. I'm already out of my depth – but it suffices to say that General Relativity remains central to modern astrophysics and cosmology.

Einstein states that the whole of science is nothing more than a refinement of everyday thinking. He simplifies the issues by saying, "When a man sits with a pretty girl for an hour, it seems like a minute. But let him sit on a hot stove for a minute – and it's longer than any hour – That's relativity."

There's a story about how Albert Einstein, expounding his theory of relativity, travelled to many of the smaller universities and colleges in the USA, delivering lectures on this subject. During one journey, in his chauffeur-driven car, the chauffeur remarked "Dr Einstein, I've heard you deliver this lecture about 30 times. I know it by heart and bet I could give it myself." Well, I'll give you the chance," said Einstein. "They don't know me at the next college, so when we get there I'll put on your cap and you introduce yourself as me and give the lecture." The chauffeur delivered Einstein's lecture flawlessly. When he had finished he started to leave, but one of the professors stopped him and asked a very complex question filled with mathematical equations and formulas. The chauffeur thought fast – "The solution to that problem is quite simple," he said. "I'm surprised you have to ask me. In fact to show you just how simple it is, I'm going to ask my chauffeur to come up here and answer your question".

In Trinity College, Cambridge, there is a manuscript dated 1530 which, translated into modern English reads, If your lips would keep from slips, five things observe with care! To whom you speak, of whom you speak, and how, and when and where. It is no uncommon experience in life to be talking both to a person and of him. Sir Arthur Sullivan was standing at the back of the stalls at one of the D'Oyley Carte performances and began to hum one of the tunes being sung on the stage. An irritable old gentleman turned to him with the remark, "I paid to hear Sullivan's music not yours." James Agate, the writer and critic, once wandered into a bookshop at Leamington and found there a volume of his literary offspring. Feigning an airy unconcern he asked the bookseller whether he had much sale for this author. The answer came promptly and emphatically that there was no sale at all. "But yet you stock him?" said the crestfallen author, unwilling to believe the truth. Then came the knockout blow! "No, sir, we do not stock him. That is a copy ordered by a chance customer and never collected."

The Bible has many instances of talking to and of; the famine-stricken sons of Jacob, when they went down into Egypt and had an interview with the Grand Vizier, told him of their long-dead brother, Joseph. They did not dream that this lordly person whom they were addressing, the controller of Egypt's corn, was he. At Eastertide we recollect that in the Arimathean's garden in the half light of dawn, Mary accosted the gardener and asked him where the body of Jesus had been laid. She found that the 'gardener' was the Risen Lord Himself. Later that same day two wayfarers on the Emmaus Road fell into step with a stranger to whom they spoke of "a Prophet mighty in deed and word." By evening they knew who their fellow-traveller had been.

Quote

Science without religion is lame. Religion without science is blind.

(Albert Einstein 1879–1955)

Irish Logic

The railway station at Ballyhough had two clocks, which disagreed by some six minutes. When an irate traveller asked a porter what was the use of having two clocks if they didn't tell the same time the porter replied – "And what would we be wanting with two clocks if they told the same time?"

114. 1997

Measurements? Christian Standard – The Measure of the Stature of the Fullness of Christ – Ephesians 4 v13

Checking some facts in Cruden's Concordance recently I came across the cubit – length of Ark – 300c, Goliath's height 6c. Intrigued I consulted my Random House Dictionary

– "An ancient linear unit based on the length of the forearm, usually from 17-21 inches". There was a time when there were no measures, and the first measure was the breadth of the finger – a 'digit'. A piece of wood was measured by so many finger breadths. To make it easier a 'palm' was four fingers-breadth. Then followed the cubit which originally was two 'spans' equal to six 'palms'. In the Bible the King was measured by a 'Royal cubit' i.e. 'seven palms' (lucky for him). Then the foot was introduced, not 12 inches but your own foot. (I would have fared badly with small feet, unlike a policeman's). The yard at first meant a step, but everyone's paces were different. King Henry I began to rectify matters – a yard was to be the length of his arm – thus the first effort for standardisation! A pound was the amount of bread a man could eat in a day. An acre was the amount of land an ox could plough in a day. A bushel, the amount of seed to sow an acre. Some people ate a lot and some little and different oxen ploughed more or less. In Leviticus 2 we read about when they were sharing out flour – everyone was to take a 'handful' – what an advantage if you had a big fist!

Today we've gone metric – I still mentally convert everything back to feet and inches. Pity us old 'uns! An old man who did the sweeping up in a saw mill was asked what he thought about the change over from feet and inches to metres, centimetres and millimetres. He thought for while and said, "We're getting a lot more sawdust." The days of ft, in, yd, lb, cwt, fl oz and teaspoonfuls are gone forever! In their places we have mm, ml, kg, gsm, (g/m^2). Everything of a metric nature is governed by the requirements of the SI system, which covers a whole range of both simple everyday units and fiendishly scientific terms. Some of the units are named after great scientists, such as James Watt, Isaac Newton and Andre-Marie Ampère, for whom the respective symbols are WN and A. For example the Newton is a unit of force equivalent to about 10g which just happens to be the weight of a medium sized apple.

The older we get the more life becomes complicated. I long for the furtherance in life of Thomas à Kempis great beatitude – "Blessed is Simplicity". On reflection, standardisation has some advantages, the billion meant different things depending on where you lived. It is one thousand million in America but, until a few years ago, it was one million million in Europe. We have now settled with the United States for their standard. But again there was never really any confusion between the big billion and the small billion; as the difference was only 999,000 million! A mere bagatelle when you are counting your blessings!

If (After Rudyard Kipling)

If you can stand before false accusations and lift your head in grace and face the lies; if you can join in another's celebrations, while your life falls in ruins before your eyes. If you can grieve with others who are grieving, yet find in Christ a peace beyond all griefs; if you can love those who are unbelieving, and yet stand firm and sure on your beliefs. If you can lose all wealth and earthly treasures, and count it as the loss of so much dust; if you can scorn success by mortal measure, striving for reward that cannot rust. If you can put your hand to Christian labour, be buried with Christ, your sins all put to end; if every day you can love your neighbour, you will receive the crown of life, my friend.

Teacher – "The man named Lot was warned to take his wife and flee from the city, but his wife was turned to salt."

Small Boy – "What happened to the flea?"

Just a Thought!

A free thinker is a man who isn't married

115. 1997

Tolerance

"If you cannot mould yourself as you would wish, how can you expect other people to be entirely to your liking? (Thomas à Kempis, 1380–1471 – 'The Imitation of Christ'). If I were to be marooned on a desert island I would like the above book for a companion: plus the 'Conversations of Goethe with Eckermann' (Everyman Library) and; for good measure 'The Fables of Aèsop! The latter's life was a paradox (620–560 BC) illiterate yet intellectual, born a Phrygian slave, becoming a freeman, birthplace uncertain, slave of Ladmon of Samos, described as ugly and deformed. Tradition states that he met with a violent death in the hands of the inhabitants of Delphi – they didn't like what he thought about them! From his fable of the Fox and the Grapes, we understand the meaning of the term 'sour grapes' and from the fable of the Lion and the Mouse, the moral lesson that without good nature and gratitude, we would live in a wilderness of indifference and selfishness. In life the great and the small, the rich and the poor have need of each other. Life entails a caring and a sharing for each other in mutual help and co-operation. The fables of Aèsop, in which he used animals as his examples, help us to understand this.

The story of his life tells us that one day Aèsop, then living in Argos, set out to visit Corinth, some fifteen miles away, for the first time. The journey took him up hill and down dale, through wood and lonely paths. For a long time he met no one, but about half-way he met a man who was coming from Corinth. The stranger asked the way to Argos and Aèsop gave him directions. The man asked the question, "Can you tell me what kind of people live there?" Before answering Aèsop said, "You've never been to Argos and I've never been to Corinth, can you tell me what kind of people live in Corinth, where I'm going? The man replied "Oh, I'm sorry for you, they are a wretched crowd at Corinth, selfish and mean. I'm glad to leave them and I only hope the people in Argos will be better." Aèsop said, "I'm sorry to hear that, because you'll find just the same sort of people there in Argos." They parted, and the man walked slowly on his way to his destination with heavy step. A little later Aèsop met another traveller coming from Corinth who also asked him for directions to get to Argos, which were readily given. The man thanked him, and also asked the question, "What sort of people will I find there?" "Well," said Aèsop, "I go to Corinth, what kind of people did you leave there?" The answer was, "Oh, I'm sorry to leave there; I don't suppose I shall ever find better people than they are, so kind and friendly. If only I were not seeking work I should never leave Corinth. I only hope that the people of Argos will be a little like them." "Never fear," said Aèsop, "I'm glad to tell you that you will find the same sort in Argos." The man, with keen anticipation, went on his way with joy and thankfulness. The moral is that in life, we generally find what we look for, good or bad, so often if we expect to find apathy, selfishness and indifference, we find what we anticipate. If we seek that which is genuine, reliable and honest, these are the qualities we find, appreciate and value.

My granny, a wise old girl of blessed memory, had her own rule of life and behaviour in often saying, "There is so much good in the worst of us, and so much bad in the best of us, that it ill becomes any of us to talk about the rest of us!" Jesus put all this in correct perspective in Matthew 7 v 3 – "Why do you look at the speck of sawdust in your brother's eye, with never a thought for the great plank in your own?" Bertrand Russell, in his Sceptical Essays, states that there are two kinds of morality side by side; one which we preach but do not practise and the other which we practise but seldom preach – the latter is to be preferred!

An Early Start

Small girl – "Why doesn't baby talk?"
Mother – "He can't talk yet, small babies never do."
Small girl – "Oh yes they do. Teacher read the other day from the Bible how Job cursed the day he was born."

Tit for Tat

A dead donkey, partially covered over, had been left in a field near the minister's house, from a previous gypsy encampment. The minister of the church wrote to the local council about it and they replied facetiously, that they understood that it was a minister's duty to bury the dead! He replied that he knew that, but he wanted first to let the relatives know!

116. 1997

Again in Retrospect

John Ruskin, MA, LLD, my favourite Victoria author, in writing "Sesame and Lilies" – a. of King's Treasure, and b. of Queen's Gardens, dedicated this volume to the influence of good books and of good women in his life. I endorse whole-heartedly his dedication. As one having 'many books' and probably the same number of the latter! who have, and will continue to influence me ad infinitum. Often surveying my bookshelves I reflect that tempus fugit and I must read 'that' book which challenges me, like Saint Augustine, "to take up and read". One such book was Candide by Voltaire. The book is subtitled 'Optimism' and tells the tale of the woes that befall a naïve simpleton who is brought up to believe that the world is the best of all possible worlds. The point of Voltaire's story is to show how Candide's optimism is foolish in a world in which people's lives are shaped for the most part by cruel and sometimes incomprehensible forces. The story takes the form of a quest; the young man's quest for union with his beloved Cunegoude. They go through many separations and reunions, but some how the two lovers survive. The tale is told with great verve and hilarity and, like life itself, the journey involves much suffering, trial and tribulation intermingled with joy, happiness and hope. Voltaire had little patience for purely metaphysical speculation, his attitude to life was 'down to earth' and practical, reflected in the last page of Candide – "Let us work without arguing... It's the only way to make life endurable."

Voltaire (1694-1778), whose full name was François-Marie Arouet de Voltaire, was a writer who believed in writing the truth. He criticized the wastefulness of war, religious intolerance, and the unnecessary poverty and powerlessness of the average citizen. As a result of his frankness he was twice imprisoned, once exiled from Paris, had his books and pamphlets banned by the French government, and was denied burial by the Parisian Clergy when he died. Yet the spirit of his writings prevailed and 13 years after his death, the new post revolutionary government brought Voltaire's remains back to Paris with great ceremony and thousands of people lined the streets to see the funeral procession. I cherish his 'Philosophical Dictionary' (selected and arranged by H.I. Woolf). His reflections on God, friendship, etc. are most revealing. I append a brief selection of the wisdom of Voltaire.

    a. Work banishes those 3 great evils – boredom, vice and poverty.

    b. I disapprove of what you say, but I will defend to the death your right to say it.

    c. Faith consists in believing when it is beyond the power of reason to believe. It is not enough that a thing be possible for it to be believed.

    d. If God did not exist, it would be necessary to invent Him.

Press Cuttings

Essex County Council, which is currently seeking to cut costs by £25 million, has authorised £7,000 to be spent on the number plate for its official car.

A Lotus Elite sports car, brought in for service more than 30 years ago but never claimed or collected by the owner, is being sold by a Buckinghamshire garage for £30,000.

A Shrewsbury vicar won first prize in a local quiz. His prize was a copy of Teach Yourself Christianity.

Colour Blind

I am black, I was born black. When I go out in the sun, I'm still black. When I am sick, I am black; when they bury me, I am black. You are white, you were born pink. When you go out in the sun, you turn red, then you go brown. When you are sick, you turn white. When you are dying, you go grey. When they bury you, you are purple. And you have the nerve to call me coloured! (West Tanfield Magazine)

117. 1998

The "Christmas Spirit" and the Christian Life

Except for a small minority, Christmas is no longer primarily a religious festival. For so many, the spiritual emphasis of Christmas – carols, nativity plays, church services, is an optional extra which doesn't interest them. First and foremost it is now a time for family celebration and of consumerism. As a nation we now leave out, or neglect, the religious content of Christmas. In recent decades we have manufactured Christmas into an idealised dreamtime of happy family life sandwiched between spending sprees. We live in an age of consumerism; personal affluence and keeping up with (or bettering) our neighbours, motivates society. Thus, as a nation, we respond to the trappings of inclusiveness – the television and radio laden with seasonal goodies, saturation advertising, decorations, etc, all inviting us to spend more and more. This must sharpen the misery of those left out, the poor, the destitute and homeless, the single and the childless. The 'Festive Season' and its aftermath is the busiest time of the year for the Samaritans, dealing with the concerns of the steep rise in the victims of domestic violence, suicides and the sheer destitution and misery of the have-nots of society. This Christmas is the time when we should reassess our values – our giving and our service to others in the light of Him who came that all of us might have more abundant life. It has been well said that there is enough in the world for everyone's needs, but not for everyone's greed. Some 12 years ago the Church of England published 'Faith in the City', based on the simple assumption that, in a decent society, eliminating poverty is a moral obligation. The Beveridge Report, of blessed memory, was a scholarly account of how the four horsemen of the post-war apocalypse – poverty, unemployment, ignorance and disease, could be dealt with. Complacent self-interest must be superseded for the common good. The recent publication by the Rowntree Foundation stated that the creation of an underclass, permanently alienated from the rest of society, is certain to end in disaster, creating conditions which end in unrest, leading to riot, arson and looting. In a decent society people should be helped according to need, not desserts. Our concern should be with remedies rather than with blame.

At Christmas, the season of goodwill, we should remember that Jesus in His ministry took many old laws by which society had lived, and filled them full of new meaning. But there were also some new laws which He framed. One of them was the law of forgiving love and another, the law to 'bear one another's burdens'. These laws embrace and further the true and really worthwhile Christmas spirit.

Updating Scripture

At a school nativity play in Derby, three six-year-old boys were cast as the Kings. Presenting their gifts at the stable the first said, "Gold your Majesty," the second, "Myrrh your Majesty," and the third, "And Frankie sent this."

Pass it on

If you see someone without a smile – give them one of yours.

Upward an Onward

Why not go forward singing all the way, it makes the journey through life easier.

(Virgil)

118. 1998

Songs of Praise

This 'new introduction', held every two months, is very popular with the membership! Perhaps it is a wee protest against the everlasting 'preaching of the Word' – the preacher; six feet about contradiction, often out of touch with reality, pontificating and indulging in flights of forensic fancy – just to show how clever and informed he (she) is! Recently, at an evening service in Stockport, I was challenged from 'the floor' during the address. There followed an interchange of views, which at least kept the congregation awake!

So often our services are stereotyped and formal, packed with strange words and terms like incarnation, redemption and the need to be 'saved'. The disciples asked Jesus to teach them to pray and He gave them a simple formula known as the Lord's Prayer, and He also told them to chat to God, as a child would to a loving parent. Today we receive leaflets advertising courses in prayer and spirituality – held at 'retreat houses', costing quite a large sum of money. The impression is given that prayer is a technique that only intelligent, well-informed people can assimilate. The same applies to the Bible. The four Gospels were actually composed like children's books, divided into short chapters, each with a good story or some witty saying. The story of the Good Samaritan and the Prodigal Son still continue to capture our imagination and be a guide to living and behaviour. The Bible is a library of 66 books, 39 + 27, and at least half of it is virtually unreadable, full of contradictions, cruelty and behaviour at variance to the life and teaching of Jesus.

Some time ago a survey was conducted to discover who was the most popular religious figure in Britain today. It wasn't a bishop or cleric, but Thora Hird, who was associated in the public mind with loving and putting into practical living, the sentiments expressed in our hymns. It is our hymn writers who, over the centuries, have most successfully reached the hearts and minds of ordinary folk. Charles Wesley, Isaac Watts and the great army of hymn writers took the tunes sung in the taverns and gave them simple Christian words. They, with the compilers of our hymn books, had a genius for marrying vivid poetry with stirring melodies. Small wonder that at least five times more people watch Songs of Praise each Sunday than attend a live worship in church. We shall sing our hymns and read our Bibles with one aim in view – to help us to know Jesus better and to strive to follow His example in the living of our lives. Regarding the latter, Paul reminds us that we have this treasure in earthen vessels!

Value for Money

In 1274 the Bible was in nine volumes. To own one it cost £33.6s.9d. to purchase. The average wage of a labourer was 1s.5d. per day. Thus for him to own a Bible he would have needed to work 5,333 days to get one. Consequently the poor were Bibleless.

Irishism

One Irishman was telling another how God always ensures people's misfortunes are compensated in some way. If someone has bad eyesight, the sense of smell is heightened. If the hearing is poor, the sight is better. "To be sure," says the listener, "I've always noticed that whenever someone has a short leg, the other is always a bit longer."

119. 1998

Things Immemorial and Discovery

When I was a small boy my constant companion lived with his mother next door. She was a teacher, always asking questions, and I tried to give her a wide berth, but not always succeeding. One day she asked me, "What was the largest island in the world before Australia was discovered?" The answer was 'Australia' because it had always been there before it was 'discovered'. When Sir Isaac Newton sat in his garden that day long ago and a falling apple attracted his attention, we know what followed. He discovered the law of gravitation. The law had always been at work in the universe, Newton only discovered it. When wee James Watt, in his humble Scottish home, watched the kettle-lid jumping up and down, he also made a discovery. The fire had generated steam, and steam meant power. Yet that power had always been there, mankind had not seen how it could be used. From that simple beginning came the steam engine, then the loco-motive, then the great ocean liners. When the Wright Brothers started to build a machine which, though heavier than air, could fly, they did not create new laws but found certain laws governing such a project, and so the science of aviation developed. So with electricity and magnetism, electromagnetic waves, which caused a travelling disturbance in space, a discovery leading to radio, television, computers, etc. there from the beginning of time! We progress from the relative to the absolute. As Pippa reminds us, "God's in His Heaven, All's well with the world."

A Good Man

Not all Presidents of the United States, past or present, qualify for the term 'good'. One is outstanding with Abe Lincoln, and he's still around – Jimmy Carter, who today is still a Sunday school teacher and preacher (Baptist). He likes to tell an old joke to explain his faith – A man has just died and stands outside Heaven's gate. He has been a successful businessman, who regularly attended church, even taught in Sunday school from time to time. Saint Peter asks the man what he has done to help others. The man answers "Back during the Depression a group of hobos came to my house and my wife fixed them sandwiches. Even in depressed dollars that was worth at least 50 cents." Saint Peter asks, "What have you done more recently?" He replied, "Matter of fact, just last year my neighbour's house burned down. I found a little table on my porch and gave it to him. That was also worth 50 cents." Saint Peter then sent an angel to verify the prospective entrant's claims. The angel reports, "What he says is absolutely true, what shall we do with him?" Saint Peter replies, "Give him back his dollar and tell him to go to Hell."

A Duty-ful Wife

A recent press report in the *Guardian* stated that a woman, whose husband died while they were on holiday abroad, phoned Manchester Airport information desk to ask if he was still entitled to his duty-free allowance for the return flight.

Church Notices

Don't let worry kill you – let the church help.

This being Easter Sunday, we will ask Mrs... to come forward and lay an egg on the altar.

Requiem

When Jesus Christ was four years old, the angels brought Him toys of gold; But with these He would not play – He made Him wild fowl out of clay. And blessed them till they flew away. Oh! Jesus Christ, Thou child so wise – Bless my hands and fill my eyes – And bring my soul to Paradise.

120. 1998

Length of Days

Of the many books for Lenten reading now available, I still return to one published in 1935 by W.R. Inge, the Dean of St Paul's 1911-1934, entitled 'The Gate of Life'. In his last sermon before his retirement from St Paul's Cathedral, he said that length of days was the boon for which many have always prayed and longed for, and then reminded the congregation that Solomon was sensible enough to pray for wisdom above all else. "We ought," he said "neither to fear death nor to wish for it." We ought to feel that death simply does not count. All that matters is that a life should be lived in service and fellowship till the time of its close. Thus the wisdom of the Dean, miscalled Gloomy. There is no gloom for those who accept that life is for living, accepting the challenge that each day is a new beginning, which we have to live and use to the full. We must admit and realise that physical wellbeing alters with the years. Brawn is no doubt pretty well exhausted at 50, but much of the best brain work of the world has been done after that age, even up to 80 and 90 years, some are still mentally young! Darwin was 56 when he published the Origin of Species; Bacon was 61 when he wrote the Novum Organum; Faraday was 53 when he made his great discovery. Kant was 64 when he wrote his Critique. Again Michelangelo was doing his superb decorations at St Peter's, Rome, at 82 and Voltaire made his triumphant entry into Paris when he was 84.

Confucius, who was no fool, used to say that until 30 a man is like a vine or ivy, with no inherent strength. At 40 he is a bare tree. At 50 he puts forth leaves. At 70 he begins to bear fruit!

Barbara Holden, on one of the cards received on her 80th birthday, read the following observation. "Every culture enriches our lives with its own unique beauty and wisdom; yet we all share the same hopes and dreams; the same need for love and home and kinship. These are the common threads that bind us together as one family in one world. A birthday is not a measure of how old we've become, but a celebration of where we are in the magical circle of life."

For many years we have misunderstood the saying, "Those whom the gods love die young." It does not mean, as we have long supposed, that if the gods love you your life will be short, but that however long you live, you will still be young! The saying is obviously Greek, the author is assumed to be Menander, an elegant writer of play and comedies, whose works have survived only in fragments over the intervening years. The secret of living is interest – continued interest in the present and the future. Old age can be defined as loss of interest in life, and there comes a time as in life, when we stand at the crossroads between old age and youth. Both roads lead to age counted in years, but one road leads to real old age, and the other leads to age that retains its youth. We note the changes about us, sometimes the past seems a golden age and we regret its passing. But whether we regret or approve, we must retain our keen interests, realising that life is more in living than in any theories about it. These may be superseded but the living of life to the full must go on. To revert to old Menander, the love of the gods shows itself in the temperament and character which makes the right choice when we come to the parting of the ways. Down one road the world merely recedes and marching becomes dull and difficult. Down the other road there is much to do and to look forward to achieving. This keeps us youthful to the end – the best is yet to be!

A sermon helps people in different ways. Some rise from it greatly strengthened, others awaken from it greatly refreshed.

121. 1998

Fiddlers – Acts Chapter 5 v 1 Ananias and Sapphira

Husband and wife withhold money for themselves that had been dedicated to the common good of the early church. When Peter confronts Sapphira with her falsehood, she lies to him about it. Like her husband Ananias, she falls down dead, as he did when he came before Peter three hours earlier. The love of money was their downfall. They were members of the early Christian Community at Jerusalem, who all agreed to share all that they had with one another, and to contribute to a common treasury to meet the common need (Acts 2 v 44 & 45, Acts 4 v 32). They entered into the agreement voluntarily and this agreement had become a sacred pledge for the faithful. Ananias and Sapphira desired credit for giving all to the church, without actually doing so. They coveted some of the money for themselves and resorted to dishonesty and untruthfulness to keep it. According to early Hebrew records, the name Sapphira means 'beautiful' and the name Ananias means 'Yahweh is gracious'. God had been gracious to them, but greed leading to dishonesty was their undoing. Yet like all other Christians they would be familiar with Christ's own words, "Ye cannot serve God and mammon." (Matthew 6 v 24).

Today we read about a happily married couple who get divorced and continue to live together – because it lowers their taxes. A nightclub performer who specialises in 'feats of memory', sheepishly told a judge that he 'forgot' to declare his income. An electrician routinely reducing his fees for customers who pay cash, so he can avoid paying VAT and income tax. Tax dodging is, perhaps, Britain's main growth industry. While tax dodging in executive suites is nothing new, the number of ordinary Britons involved in 'the tax fiddle' continues to grow, the loss to the Treasury in uncollected taxes is enormous and estimated in billions of pounds. The nation once prided itself as a law-abiding civic-minded citizenry. The change is blamed on the fact that tax rates are amongst the highest in the world and the gap between rich and poor continues to widen. The attitude is, "I have to look after my wife and kids, and if I can do it best by fiddling then I'll fiddle" – "It's the system that makes you do it" – so says a man on the dole while picking up some £80 a week in undeclared income by laying carpets. For the poor, fiddling usually means moonlighting and not declaring the income, or collecting unemployment benefit while secretly doing casual labour. Wealthier Britons have devised more elaborate schemes to fool the tax collector, often aided and abetted by 'professional' help. Traditional British integrity continues to be undermined. "How else do you expect people to live?" – asked an accountant, "many people can't 'live' on present dole, relief grants, wages or salary."

Where stands the Christian church in these matters? We know that we represent less than ten per cent of the population, but the answer is most surely found in the Life and teaching of Jesus Christ who came that all might have Life and have it more abundantly.

Torah and Talmud Truths

I went and sowed corn in my enemy's field, that men might know the ways of God. The greatest of all heroes is he that turns an enemy into a friend. (The Talmud). The Torah and Talmud contain the fundamental codes of Jewish laws and behaviour. Jesus was a Jew and there is, we trust, a lot of Him in all of us. The Benediction, which with curious misinformation many Gentiles imagine to be of Christian origin, reflects our universality – "May the Lord bless you and keep you, may the Lord make His face to shine upon you and be merciful unto you; may the Lord lift up the light of His countenance upon you, and give you peace." Amen.

Over-Due

A book borrowed from Stafford Library, in England, in 1863 has been returned by the honest librarians of the University of Chicago, USA, when they discovered who it belonged to. They cancelled the fine of £4,000 that had accrued over this period of time. The book was 'De Naturis Rerum' by Alexander Neckham.

122. 1998

Love and Marriage

W.H. Auden (1907–73) the well-loved British poet and man of letters, musing on the theme of Love wrote –

> When it comes, will it come without warning, just as I'm picking my nose? Will it knock on my door in the morning; or tread in the bus on my toes? Will it come like a change in the weather? Will its greeting be courteous or rough? Will it alter my life altogether? O tell me the truth about love.

A Swedish writer, Ellen Key, observed – "Love is moral even without legal marriage; but marriage is immoral without love." Victor Hugo, in a moment of enlightenment, stated, "The greatest happiness in life is the conviction that we are loved, loved for ourselves – say rather loved in spite of ourselves," and Avebury, of blessed memory, reflected, "Love is the light and sunshine of life. We cannot fully enjoy ourselves, or anything else, unless some one we love enjoys it with us". Finally, the sublime thoughts of Bourdillon – "the night has a thousand eyes, and the day but one, yet the light of a bright world dies with the dying sun. The Mind has a thousand eyes, and the heart but one; Yet the light of a whole life dies when its Love is done".

Mixed faith marriage has become an increasing trend, changing the face of all religious communities over Britain. Some see it as the triumph of love over tradition, others view it as a religious disaster. Dr J. Romain, a rabbi of the Jewish faith, author of 'Till Faith do us part', states that it has been estimated that some 67 per cent of all Catholics marry out of their faith, as do 44 per cent of Jews. The Church of England has issued special guidelines for the increasing number of mixed faith marriages. Muslim, Sikh and Hindu leaders are also alarmed at the increase of such marriages. The classic objection is that a dual faith household ends up as a no-faith household and children are brought up without any religious guidance. Also from a Jewish viewpoint, there is the additional concern of numerical survival for the 330,000 strong community in Britain which, like most Christian organisations, has witnessed a disturbing decline in adherents during the last decade.

But all is not gloom and doom! A recent seminar for mixed faith couples revealed the opposite to opting out. Many in a mixed faith relationship are still deeply attached to their religious tradition, maintaining it for themselves and passing it on to the next generation. The vast majority did not consciously seek out an other-faith partner – it just happened that way through a chance encounter, be it at college or university, through working together in the office or workshop, or at a social gathering etc. In a tolerant multicultural society, people are judged as individuals rather than by the religious or racial group to which they belong. It is inevitable that once they mix together, relationships will be formed and very often social and cultural common interests outweigh the religious differences that divide them. We are part of one world and God is our creator and sustainer. John Masefield, the poet laureate of yesteryear, expressed it well – "So by the bedside of the dying black, I felt our uncouth souls subtly made one; Forgotten the limits of each others lack, forgotten the petty deeds of ill-things done. We were but men, who for a spate of years, sort the one city by a thousand roads."

Legend

Up in Heaven, God had just made all the animals, and they held a raffle to see who would get what. So the lion got a mane, and the leopard got spots and the cat got a meow, etc. Then at the end, God came down and all the animals lined up to shake his hand. And God said, "Where's the camel?" And St Peter said, "The camel's not coming. He's got the hump!"

Conversation Piece

"You know her hair's dyed?" said the lady discussing a mutual acquaintance.
"Dyed!" replied her friend. "By the look of it, it's committed suicide."

Epitaph on a Tombstone

Here doth lieth Walter Pryet, Reason whyeth... Fast-food diet...

Full Circle

A man who bought £5.00 worth of books from a church jumble sale in Lewes, Sussex, returned home to discover that they had been donated to the organisers by his wife. Moral – (Matthew 6 v 3) "When you do some act of charity, do not let your left hand know what your right is doing."

123. 1999

Bedside Reading

It was William Ross Wallace (poet) who said, "The hand that rocks the cradle, is the hand that rules the world" and my experience at Morley, and elsewhere, is that the same hand maintains the life and witness of our churches and without our women-folk, the churches would fail to function and witness! I'm indebted to Harry Mitchell for presenting to me a book in the recent Penguin Classics of their edition of Geoffrey

Chaucer's The Canterbury Tales. I was 'taught' Chaucer and Shakespeare in my schooldays and found them 'no go' areas of interest! Now in my old age I realise that Chaucer was the father of English poetry and Shakespeare the father of the English language!

Chaucer (1342–1400) was a well-educated man who knew French and Latin and was also familiar with contemporary, as well as with classical, literature. He had a remarkable broad experience of life. In his teens he served as a page or messenger-boy to royalty and later held important positions in the King's service as a customs officer, a Justice of the Peace, a Clerk of Works to the King, and a member of parliament. These posts brought him into close contact with people from all walks of life – rich and poor, and an understanding of human nature with all its follies and frailties.

He began his famous work, The Canterbury Tales, in 1387. His plan in writing the story was to present a group of men and women, representing all levels of society, as they travelled on a pilgrimage to Canterbury and each pilgrim was to tell two stories on the way to Canterbury and two on the way home. One such story was The Wife of Bath's Tale. She delivers, to start with, a very candid autobiography! The unmarried life she contends, may be fine for some, but not for her. She goes on to assert that the marriage is happiest when the wife holds sway over the husband. As proof she tells of her five marriages; and particularly the fifth to a younger man named Johnny. He made her miserable until they had a fight in which she pretends he had killed her. After that he submitted to her, and the couple never quarrelled again, but lived happily as equals. Her story, based on good King Arthur's days ends thus:

> So they lived ever after to the end
> in perfect bliss, and may Christ Jesus send
> Us husbands meek and young and fresh in bed,
> And grace to overbid them when we wed.
> And – Jesu hear my prayer! – cut short the lives
> Of those who won't be governed by their wives:
> And all old, angry niggards of their pence.
> God send them soon a very pestilence!

So girls you see what power and influence you have over the weaker sex. Abraham Lincoln meeting Harriet Beecher Stowe, author of Uncle Tom's Cabin, said, "So you're the little woman who wrote the book that made this great war!" Truly the hand that rocks the cradle – rules the world and our churches!

The Epicure's Christmas Litany

> Hark the herald angels sing
> Beecham's pills are just the thing.
> Work you gentle, meek and mild
> Bowel and stomach reconciled!

A Fact

The world already has 25,000 golf courses, covering an area the size of Belgium.

A Thought

Get ready for eternity. You're going to spend a lot of time there.

Any Offers!

(Notice in a Welsh fishing village) Wanted – a good woman who can clean, dig worms, sew and who owns a good fishing boat and motor. Please enclose photo of boat and motor!

124. 1999

Introspection and Self-Pity

Dr Thomas Browne, an English physician and writer of the seventeenth century, had a favourite expression, "Lord deliver me from myself." So many of us, despite our manifold advantages and circumstances in life, have developed, to an inordinate degree, the capacity of being sorry for ourselves, and failing to count our blessings!

Visitors to the Channel Island of Jersey – on a cliff overlooking the harbour, may recollect an old bench, where, many years ago, Victor Hugo, an exile from his beloved France, used to sit every evening, gazing into the sunset, giving himself up to profound meditation and melancholy. Finally he would rise and selecting pebbles of varying sizes, he would cast them, with energy and purpose, into the water beneath. This behaviour did not escape the notice of some children who played nearby, and one evening a little girl, bolder than the rest, went to him and said, "Monsieur Hugo, why do you come here to throw these stones?" The great writer was silent, then he smiled gravely and said, "Not stones, my child, I am throwing self-pity into the sea."

In this symbolic act there is a powerful lesson for us today. We easily find cause for personal grievance and complaint in the living of our lives. We are soon 'put out' and magnify a personal idiosyncrasy until it becomes an unalterable habit and way of life. So often with this comes a growing indifference to our interest and concern in the welfare and wellbeing of others. In essence, the basis of self-pity is selfishness. People who are sorry for themselves can never be truly sorry and sympathetic of others.

Victor Hugo (1802-1885) had a tremendous physical presence. He was a man of legendary strength, energy and appetite. He was also a man of enormous vanity, who said at one point, that Paris should be renamed 'Hugo'. He certainly had great talent and was a perfectionist with amazing stamina. Within 2 years, between the ages of 17–19, he wrote 272 articles for a journal he edited with his brother and published his first collection of poetry in 1822 (aged 20). By the time he was 38 he had published 8 plays, 7 volumes of poetry, and novels including the Hunchback of Notre Dame (1831). At 40 he was the most popular and respected author in France and elected to the French Academy.

In 1843 came tragedy, his first failure in the theatre, and the death of his favourite daughter and her husband drowned in a boating accident. His grief and self-pity was colossal, he wrote nothing for the next 10 years. He was exiled, as a political rebel, in 1852 to the Channel Isles for 18 years and when Napoleon III fell from power in 1870, Hugo returned to his beloved France. His funeral (1885) was attended by more than a million people. The funeral parade was miles long, led by entire regiments of cavalry. Behind them followed carriages filled with the greatest dignitaries of Europe. The French people felt that they were burying not just a writer, but a national hero.

On Reflection

It was whilst in exile that he wrote many of his greatest poems and the splendid protest novel Les Misèrables (1862).

A Thought

I avoid looking forward or backward, and try to keep looking upwards. (Charlotte Brontë)

Toilet Crisis for the Police

Comment made by Harrogate Police Inspector, Nigel Boynton, on the reported theft of 30 potties – "We have got nothing to go on!"

125. 1999

Question! – How Old is Old?

There is a rumour going around that somebody – you know who – will be – on 21.4.99 sharing a birthday with the Queen (God bless her). Malcolm Muggeridge always said that his seventies were his best decade, busily planning for the future. The same can be said of people in their eighties as well, and even people in their nineties. My grandmother, in her long black dress and cap, was old at seventy, which was then regarded as being 'very old'. Today, if people want to set an age that most people regard as old, the ninety onwards is probably a safe bet. Fiddlesticks! One should strive not to contemplate one's age, even less try to 'be' it. Worse still is to pre-empt it by adopting prematurely senile mannerisms, as some men do. The thing is to behave as if one is going to live for ever.

In 1369 Tamburlaine the Great (Timur the Lame) became ruler of Samarkand, a wealthy oasis town on the great Silk Road in Central Asia. Its historic architecture and temples are still one of the wonders of past civilisations. I'm still anticipating a journey there to compare it with the many interesting places visited in Europe, Africa, Asia, America and the Far East. Like James Elroy Flecker's (Hassan) pilgrims, with them I say,

"For lust of knowing what should not be known – we take the Golden Road to Samarkand." Also the books unread, or started and never finished! I must tackle, not only the abridged version by D.M. Low, often dipped into, but the full text of Edward Gibbon's 'The Decline and Fall of the Roman Empire', also the finest book in the German language 'The Conversations of Goethe with Eckermann'.

According to the Annual Abstract of Statistics, and recent health studies literature, there are three categories of 'old', the 'young old' are between 65-74 years, 'old' are between 75-84 years; and 'very old' are 85 years and over. So much for statistics!

> Age is a quality of mind. If you have left your dreams behind – if hope is
> lost. If you no longer look ahead. If your ambitions' fires are dead.
> Then you are old! But if from life you take the best
> And if in life you keep the jest. If love you hold
> No matter how the years go by. No matter how the birthdays fly –
> You are not old!

Helen Keller, born blind, was asked – "Is there anything worse than being blind?" She answered, "Yes, to have sight but no vision."

Mistaken Identity

Sergeant Watling – Officer in charge of the Muswell Hill School Truancy Patrols, stopped an obvious 'class-bunker' on the street. He asked the boy, "What school do you go to young man?" Reply "I am not a young man, I am a lady and I don't go to school because I'm 38."

The Danish philosopher Kierkegaard said of death, "That it is the road we all have to take – over the Bridge of Sighs into eternity." Our own Samuel Johnson observed, "It matters not how a man dies, but how he lives. The act of dying is not of importance it lasts so short a time."

The man who lives by himself and for himself is apt to be corrupted by the company he keeps.

126. 1999

Time

The coming millennium makes us think of the mystery of time. Luke and Matthew both agree that Jesus was born before the death of Herod the Great, which can be placed confidently in the spring of 4 BC. The first century Jewish historian Josephus stated that a lunar eclipse occurred shortly before Herod's death and this can be dated March 12-13 4 BC. The error which misdated Jesus' birth was perpetrated by a monk called Dionysius Exiguus, who lived in the AD sixth century and worked out his chronology without the benefit of sources now at our disposal.

J.B. Priestley is one of my favourite authors. He wrote some very interesting and thought-provoking plays including 'Tim and the Conways' and 'I have been here before'. The latter play, in particular, reveals Priestley's interest in Time and Recurrence in which he acknowledges his debt to the writings of P.D. Ouspensky. A dictionary definition of time is "a point at which, or period during which, things happen; or the state of things at any period." Canon Henry Twells in his poem Time's Paces wrote:

> When as a child I laughed and wept, Time crept.
> When as a youth I waxed more bold, Time strolled.
> When I became a full grown man, Time ran
> When older still I daily grew, Time flew
> Soon I shall find, in passing on, Time gone
> O Christ wilt thou have saved me then?

'Time' – The supply of time is a daily miracle. You wake up in the morning and your purse is magically filled with 24 hours of it. No one can take it from you, it is unsaleable, and no one receives either more or less than you receive. In the realm of time there is no aristocracy of wealth or intellect, for genius is never rewarded with even an extra hour in the day. You cannot borrow time, so it is impossible to get into debt. You can waste time today, but not tomorrow, for that is kept from you. One must arrange everything within the income of 24 hours. We can never have any more time, for we have, and always have had, all the time there is. So – TAKE TIME.

> Take time to think – it is a source of power
> Take time to play – it is the secret of perpetual youth
> Take time to read – it is the fountain of wisdom
> Take time to pray – it is the greatest power on earth
> Take time to love – and be loved
> It is a God-given privilege – take time to be friendly
> It is the road to happiness – take time to laugh
> It is the music of the soul – take time to give
> It is too short a day to be lazy – take time to work
> It is the price of success – take time to be charitable
> It is the key to Heaven.

Russian Proverbs

Free cheese is only found in mousetraps.

Even in another world we shall have to serve the gentry, for they will be in the cauldrons, and we shall have to stoke the fires.

Fleet Street Barons and the Prostitution of the Press

Sir Walter Scott to his nephew on hearing that he was thinking of becoming a journalist – "I'd sooner that you sold gin to poor people and poisoned them that way."

127. 1999

===

Reverie

Can progress and advancement in science and technology always be an advantage? Does development in the Internet and e-mail mean the demise of communications by letter writing? A late spell of 'spring-cleaning' caused me to re-read a bundle of letters written to me over seventy years ago by my mother when, as an immature youth of 16 years, I had left my native village to seek fame and fortune via work and education in the great metropolis of Manchester. The letters, written in a beautiful handwriting, were all signed "Your loving mother." That was what she was, and in memory always will be.

The philosopher Hubbard has observed that growth of intellect is Progress, that Progress is Evolution, and Evolution is Progress. I favour John Ruskin's comment that – He only is advancing in life whose spirit is entering into a living peace with collective life and the environment, through fellowship, compassion and service.

One of the great and moving letters of the last century was written by Friedrich Wilhelm Nietzsche (1814-1900) the German philosopher (who rejected absolute moral values and the 'slave morality' of Christianity) when the long friendship he had enjoyed and valued with Richard Wagner, to whom he had been both friend and advocate, came under strain and was terminated. The letter is a masterpiece reflecting all that is best in good wishes for the future when they go their separate ways. In this century, now drawing to a close, one of the most moving and beautiful letters was written by Earl Balfour to Lady Desborough when, in the early days of the Great War, 1914-18, her two elder sons, Julian and Riversdale Grenfell, were killed on the Western Front.

He wrote – I do not pretend to offer consolation; In one very real sense there is no consolation to offer the blow, the double blow has fallen, and the shock which threatens the very citadel of life can be softened by nothing that I or perhaps any other can do or utter. Who can measure the pain of separation? Who can deny that, normally at least, death means separation. Nevertheless, (he went on to say) this severance, though complete, is but temporary. For myself, I entertain no doubt whatever about a future life. I deem it at least as certain as any of the hundred-and-one-truths of the framework of the world, as I conceive the world. It is no mere theological accretion, which I am prepared to accept in some moods and reject in others. I am as sure that those I love and have lost are living today, as I am that yesterday they were fighting heroically in the trenches. The bitterness lies not in the thought that they are really dead, still less in the thought that I have parted with them forever, for I think neither of these things. The bitterness lies in the thought that until I die I shall never again see them smile or hear their voices: The pain is indeed hard to bear, too hard it sometimes seems for human strength yet, measured on the true scale of things it is but a brief time – death cannot long cheat us of love – we part to meet again.

Mark Twain's Comment

Let us endeavour so to live, that when we come to die even the undertaker will be sorry.

Garden Woes

My radishes are puny things; my peas and beans are dying; And as for the potatoes, well, the things aren't even trying: And that's the way my garden grows – I tell myself "who needs it?" But down inside it hurts to know – it bites the hand that weeds it.

Royally Entertained

It is reported that the Queen doesn't drink much alcohol; but she enjoys a gin and tonic. Once when she was staying at a British Embassy abroad, the ambassador apologised because he had not been able to get the Queen's favourite brand of tonic water. "Never mind," said the Queen, "it's the spirit that counts."

128. 1999

The End of an Era – 31 December 1999

It is a sobering thought that the next issue of this newsletter will be in the third millennium – the year 2000! I recollect, with some amazement, that my maternal grand-father was a child of the Industrial Revolution, a time when a man known as a 'knocker up' tapped before dawn on the windows of workers' terrace houses in our mill towns. Thin, pale faced children were dragged from their beds to hasten out, with the women and men folk, into the cold streets. Many of the children went barefoot. All made their way between soot-blackened rows of brick-built houses to the multistorey mill. In those days, in the nineteenth century, they worked 12 to 16 hours a day, in cramped, airless, conditions, so deafened by machinery that they had to lip-read. Lungs became clogged with cotton dust, and life was short and certainly not sweet. A doctor, writing of con-ditions in Manchester in the Textile Industry, observed, "The mills produced a degenerate race of human beings, stunted, enfeebled and depraved, men and women with no future and children that would never be adults." In those early days children were employed in the mills from the age of six or seven. Mill owners would get children in batches from parish workhouses, treating them as little more than slaves, kept on star-vation diets, at the mercy of overseers armed with whips and straps. (Unfortunately these conditions still exist today in India and Pakistan in the carpet and other industries). Reformers like Robert Owen, an enlightened mill owner and a Christian, changed these conditions, and the Factory Act 1847 limited children to half-day working. Hardship and poverty were widespread in the nineteenth century but human dignity often survived in the most squalid conditions.

The twentith century pointed to the new age in human relationships. In 1901, the President of the United States entertained a black man to dinner in the White House for the first time. Marconi transmitted the first wireless signal across the Atlantic – the forerunners of all our far-reaching developments in communications. The first motor cars became luxury objects, and in 1908 Henry Ford produced his first Model T, a car for the multitude, and by 1927 more than 15 million Model Ts had been built. The term 'global village' was coined to signify the breaking down of barriers between people of different cultures and the unifying of the ways of life as the world was brought closer together by transport development, electronic and communications progress. The twentieth century was hailed as 'the century of the common man' with a global outlook for worldwide co-operation! This was not to be realised. The heavy price of the First World War, which grew out of Europe's divisions, jealousies and selfishness, was 10 million dead. The Second World War lasted longer, cost 64 million dead and brought about more profound changes, affecting people's lives not only in Europe's cities but in tropical islands, and ended with the explosion of an atomic bomb on Japan, ushering in a nuclear age, which can be traced back to the beginning of the twentieth century, when the science of physics underwent a radical revolution. Medicine was also developed scientifically, with new drugs, including the contraceptive pill, an innovation with potentially far-reaching consequences in a world whose population had risen at an unprecedented rate from 2,000 million in 1930, 3,000 million in 1960. Today China's population alone is well over 1,000 million and India has now reached the 1,000 million mark.

A triumph for mankind was in 1961 when a Russian astronaut orbited the earth and 8 years later when an American set foot on the moon – this a mere 60 years after Louis Blériot had become the first man to cross the English Channel in an aeroplane. When I was a schoolboy, the idea of a moon landing witnessed by millions of people on television and radio, with a global audience, would have been regarded as the hallucinations of a crank! History never stands still, we progress from the relative to the absolute, and the twentyfirst century will present a challenge to all of us in our human relationships. Each day is a new beginning. William Blake reminds us that "Man's desires are limited by his perceptions, none can desire what he has not perceived." Margaret Mitchell, the schoolteacher from Atlanta, who died aged 40, killed in a street accident, wrote the twentieth century classic 'Gone with the Wind', and ended that great book with the words "After all, tomorrow is another day". May the twentyfirst century be a new beginning for world peace and co-operation in which the principles for which Christ lived and died, are put into practice. This can be achieved if the will is there to succeed.

A Thought

Consistency is not an absolute virtue.
People that never change their opinions love themselves
more than they love the truths. Source unknown
(quoted by Winston Churchill)

Nodding Acquaintance.

A businessman suffering from insomnia asked a friend how he managed to sleep soundly every night: "Do you count sheep" he inquired,
"No" replied the friend, "I talk to the shepherd".

2000–04

129. 2000

Reflection on Criticism

> Let your speech be always with grace, seasoned with salt, that you may know
> how you ought to answer every man.
>
> (Advice from St Paul – Colossians 4 v 6).

For me, the highlight of 1999 was attending, by courtesy of all my friends in our Fellowship, as a birthday remembrance gift, the concert at the Bridgewater Hall, Manchester, on Friday, 4 June 1999. The conductor was Yuri Temirkanov with the St Petersburg Philharmonic Orchestra (120 strong). The second half of the programme was Tchaikovsky's Symphony No 6, the *Pathetique*. I heard this great symphony many years ago in Russia, when St Petersburg was then known as Leningrad and the orchestra the Leningrad Philharmonic. The conductor on that occasion was Riccardo Muti, who, like Sir Thomas Beecham of blessed memory, was an autocrat on the rostrum, and a superb conductor – in my humble estimation! Muti, last year, conducted a performance of Mahler's Fourth Symphony with the Vienna Philharmonic at the Festival Hall. Two critics reported on the rendition. The first from the *Independent* – "The opening jog-trot was too fast, the principal first theme too heavy and phrasing thereafter was prosaic; even a mite jerky. Natural pauses seemed like awkward rests, rustic instrumental solos were accurate but irritable, and the sum effect was a tense efficiency, polished in part but oddly soulless!" Then from the *Financial Times* "The playing was scrupulously prepared and Muti's care for lean, clear textures enhanced the orchestra's natural balance. The result was a streamlined performance, fresh-air Mahler, which moved keenly and naturally. After an opening movement light on its feet, the scherzo was swift and graceful; and the long slow movement breathed a pure mountain air, thanks to the ethe-real nature of the Viennese violins."

So much for 'personal opinions'. Thomas Haemmerlein, born in Kempen, Germany in 1330, the monk known as Thomas à Kempis who devoted his life writing and living that world's classic masterpiece 'Of the Initiation of Christ' (four books) said something very profound in its wisdom of life, "Often times I could wish that I had held my peace." An old proverb states "speech is silver, silence is golden," Jesus in Matthew 7 v 3 said "And why beholdest thou the mote that is in thy brother's eye, but considerest not the beam in thine own eye?" Rossini, said of Wagner, "He has lovely moments but awful quarters of an hour." Which reminds me of Alexander Pope's remark – "Damn with faint praise, assent with civil leer; And without sneering teach the rest to sneer."

Nevertheless, as human beings we realise that it is not always possible to agree with each other! As Christians we are asked to "speak the truth in love" and the strange paradox of life is that so often through aggression and disagreement something worth-while can result. St Paul's 18 months ministry in Corinth (Sept 51 – Feb 53) ended abruptly arising from the criticism and hostility he received there. But out of it we ben-efit from the treasure of two great letters – 1 and 2 Corinthians for which we are eternally grateful. We face the year 2000 and the new millennium with a degree of concern and apprehension. I leave with you the words of Epictetus (born AD 50 in Phrygia) weak in body, a cripple, born a slave – "If death shall find me in the midst of these studies, it shall suffice me if I can lift up my head to God and say, The means which thou gavest me, I have not neglected."

At midnight on 31 December this twentieth century ends, and we face the challenge of the twentyfirst century. May it bring with it peace and prosperity universally with increased health, happiness and friendship worldwide.

> Ring out the old, ring in the new,
> Ring happy bells, across the snow:
> The year is going; let him go;
> Ring out the false, ring in the true.

(Tennyson)

Any Offers

The minister at the end of his 'Children's address' cheerfully asked if there were any questions! A small girl piped up – "Please sir, why did the angels walk up and down Jacob's ladder when they had wings?" "Ah, I see," said the minister, breathing deeply. "Now is there anyone who would like to answer that question!"

130. 2000

'Big Mac' Problems

The surprise of my first visit to America some 30 years ago was not its skyscrapers and free-ways, but the 'size' of men, women and children – sheer obesity! More recent visits reveal a 'size consciousness' – dieting and exercising having become a way of life. In Europe dramatic increases in diabetes, heart disease, etc. are now forecast as a result of the epidemic of obesity sweeping Europe. Since 1980 obesity rates in England have risen from 8 to 20 per cent for women and from 6 to 17 per cent for men. The reasons given include sedentary lifestyles and a richer diet, both linked to growing prosperity and fast food eating habits. The greatest cause for concern is the number of overweight children – tele-addicts, driven by car to and from school by mum or dad – neglecting the means of locomotion – two good legs, which God has provided for our use and mobility in life.

Generosity

Asked to name the outstanding 'Christian' of the twentieth century I have no hesitation in naming Mother Teresa, (Agnes Bojaxhiu of Skopje, Albania) who, in 1928, when she was 18, felt the missionary calling; going to Ireland to join the Sisters of Our Lady of Loreto and, in 1929 was sent to Calcutta, India, to fulfil her destiny there. She was bestowed many awards in her long life of service to the poor, including Nobel Peace Prize in 1979. Other awards included doctorates, honoris causa by many universities, and large cash prizes. She never considered any of these prizes and cash awards as personal property, but merely accepted them in the name of the poor, and spent every cent of them, for the poor. She had many stories to tell, including the following – "One night a man called to tell me that a Hindu family, a family of 8 children, had not eaten anything for days. They had nothing to eat. I took enough rice for a meal and went to their house. I could see the hungry faces, the children with their bulging eyes! The mother took the rice from my hands, divided it in half and went out. When she came back a little later I asked her "Where did you go? What did you do?" She answered, "They also were hungry". "They," were the people next door, a Muslim family with the same number of children to feed and who did not have any food either."

That mother was aware of the situation. She had the courage and the love to share her meagre portion of rice with others of a different faith. In spite of her circumstances, I think she felt very happy to share with her neighbours the little I had taken her. In order not to take away her happiness, I did not take her any more rice that night. I took her some the following day."

Matthew 5 v 42 "What is a Christian?" someone asked a Hindu man. He responded, "The Christian is someone who gives."

True Answers from a 1999 GCSE Examination Paper

1. The Bible is full of interesting caricatures. In the first book of the Bible, Guinessis, Adam and Eve were created from an apple tree. One of their children, Cain, asked, "Am I my brother's son?"

2. Moses led the Hebrew slaves to the Red Sea, where they made unleavened bread, which is bread made without any ingredients. Moses went up to Mount Cyanide to get the Ten Commandments. He died before he ever reached Canada.

131. 2000

Spring 2000

My beloved spake and said unto me. Rise up my love, my fair one, and come away. For, lo the winter is past, the rain is over and gone. The flowers appear on the earth, the time of the singing of birds is come, and the voice of the turtle is heard in our land.

(Song of Solomon 2 v 10-12)

When all the world is young lad
And all the trees are green;
And every goose a swan lad,
And every lass a queen;

Then hey for boot and horse; lad.
And round the world away;
Young blood must have its course lad.
And every dog his day.

(Charles Kingsley 1819-75)

Spring

When the sap rises and when, we are told, a young man's fancy turns to thoughts of love and romance! For others it can also be a time of memory and looking back to the yesteryears which will never return. In one of the great autobiographical books of English literature, George Borrow, (1803-1881) in Lavengo, is suffering from 'self-pity', feeling very sorry for himself. He enters into conversation with his gypsy friend, Jasper Petulengro, voicing his state of mind. Jasper replies:- "Life is sweet, brother." "Do you think so?" "Think so! There's night and day, brother, both sweet things; sun, moon and stars brother, all sweet things; there's likewise a wind on the heath. Life is very sweet brother, who would wish to die!" "I would wish to die." "You talk like a fool, were you a Romany, you would talk wiser: Wish to die indeed! A Romany would wish to live forever." "In sickness, Jasper?" "There are the sun and stars, brother". "In blindness, Jasper?" "There's the wind on the heath, brother, if I could only feel that I would gladly live forever."

George Henry Borrow was a scholar, translator and, above all else, a traveller. His autobiographical experiences are told in his superb writings in Lavengo (his Gypsy name), The Romany Rye, Wild Wales, The Bible in Spain, etc. and are amongst the treasures of English literature. His journeying recorded in Wild Wales, is still a master-piece of observation and experience. No travel book on Wales published since, can equal it. His companion in many of his travels there was Isopel Berners the splendid road girl, workhouse born. Like Barrow, she was of magnificent physique, a handsome six-footer plus being also intelligent, honest and reliable. On one occasion she floored, with a single blow, a 'gentleman' who made lewd suggestions to her! If ever I get 'up yonder' (which is doubtful), an item on 'my agenda for Heaven' will be to seek out George Borrow to ask him why he never married Isopel Berners? What a life companion she would have made! He did marry when 37, Mary Clarke, the widow of a naval officer, and subsequently toured in Wales and elsewhere with his step-daughter. In his active and very full life he also worked as a language translator and translated parts of the Gospels into several dialects for the Church of England.

Grandma Anna Moses (1860-1961) who was, late in life, a remarkable self-taught painter in the USA. She wrote her autobiography (died when 101 years old) entitled 'For Whom the Bell Tolls'. In it, she observed – "What a strange thing is Memory and Hope. One looks backwards, the other forward. The one is of today, the other is the tomorrow. Memory is history, recorded in our brain; memory is a painter, it paints pictures of the past and of the day."

Any Answers

Attending a wedding for the first time, a little girl whispered to her mother, "Why is the bride dressed in white?" "Because white is the colour of happiness," her mother replied. "And today is the happiest day of her life." The child thought about this for a moment and then said, "So why is the groom wearing black?"

A husband and wife drive for miles in silence after a terrible argument in which neither would budge. The husband pointed to a mule in a field. "Relative of yours?" he asked. "Yes," she replied, "by marriage."

132. 2000

Take Time

The past has gone, the future has yet to come, the present is all we have. We cannot change the past, nor can we draw upon the future, but we can use the present. So let us touch the philosopher's stone, for it is the foundation for successful living.

Take time to look – it is the price of success
Take time to think – it is the source of power
Take time to play – it is the secret of perennial youth
Take time to read – it is the source of wisdom
Take time to be friendly – it is the way to happiness
Take time to laugh – it is the music of the soul

It is possible that the chief harm done by organised religion has been the idea that we live in three worlds at once – past, present and future. To drag our past behind us and look forward to sweet rest in heaven, is to spread the present very thin! The person who lives in the present, forgetful of the past and not too concerned for the future, shows a high degree of wisdom! The best preparation for tomorrow's work is to do our work as well as we can today. The best preparation for a life to come, is to live now and here. We should live always striving to follow the highest and the best. If we have made mistakes in the past, reparation lies not in regrets, but in thankfulness that we now know better. We are punished by our sins, – not for them, and they can be a blessing and a benefit, if, having tasted the bitterness of error, we can avoid it in the future. If we have withheld the kind word and the look of sympathy in the past, we can today give doubly, and thus, in degree, redeem the past. And we best redeem the past by forgetting it and losing ourselves in useful work here and now. Life is a great privilege. We should thank God that we are here to live it to the full. Avebury, one of the wisest of philosophers, reminds us that whether a life is noble or ignoble depends, not on the calling which is adopted but on the spirit in which it is followed. The humblest life may be noble, whilst that of the most powerful monarch or the greatest genius may be contemptible. It is not so much the hours that tell, as the way we use them, life must be measured by the thought and action rather than by the time. Remember Lord Byron's sad lament:

"Through life's long road so dim and dirty. I have dragged on to 3 and 30. And what have these years left for me – nothing except 33."

A Thought

Prayer can never supplant work. When we pray for God's will to be done on earth, we ask for his nature to be revealed in deed, for his rule to bring unity, justice and love. Faith without action is dead. Prayer without work is hypocrisy.

(Eberhard Arnold).

Cast a cold eye on life, on death; horsemen pass by

(W.B. Yeats)
(Epitaph on his tomb)
(Sligo Churchyard)
(Republic of Ireland)

Did you know

In Shakespeare's time, mattresses were secured on bed frames by ropes. When you pulled on the ropes, the mattress tightened, making the bed much firmer for sleeping on. Hence the well-known phrase, "Good night, sleep tight."

133. 2000

On Boredom

The state of being bored (noun). The English language abounds in anomalies – bore can mean to piece a solid substance with some rotary cutting instrument or again bore can mean a dull, tiresome or uncongenial person, etc. Boredom throughout history has certainly been responsible for a number of deaths. For instance Louis XIV regularly started a number of wars out of sheer boredom. George Sanders, whom I seem to remember as a suave film actor in my days of cinema-going, did away with himself with a lethal cocktail of Nembutal and vodka. In one of the three suicide notes found after his death, he wrote, "Dear world, I am leaving because I'm bored. I feel I have lived long enough. I am leaving you with your worries in this sweet cesspool – good luck." He had been suffering for some time from a screwed-up private life with severe financial problems and deteriorating health. We are also given to understand that chronic boredom is closely linked with mental depression, isolation, a feeling of being inadequate and unwanted, also a feeling of frustration in life.

Children, since the mid-1970s have grown up in a society where education and their urge to work and provide, to win respect from their community, to bring up and rear children loving families, has been undermined by unemployment, lack of incentives and opportunity in planning their careers. Thus many, with no future prospects, plunged headlong into the now, seeking immediate excitement and pleasure, following a doctrine of hedonism, leading to the misuse of drugs, and the gaining of peer respect and fear through criminal activities. Role models for them were not found in Christianity, but in such characters as the Gallagher brothers, and others. A Scottish Executive survey reported in the *Glasgow Herald* – revealed that 85 per cent of teenaged boys and 67 per cent of girls committed crimes during the past year – which included damaging property, stealing from shops, car thievery, and stealing from school. In London, street robbery is up by an alarming 36% – a third being school children robbing other school children, often grabbing each others mobile phones with menaces.

The antidote to boredom is a practical interest in life and living. A well-known saying is, "The devil tempts all, but the idle person tempts the devil." Thomas Carlyle (The Sage of Chelsea) (not the football team) wrote in Sartor Resartus (The Tailor Re-Patched) "Blessed are those who find joy and satisfaction in their work, let them seek no other blessedness." To which we say. Amen!

A new 'If' for a Christian (After Kipling)

If you can stand before false accusations, and lift your head in grace and face the lies; if you can join in another's celebrations, while your life falls in ruins before your eyes; If you can grieve with others who are grieving, yet find in Christ a peace beyond all griefs; if you can love those who are unbelieving, and yet stand firm and sure on your beliefs; If you can lose all wealth and earthly treasures, and count it as the loss of so much dust; if you can scorn success by mortal measure, striving for reward that cannot rust. If you can put your hand to Christian labour, be buried with Christ, your sins all put to end; if every day you can love your neighbour, you will receive the crown of Life, my friend.

Too True!

A teacher (young, brash and foolish) announced to her class, "I am an atheist, are any of you atheists too?" All the children put up their hands, except for one little girl. "So what are you, if you are not an atheist?" asked the teacher. "My mother is a Christian, my father is a Christian and I am a Christian, too," said the girl. "Oh, and if your mother were a moron and your father were a moron, what would you be?" sneered the teacher. "An atheist," she replied.

Quote

Kindness is the oil that takes the friction out of life.

If you are all wrapped up in yourself, you are overdressed.

(Anonymous)

John Paton, the missionary, brought Christianity to the Pacific Islands. Years later the communists arrived – saying "You have listened to fables and lies, there is no God." The chief, retorted, "You should thank the God you do not believe in – for if you had arrived before Paton, we would have eaten you!"

134. 2000

Life's Paradox

Take my yoke upon you and learn from me. For my yoke is easy and my burden is light.

(Matthew 11 v 29-30).

The influence of words should never be underestimated; they fall like dew upon a thought, producing that which makes us think. Thus Archimedes – "Give me a standing place and I will move the earth;" and Oliver Cromwell, "Not only strike while the iron is hot, but make it hot by striking." W.S. Gilbert in the libretto to the 'Pirates of Penzance' reflects, through Frederic, "How quaint the ways of Paradox! – at commonsense she gaily mocks us."

Our Lord, in his teaching, relied mainly upon self evident truth, simply stated and not argued – a practice which is just as consistent with profundity as it is with simplicity. This paradoxical character of Our Lord's main teaching blend that teaching with the very universe itself which, in the eyes of today's science increasingly seems to be built of paradox. If the universe appears to be stable in any degree, it is only because of a most delicate equilibrium of opposing forces persistently maintained and renewed. This is true of the microscopically small as of the colossally great in nature. A scientist or philosopher looking for a teaching principle adequate to the universe now known, finds that teaching shot through and through with paradox; and this too is found in the teaching of Jesus.

One definition of a paradox is "a tenet or proposition which seems to be at variance with common sense or contradictory to received opinion". Thus St Paul's "When I am weak then I am strong." Reflection reveals a way of reconciling the seemingly contradictions creating a new synthesis of a more stable and enduring truth. Thus with St Paul, the realised weakness leads him to lay hold on new powers. History is, in general, a record of progress. In the conquest of the sea, the limitations of the oar, led on to the development of the sail, and the inadequacy of the sail led on to steam-driven vessels and then the modern ocean liner – shortcoming and inadequacy becoming the door to strength. Thus Paul is arguing in effect, "When I realise and confess my weakness, I lean on divine strength and become stronger in deed."

Jesus was a carpenter, and knew all about yokes. He had fashioned many with his hands and lucky were the folks fitted with yokes from that workshop in Nazareth. Often when supplying yokes, he would have to say on occasion, "My yokes are easy, they do not chafe the neck of the beast, they fit comfortably." He probably spoke thus many times to his customers. Now, with the enlarged horizon of everyone's needs, he recalls the old phrase and gives it a richer meaning.

The yoke is a common figure in scripture, never to be regarded lightly. Proverbs says, "Learn to bear the yoke in youth." There is always the hint of stress and strain. The very purpose of a yoke was to make it possible for heavy loads to be drawn. It is essentially the symbol of service – often hard to bear. But it is the service Christ himself rendered, and to which he called all who would follow him – as well as pulling one's own burden he asks us to pull other's burdens also. Thus the paradox – his harder yoke is the easier. His heavier burden is the lighter. For as we "come to him" we find we are not alone in the yoke or beneath the burden. He, the strong Son of God, increasing the weight upon our yoke piling up the burden upon our backs, places himself by our side to pull and lift with us and lo! – "In His service the yoke is easy and the burden light."

The Challenge

The church is here to comfort the disturbed and to disturb the comfortable.

Anyone who thinks they are too small to make a difference, has not been in bed with a mosquito!

135. 2001

What does Christianity Mean?

In the home – kindness. In business – honesty.
In society – courtesy. In work – thoroughness.
In play – fairness. To sin – resistance.
To the unfortunate – pity.
To the weak – help.
To the strong – trust and goodwill.
To the penitent – forgiveness.
To all people – reverence, love and service.
To God – worship, service and trust.

Life Begins at 60 plus

Don't worry if you haven't made your mark! There's plenty of time yet! Research workers who have looked into the histories of some 400 famous people – each one outstanding in their special field of endeavour – politics, painting, poetry, writing, etc. found the following:-

- For 35 per cent of them their greatest achievement came between the age of 60 and 70 years
- 23 per cent when they were between 70 and 80
- And 8 per cent when they were more than 80

Thus 66 per cent of the work and effort that has benefited the world has been done by folk passed 60. So cheer up and go to it!

Look forward, with keen anticipation to the New Year (2001). The best is yet to be! One of the most obscure prophets of the Old Testament was Habakkuk. Yet he was the one who stated the finest avowal of faith and trust ever penned: "Although the fig tree shall not blossom, neither shall fruit be on the vines, the labour of the olive shall fail, and the field shall yield no meat, the flocks shall be cut off from the fold, and there shall be no herd in the stalls, yet I will rejoice in the Lord, I will joy in the God of my salvation."

Great Thoughts

The night has a thousand eyes, And the day but one, Yet the light of a bright world dies with the dying sun. The mind has a thousand eyes, and the heart but one, yet the light of a whole life does when its love is done.

(Bourdillon).

The soul's dark cottage, battered and decayed
Let's in new light, through chinks that time hath made,
Stronger by weakness, wiser we become,
As we draw near to our eternal home.
Leaving the old, both worlds at once we view,
And stand upon the threshold of the New.

The poet Keats chose as his epitaph "Here lies one whose name was writ in water." He believed that his life would be viewed without consequence, and that he would be but one more transitory figure among the yearning and striving masses. How wrong he was!

Longfellow, in his 'Tales of a Wayside Inn' expressed so well our feelings on the sad occasions of parting. "Our ingress into the world was naked and bare; Our progress through the world if often full of trouble and care: Our egress from the world, will be to nobody knows where; But if we do well here, we shall do well there." The Christian Hope is that the best is yet to be.

True love is drowned by no billows of mischance. True love fears no thunder-bolts of fate. True love abides, immortal, firm, unchangeable. To have loved once is to have loved for aye.

(Wishart's 'Deeds of Montrose')

Service to others is the rent we pay for our room in the world.

Addison said, on the death of a loved one, "When we meet hereafter, we shall meet in happier climes and on a safer shore." Thus the Christian Hope!

136. 2001

The Golden Rule

When this little homily is read, I will be preparing to travel to Bangladesh. The visit is to participate in the wedding of an 'old student's' daughter (aged 21) who is to marry a doctor in Sylhet, which is some 80 miles from Dacca, the capital city. Since retiring from a position of higher education, I have 'attended' many such functions for 'overseas' ex-students in England, India, Pakistan and Nigeria. I had, and still have, a special relationship with 'my boys' which we mutually share. Bangladesh is 87% Muslim, 9% Hindu and 4% Christian. Whilst there I'll pray in a mosque, a temple and I trust, if I can locate one, a Christian church.

Human nature is the same worldwide; the colour of the skin is but incidental. The poet and writer John Masefield was inspired to pen these words, "So by the bedside of the dying Black; I felt our uncouth souls subtly made one; Forgive the meanness of each other's lack; Forgive the petty tale of ill things done; We were but man, who for a tale of days seeks the one city by a million way." Again, one of our great epic poems ends with the words, "There is neither East nor West, border nor breed nor birth, when two strong men stand face to face – though they come from the ends of the earth". The oldest of the world's monotheistic religions is Judaism (belief in one God). God revealed His law (the Torah) to the Jewish people and choose them to be a light and an example to all mankind. It is a fact that all the world's religions subscribe in principle. If not in practice to The Golden Rule of Life:-

Buddhism
Hurt not others with that which pains yourself.   (Udanavarga 5:18)

Christianity
All things whatsoever ye would that men should do to you, do ye even so to them; for this is the law and the prophets.   (Bible, St Matthew 7,12)

Confucianism
Is there any one maxim which ought to be acted upon throughout one's whole life? Surely the maxim of loving-kindness is such – Do not unto others what ye would not they should do unto you.   (Analects 15. 23)

Hebraism
What is hurtful to yourself, do not to your fellow man. That is the whole of the Torah, and the reminder is but commentary. Go learn it.   (Talmud)

Hinduism
This is the sum of duty; do naught to others which if done to thee, would cause thee pain.   (Mahabharata 5,1517)

Islam
No one of you is a believer until he loves for his brother what he loves for himself.   (Traditions)

Jainism
In happiness and suffering, in joy and grief, we should regard all creatures as we regard our own self, and should therefore refrain from inflicting upon others such injury as would appear undesirable to us if inflicted upon ourselves.   (Yogashastra 2. 201)

Sikhism
As thou deemest thyself so deem others. Then shalt thou become a partner in Heaven.
(Kabir)

Taoism
Regard your neighbour's gain as your own gain; and regard your neighbour's loss as your loss.
(T'ai Shang Kan Ying P'Ien)

Zoroastrianism
That nature only is good when it shall not do unto another whatever is not good for its own self.
(Dadistan-I-dinik 94. 5)

'Non Compos Mentis'

1. A woman in Bristol phoned the local authority to say that she had found a large hole in the road. She was immediately put in contact with the Lost Property Office!

2. In a field in West Yorkshire there is a sign saying, "Beware of the Bull – Entry free, the bull will charge later."

3. The NSW Public Works Dept, have a portable toilet with the sign – "Please do not place your handbag in the urinal."

137. 2001

"Work Like Billyhoe"

When I was a child this was one of the favourite expressions of my mother, and if anybody "worked like Billyhoe" it was my mother, a war widow of the 1914-18 war, left with six young children to feed and clothe and bring up. It was many years later that I found out that there was a 'Billyhoe' – a Norfolk curate of some centuries ago – the Revd John Billyhoe. Apparently everybody knew him as a man who worked untiringly, one always running because he could not stay to walk. Whenever he was sent for he was there right away, and whatever he was doing he worked as if it was the last hour he had to live. Everybody admired and loved him. If mothers wanted their children to hurry over an errand, they said "go to the grocer's for me, and run like Billyhoe." When set to work on weeding the onion-beds, etc. they were expected to work like Billyhoe, he was the example to follow.

We know that Jesus worked untiringly, both as a carpenter and as a leader of men, as did Paul on those three great missionary journeys. Thus the challenge, "I must work while it is yet day, the night cometh in which no man can work." William Penn and the Pilgrim Fathers knew the value of initiative and exertion, thus Penn's, "No pain, no palm no thorns, no throne, no gall, no glory, no cross, no crown."

There are lots of stories in the Bible about people who worked like Billyhoe, for example Rebekah who, when Eliezer asked her for a drink of water, drew water for all his ten camels as well. Anyone who has tried to satisfy the need even of one thirsty animal will realise how long and hard she had to work. Joseph must have worked like Billyhoe when he was a slave in the house of Potiphar, and then worked like a slave to store food in Egypt, in preparation for the seven years of famine which he foresaw.

The Good Book says, "Whatsoever thy hand findeth to do, do it with all thy might" (Eccles. 9 v10) and in the New Testament we read, "Thou shall love the Lord thy God with all thy heart and with all they strength and with all thy mind; and they neighbour as thyself." Then we would be 'working like Billyhoe' (if we followed this command) and the Kingdom of God would be a little nearer realisation in this sad world.

Asylum Seekers

Contrary to what we might be led to believe there is plenty of room in this country for immigration. Last year about 270,000 people came to live in the UK. Where did they all go? Well, 230,000 people left, so that's not really a very big increase is it? Our birth-rate is declining, in contrast to the subcontinent of India, where a baby is born every two seconds.

Tail-Piece

The owner of a very valuable dog asked the vet if he would cut off the dog's tail as close to his body as possible. The vet protested that this would spoil a valuable dog, but finally agreed to perform the operation; first asking, "Would you mind telling me why you want this done?" "Yes," said the owner, "My mother-in-law is coming to visit us and I don't want a single thing in the house to give the slightest indication of welcome."

138. 2001

Bird Songs at Eventide

I find it most satisfactory and relaxing, at this time of the year, at the end of the day, to sit in the garden and listen to the calls and songs of the birds before sunset, and before they settle down for the night. Bird-life and habit have, and always will, fascinate us, and we have learned a great deal from our observations, which will continue to proliferate. They represent nature's music.

Wagner, in the 'Ring Cycle' uses for the motif in Seigfried's 'Journey to the Rhine' the clear triple call-note and song of the lovely golden oriole, a handsome but rare visitor to the UK. Here Sir Landon Ronald (musician and conductor) set to music Simpson's lovely poem 'Down in the Forrest' – a song of great beauty and lovely sentiment. Vaughan Williams has given us 'The Lark Ascending' and Frederick Delius 'On Hearing the First Cuckoo in Spring'. Vivaldi was inspired by a goldfinch to write a flute concerto and Respighi listened to a nightingale and wrote the 'Fountains of Rome'. Again the three call notes of the European quail is a motif in Beethoven's Pastoral (6th) Symphony and Mozart kept a pet starling, which is immortalized in his Divertimento for Strings and two horns (K522), a work also known as 'The Musical Joke'.

Thus the music of nature has always had a way of affecting the nature of music. Starlings can vary their songs; by adding or suppressing notes and varying patterns of notes. Mozart's pet starling died on 27 May 1784. It was buried with hymns sung at the graveside, and a poem penned in its honour! One irony and tragedy of life is that Mozart himself 'rests' in an unknown grave in a Vienna cemetery (aged 35). His death was a destruction of genius as grievous as the death of Schubert.

Why the title 'Bird Songs at Eventide'? Well, it's one of my favourite songs, evoking many memories, especially when sung by John McCormack, with the accompaniment at the piano, by Edwin Schneider, with its lovely birdlike trills. A thing of beauty is a joy forever.

Who is the Greatest?

Socrates and Aristotle each taught for 40 years. Plato for 50, Jesus for only 3. Yet His influence far surpasses the combined 130 years of teaching by these men who are acknowledged as the greatest philosophers of all antiquity. Jesus painted no pictures, yet the finest paintings of Raphael, Michelangelo and Leonardo da Vinci received their illumination from Him. He wrote no poetry, yet Dante, Milton and others of the world's greatest poets were inspired by Him. He composed no music, yet Haydn, Handel, Beethoven, Bach and others reached their highest perfection in hymns, symphonies and oratorios composed in His honour. Thus every sphere of human greatness has been enriched by the humble Carpenter of Nazareth. His unique contribution to the Race is in the salvation and saving of the human soul. (The Word for Today).

A Thought

The church is more than just a 'place' to which you go, but a living and loving community to which you belong and share with others. Archbishop Temple observed – "The Church that lives to itself, dies to itself."

Ecumenical

The newly wed husband confessed to his bride on their wedding night, that he was a somnambulist (sleepwalker). She replied, "Never mind, I'm a Methodist, we can go to my church on Sunday morning and attend yours in the evening. No problem."

139. 2001

Facts and Figures

It has been estimated that if we could shrink the earth's population to the size of a village of precisely 100 people, in it there would be 57 Asians, 21 Europeans, 14 from the Western Hemisphere and 8 Africans. Of these 52 would be female and 48 male. Again 70 would be non-white and 30 would be white and 70 would be non-Christian and 30 Christian (nominally).

Apparently it is a fact that 1,000 people per day find a new religion! Since 1945 some 400 'cults' have emerged, nevertheless only 15% of the total population in the UK attend church. Although marriages are in decline, inter-religious marriages and remarriages are increasing. For example, 65% Catholic and 45% Jews now marry outside their faith. The rate of divorces and marriages per year is now about equal in the UK. Divorces in the US total 15½ million and every night 40% of American children will go to sleep in homes where their fathers do not sleep.

It is apparent that Christian churches are in decline. The Christian Research Group state that the combined membership of churches is now less than 6 million, less than 12% of the population. It was 22% in 1970 and 31% in 1920. Among the traditional churches, membership peaked in 1905 for Baptists, in 1910 for the Methodists, 1930 for the Anglicans, 1935 for the Presbyterians and Congregationalists, and in 1960 for the Catholics. The only category to buck the downward trend in Christianity has been 'others' – including Orthodox, Pentecostal, etc. and 'new' or 'house' churches – which has risen to a record combined membership of 908,000 from 678,000 in 1980 and a previous peak of 854,000 in 1930.

The number of active membership of other religions is estimated at 1.5 million. This is double the total in 1980 and more than three times that in 1970. By far the fastest growing faith is Islam with 675,000 active members compared to 495,000 in 1990 and 300,000 in 1980. Three are now more Muslims than Methodists and Baptists put together and the number of mosques has risen sharply – to 660 today, from 350 in 1990 and just 193 in 1980. There are now 400,000 active Sikhs, compared to 250,000 in 1990 and 165,000 Hindus, up more slowly from 140,000 in 1990 and 120,000 in 1980.

As with Christianity, the Jewish faith has suffered decline. It counts its following as 88,000 heads of households, compared to 101,000 in 1990 and 130,000 in 1960. The number of synagogues is also down, although the number of distinct congregations using them is up.

Thought for the Day

Use your money while you're living.
Do not hoard it to be proud.
You can never take it with you.
There's no pocket in a shroud.
God will help you on no farther,
Than the graveyard where you lie.

And though you are rich while living,
You're a pauper when you die.
Use it then some lives to brighten.
As through life they weary plod
Place your bank account in Heaven,
And grow rich towards your God.

Good as Gold!

The Bible states that there is something that is more durable and of much greater value than gold – that perishes despite its being proved by fire (1 Peter 1 v 7). Gold is much sought after for its beauty and durability, it remains bright and untarnished seeming indefinitely. It is resistant to attack by water, oxygen, sulphur and almost anything else. Gold artefacts discovered in sunken vessels and elsewhere, still retain their lustre after hundreds of years. Tested or refined by fire and other processes it can still attain 99. 9% purity. Nevertheless, even refined gold perishes and dissolves when exposed to a mixture of three parts hydrochloric acid and one part nitric acid.

A River Rhyme

The Amazon flows on and on, regardless of the season. But a German river ebbs and flows with far more Rhine and reason.

Too True

For every one person who exclaims "Speak, Lord, for they servant hearest," there are two who say, "Hear, Lord, for thy servant speaketh."

Tit for Tat

Six Hell's Angels went into a bar and started abusing a little chap who was sitting there. They pulled his hair, spilled his drink over him and pushed him around. The little chap paid his bill and departed. One Hell's Angel said to the barman, "He's not much of man, letting us do that to him." The barman replied, "He's not much of a driver either. He's just backed his truck over six brand new motorbikes."

140. 2001

"Together in Remembrance" The State Prison, Montevideo, Uruguay

At reveille everyone was up and about, no-one had slept a wink in that immense prison yard. After a day of beatings and threats of execution, the prisoners lay awake until dawn. Rumours of a massacre were rife. Today is Easter Sunday, reported a recent arrival from Motevideo, who had not, unlike the others, yet to lose track of time and the calendar.

The Christians spread the word, we have to celebrate. They knew gatherings were not allowed for any reason and they had learned in their own flesh that the rule was no joke. Nevertheless, some thing has to be done. The other prisoners, the non-Christians, helped; several of them sat by the barred gates forming a screen; others walked about without apparent purpose, forming a human ring around the celebrants. The ceremony took place in the middle of the yard.

Miguel Brun whispered a few words. He evoked the resurrection of Jesus, which promised redemption for all captives. Jesus was persecuted, jailed, tormented and murdered, but one Sunday, one Sunday like this Sunday, he made the walls shake and tremble so that in every prison there would be freedom, and in every solitude an encounter. The prison yard had nothing. No bread, no wine, not even cups. Thus it was to be a communion of empty hands, Miguel made an offering to the ONE who offered Himself "Eat," he whispered. "This is His body". And the Christians raised their hands to their lips and ate the invisible bread. "Drink, this is His blood". And they raised the non-existent cup and drank the invisible wine.

Then they embraced each other. (Edwardo Galeano)

This Modern Age

Priests at a church in Paisley, Scotland, have tackled a drop in attendances by switching the traditional 6:30 p.m. Sunday Mass to 4:00 p.m. so that members of the congregation can get home in time to watch football matches shown live on TV.

A Child's Logic

A mother was concerned that her small son had developed the bad habit of biting his nails. She tried everything – scolding, smacking, painting his nails with bitter almond oil, etc. – all to no avail. Then she learnt that at school there was a fat boy who was the butt of all the children – and her child dreaded becoming fat. Thus the technique – "You'll become fat if you continue to bit your nails!" The subterfuge worked! Soon afterwards, with his mother in a superstore, the little boy noticed a young woman at the check-out who was very obviously pregnant. He eyed her with great curiosity and finally went up to her and said, "I don't know your name, but I know what you've been doing!"

'Where there's a will, there are relations.'
'Laugh and the world laughs with you. Snore and you sleep alone.'

141. 2002

Christmas Cards

The Inter-Church Giving of Christmas Cards was discussed at some length at the quarterly church meeting. The divided result – continue if desired, sign the large greeting card as an alternative or donate the cash involved to know charitable causes, rather than to the pockets of advertisers and printers, etc. Like many things at the Festive

Season – commercialism has taken over. It is interesting to note that it was Sir Henry Cole who, in 1843, produced the first card. Having forgotten to write his regular Christmas letter to his relations, he asked a friend to design a Christmas message which could be mechanically reproduced. One thousand copies of the first card were initially printed. Sir Henry used what he needed and gave the rest to a friend for a shilling. The first Christmas card thus had little religious or festive significance. Colour was introduced in 1863 and Adolph Tuck stimulated mass interest, launching a design competition in 1880, with a 500 guinea prize. Cards received Royal approval in 1893 when Queen Victoria ordered some from Adolph Tuck's father, Raphael. The world's biggest card was printed on the side of a Boeing 707 for Qantas, the Australian airline. It read, "Have a Qantastic Christmas". The smallest was sent to the Prince of Wales in 1929 – inscribed on a grain of rice and only read under a microscope. The most expensive card ever made was commissioned by an Indian prince over 80 years ago. It was made of ivory, decorated with 1,000 scenes of the Buddha, and had 44 diamonds around the edge. It was valued at £500,000. Alfred Lord Tennyson refused a fee of 1,000 guineas to write a dozen verses for Christmas card use. Good for him!

What a Wonderful World!

If we look at the sky on a clear, moonless, night, the brightest objects seen are likely to be the planets Venus, Mars, Jupiter and Saturn. Also a large number of stars, which are just like our own sun, but much farther from us. They appear to change their positions very slightly, relative to each other, as the earth orbits around the sun, but this is not so, we see them from different positions against the background of more distant stars. This enables the expert to measure directly the distance of these stars away from us. The nearest star is about four light years away, the light from it takes about four years to reach Earth – some twenty-three million million miles! Our sun, by comparison, is a mere eight light-minutes away!

At regular intervals I take my father's gold hunter (Waltham) watch out of its resting place and 'give it a wind'. The Swiss movement is a miracle of man's inventiveness. The balance wheel turns year after year as quickly as the driving wheel of a locomotive running at 55 miles per hour. It oscillates 432,000 times a day, the distance it covers being 12½ miles per day, or 25,000 miles, the earth's circumference, in 5½ years. All the energy is supplied by a spring of one hundred millionth of one horse-power. There are parts of a watch that have to be accurate to 0. 00004 of an inch, or one fiftieth of a hair's breadth. The life of a Swiss watch is about 20 times that of a car, and its balance-wheel makes 120 million revolutions in 6 months – the equivalent of driving a car 155,000 miles. Precision instruments in the USA are able to drill holes in hair. The drill is too fine to be seen by the naked eye – so delicate that it can be bent by accidental contact with a piece of tissue paper. Yet we cannot evolve a formula for Peace on Earth and Goodwill between all Nations!

> If there is righteousness in the heart, there will be beauty in the character. If there be beauty in the character, there will be harmony in the home. If there be harmony in the home, there will be order in the nation. When there is order in the nation, there will be peace in the world!
>
> (Chinese proverb)

Lady-in-Waiting

A lady, of uncertain age, went to the doctors because she was constipated. "Well, do you do anything about it? he enquired. "Of course I do, doctor, I sit there for hours." The doctor added, "I mean do you take anything? The reply, "Oh yes, doctor, I take my knitting!"

142. 2002

William Shakespeare

William Shakespeare (1564–1616) was recently voted to be the most outstanding English personality of all time, yet, even today, little is known about him as a person. His writings, plays, poems and sonnets have had millions of words written to clarify and explain them – but of the man himself?

Nevertheless his will has been examined and interpreted over and over again by historians, with one item in particular causing much discussion – the bequest to his wife, Anne Hathaway. He left her nothing but his second-best bed, with its furniture – i.e. the coverlets and linen. Actually this was but an afterthought. In his original will, made on 25 January 1616, his wife is not mentioned at all.

This apparent meanness and cruelty towards his wife, has given rise to the belief, in some quarters, that his marriage was a failure. This is a wrong assumption. The bard, in fact, left most of his fortune to his eldest daughter, Susannah Hall, because he considered his wife too old – she was over 60 – and too ignorant of business matters to be responsible for the handling of money. He commended her to the care of her daughter. Our William must have made a tidy sum out of his works, dying quite a rich man with a substantial estate called New Place, near Stafford and with freehold property in London.

Dowsing Updated!

My most vivid memories of yesteryears, when I was a schoolboy, were the summer holidays from school, weeks and weeks of sunshine and never a drop of rain!

Then, the most important and overworked person in the village was 'Old Charlie' – a dowsing expert. He was in constant demand by farmers and nurseries, to locate the most precious of all commodities – water!

The dowser practises his art with the aid of a Y-shaped hazel twig which deflects strongly downwards at the source of the underground water or mineral, a metal rod or a pendulum may be used as an alternative. Charlie always used the hazel twig. How comes it about that Charlie had this 'sixth sense'? Well, it has become increasingly clear, through recent scientific experiments, that the ability to dowse depends on the existence of tiny magnetic receptors – magnetite crystals in the human brain, and some of us, like Charlie, have a larger concentration of these crystals than others. When this sensor detects a magnetic anomaly, it sends a signal to the dowser's muscles which experience a small contraction causing the lightly held dowsing rod to deflect. Researchers at the California Institute of Technology have identified crystals of magnetite (Fe_3O_4), the iron oxide that helps migrating 'creatures' to navigate, in the human brain!

What a wonderful world!

Making the Best Use of Everything

Walking down a residential street in Cardiff, a man heard the telephone ringing in a public kiosk. Curious, he lifted the received and said, "This is a public telephone. "I know that," came a man's voice, "could you pop over to No 12 please and tell my wife to keep my dinner warm, I'll be home in about an hour."

Add-Lib

Advert in a London tube station. "75% of all top clergy take The Times." Scrawled below were the words, "The other 25% buy it."

143. 2002

The Riddle of Life

I love the works of Omar Khayyam:-

Up from the Earth's Centre through the Seventh Gate
I rose, and on the Throne of Saturn sate,
And many a Knot unravel'd by the Road,
But not the master knot of Human Fate.

There was the Door to which I found no key
There was the Veil through which I might not see;
Some little talk awhile of Me and Thee
There was – and then no more of thee and me.

These days I bless the man (or woman) who invented the walking stick. This third leg has become a constant companion. Its use reminds me of the Riddle of the Sphinx of Thebes.

Who goes on four feet, or two feet, or three.
But the more feet it goes on, the weaker it be?

With these mystic words she was holding the devoted land in the shadow of Death. From her seat upon a great rock that overhung the highway she pronounced her riddle to every passer-by. Ignorance of its solution involved the forfeit of life, and many of the poor Thebans were obliged to pay the penalty.

But deliverance came with the coming of Oedipus. Coming back to his ancestral home, he learned of his country's sore distress, and undertook to be her delivered. He faced the Sphinx, received the riddle, and straightway saw and declared the answer. For what did it mean but man, who goeth in infancy upon all fours, who stands in manhood upon his two feet, and who in old age must needs support himself with the aid of a staff. The Sphinx, mortified at the victory of Oedipus cast herself down from the rock, and dying at his feet, was herself the last to pay forfeit of her own fatal riddle. Thus the land was freed from the scourge of Death. On reflection, the Theban stage is, in miniature, the stage of the world, and essentially the riddle of the Sphinx is the very riddle of human life – the question is "What is Man?"

> I am, how little more I know!
> Whence came I? Whither do I go?
> A centred self, which feels and is;
> A cry between the silences:
> A shadow birth of clouds at strife
> With sunshine on the hills of Life:
> A shaft from Nature's quiver cast
> Into the Future from the Past:
> Between the cradle and the shroud
> A meteor's flight from cloud to cloud!

The answer to the Riddle of Life can come only with ONE by whose life, through experience, can explain the meaning of Death and Resurrection. Humanity has waited in the shadow, trembling with fear. Of the ancient foe Death, longing for a greater that Oedipus for the coming of a Prince and Saviour – who brings deliverance from the curse of ignorance and death by revealing the mystery of life, with the origin from which it springs, and its final destiny as revealed in Jesus Christ, Our Lord.

Tall Story

A nun ran out of petrol and walked to a garage. The owner gave her enough petrol to get her car started using the only container he could find – a beer bottle. She returned to her car and was putting the contents of the bottle into the tank when a protestant minister drove up. He watched her in amazement, then exclaimed, "We may have our differences, sister, but I've got to admire your faith."

Passing By

A lovesick bricklayer who made a spur-of-the-moment trip back from Australia to visit his girlfriend in Ilkley, West Yorkshire, discovered that she had just flown out to visit him in Sydney.

144. 2002

Comment by Dwight D Eisenhower (USA)

Any stupid person can deny the existence of a supernatural power, because man's physical senses cannot detect it. But there cannot be ignored the influence of conscience, the respect we must feel for moral law, the mystery of first life on our planet, on what once must have been a molten mass, or the marvellous order in which the universe moves about us on this earth. All of these evidence the handiwork of a beneficent Deity. For my part, that Deity is the God of the Bible, and of Jesus Christ.

My youngest daughter, Justine, spent a period of her university education in France. Whilst there she introduced me to the works of Marcel Proust (1871-1922) the great French novelist and autobiographer. Son of a professor and rich bourgeois parents, he suffered lifelong from asthma. Well educated and aristocratic, he enjoyed 'gay society' until aged 31, after the death of his parents (1903), he dedicated his life for some 20 years until his death, as a hermit-invalid-recluse in a cork-lined room, writing in 15 volumes his autobiographical novel 'In Search of Lost Time'. C.K. Scott Moncrieff made a splendid abridged English translation in 3 volumes titled 'Remembrance of Things Past' (1922–1930).

An outstanding few paragraphs from Marcel Proust are as follows:

There is nothing in the condition of life on this earth to make us think ourselves obliged to do good, to be sensitive, even polite, nor for the artist to feel himself compelled to begin a passage 20 times over again – when the praise it evoked will matter little to the body which will soon decay and die. All these obligations, which have no sanction in our present life, seem to belong to a different world, a world founded on goodness, on scruple, or sacrifice a world – whence we came – perhaps to return there and live under the rule of the Unknown Law which we have obeyed here – to which every deep intellectual labour draws us close, and which are invisible only (and not even) to fools.

Musical Scoring

Arthur Schnabel, a great pianist of blessed memory, didn't like bad reviews of his concert performances. One critic gave a poor review of his rendering of Beethoven's 'Moonlight Sonata'. Schnabel read the review in bed at 2:00 a.m. He picked up the phone instantly and shouted "Who are you to say that Schnabel played the Moonlight poorly, I say it was superb." "Who's speaking?" demanded the critic, half asleep. "This is Beethoven," snapped Schnabel – and hung up!

Ode to a Philanderer

In Brighton she was Brenda, she was Patsy in Perth, in Cambridge she's Clarissa, the sweetest thing on earth, in Stratford she is Stella – the pick of all the bunch: But on his expense account, she's Petrol, Oil and Lunch!

Whitfield to Garrick (eighteenth century)

Whitfield – "How is it that you actors are able, on the stage, to produce so great effects with fiction whilst we preachers, in the pulpit, obtain such a small result with facts?" Garrick – "I suppose it is because we present fiction as fact, whilst you, too often, offer facts as though they were fiction!"

Maths

Women have a passion for mathematics. They divide their age by two, double the price of their dresses; treble their husband's salaries, and add five years to the age of their best friends!

Good, better, best, never let it rest, until the good is better and the better – best.

145.

═══════════════════════════════════════

Hail and Farewell!

The Good Book reminds us that there is a beginning and an end, and this applies to our active life and witness in the world. The minister surprised and shocked the quarterly church meeting on 19 August last, with the announcement that he would be terminating his minister in September next 2002 after completing 30 years happy association with the Fellowship. This commenced in September 1972 and will end a period of service extending over 69 years, which commenced in 1933 at Tatton St Congregational Mission Church in Hulme, Manchester, under the auspices of calling of the then Manchester & District Congregational Board, registered at Milton Hall, Deansgate, Manchester 3. During the coming 12 months the Moderator and the district council will, with the Church Fellowship, consider the future leadership and witness of the church in Morley Green.

The tree which needs two arms to span its girth, sprang from the tiniest shoot. Yon tower, nine stories high, rose from a little mound of earth. A journey of a thousand miles began with a single step (LAO-TSE)

It was on the 30 July 1972, after a unanimous vote in favour from a special church meeting, that Charles Boyer, wrote to me asking if I would accept the call to assume the pastoral oversight of the Fellowship of Morley Green, this, with my wife Marjorie's assent, I was honoured and pleased to accept, and the oversight commenced on Sunday, 10 September 1972. With my then commitment to my job in Higher Education (retirement due in 1974) I anticipated serving the church until 1980, when I would gracefully 'retire'! Twenty-two years 'on' the curtain will finally fall! It's been a privilege and a pleasure to work with such wonderful people. As long ago F. Bacon observed, "I love my friends, they half my sorrows and double my joys."

Morley Green had a special relationship with Wilmslow Congregational Church for over 100 years, and my calling to Morley had the full support and blessing of Wilmslow. Initiated by their minister the Revd R.W. Courtney. At 3:00 p.m. on the afternoon of 17 September 1972 saw the formation of Morley Green Congregational Church as a separate church in its own rights.

In my first letter to the congregation I said – "Mankind appears to have an in-built urge to self-destruction, and there is a growing unrest and mistrust of established institutions and the conventional wisdoms. People, especially the young, are looking for the new guidelines, new sheet-anchors, for a belief in a purposeful existence. The growing influence of many, plus increased leisure time of the young and unemployed, finds many bored with life, craving excitement and interest. The answer to all these problems are found in the life and teaching of Jesus."

Obviously things haven't changed much over the years. Nothing in life is sure, not death, not victory, but we must never abandon Hope – the best is yet to be! In that great Hindu book the Bhagavad-Gita (Song of the Lord dated 300 BC-AD 300) Krishna confronts the doubts and fears of the young Arjuna – He points out to his young companion that victory in life is never guaranteed beforehand – "We must ever attend to the overwhelming duty of the moment, in a spirit of emancipated understanding." "Counting gain and loss as one, prepare for battle!" In life so often gains are losses and losses are often gains. Our destiny is a great one, because the essence of it is tragic. All that we build crumbles, all that we embody turns to dust, all that we love we must one day leave behind. That which alone endures is the spirit and the character in which we understand and meet our destiny. This we pass on to our children and our friends, only a breath indeed, but the very breath of Life. The words of Jesus are ultimate in their wisdom – "He that loseth his life shall find it." When we die we face ourselves, thus we should seek to enter into immortality before death. The Kingdom of Heaven is on the earth within us and we should enter therein.

> Grant, Lord God, that we may cleave to you without parting,
> Worship you without wearying
> Serve you without falling
> Faithfully find you, for ever possess you, the one only God
> Blessed for all eternity." Amen

(St Anselm)

The Wisdom of Shakespeare (1564-1616)

> Neither a borrower nor a lender be,
> For loan oft loses both itself and friend,
> And borrowing dulls the edge of husbandry.
> This above all, to thine own self be true,
> And it must follow, as the night the day,
> Thou canst not be false to any man.

146.

===

A Post-Ministerial Involvement

January 2004
The Eternal Quest and its Problems

A letter received 31.12.2003

Dear Eric

I hope you will excuse my burdening you with a letter but ever since we had our brief conversation, after John's Christmas lunch, I have felt an increasing need to tell someone who would understand my struggle to come to terms with my loss of faith.

It is forbidden to me to admit this to anyone who possesses a strong, untroubled, faith and not given to doubts, like John, who happens to be my oldest and closest friend over the past 67 years. Nor to Mavis either. But in a brief conversation I sensed that you would accept my rather outrageous question which, if you can recall was, "Eric, have you ever had doubts about your faith," and you told me that you now called yourself a 'Christian Agnostic!'

I suppose I could call myself a Christian Agnostic but I'm not sure. You said that you did not believe in the Virgin Birth and with that admission, surely out goes the Divinity of Christ. You did not tell me how much else you did not accept. I do not believe in the existence of God. Recently it was reported in the press that a team of astrologers had discovered a new star which was so far away in the Universe that its light took five years to reach us. Where is God in all this? Primo Levi wrote in his book – "If this is a man." Auschwitz existed therefore God does not! Like you I do not believe in the Virgin birth, nor do I believe in the Resurrection. That idea appals me. I do not accept that any bible to have reproduced the authentic words of Jesus. Whose translation are we consulting? Jesus may, just may, have made some statement which the gospel writer put into words to reflect that statement. How many sermons have you listened to where the preacher claimed authority by taking just one word from a biblical phrase. That's OK by me and I get the message, that's if I'm still awake at the end of the sermon! Without a God I do not pray, what's the point. When I should be praying I remember and call to mind the many folk who should be in my thoughts but out of reach of my compassion or love or help.

All these doubts have been with me for some time so you can see with my faith in tatters a big gap now exists in my life to join the other bigger gap which will never be filled when my wife died some eight years ago. I still go to church but feel a bit of a fraud. I recite the Creed. I love the ritual of the Book of Common Prayer and really do say the Confession fervently and humbly. What an admission all this is. I go to church because I've always gone to church... I was taken, as a babe in arms, by my mother to her methodist church and from there to Sunday school, to youth services, to confirmation and so on!

It is an immense relief (although unasked) to be able to tell someone this sorry tale and someone who, I think, will understand and sympathise. So there it all is. I've committed it to paper. You must be vexed that I have used you as some sort of sounding board based on that one simple phrase – 'Christian Agnostic'. I do not expect a reply but I am so relieved to have told someone. I will end by saying – thank you for listening and my apologies for having the nerve to claim that privilege.

    Yours sincerely
      Wilfrid

147.

Reply and acknowledgement to letter sent 1.1.2004

Saturday, 10 January 2004

Dear Eric

Thank you for your letter, full of wisdom and with some nice quotations none of which I knew. I do not wish to prolong this correspondence but you have raised two points. My non-belief about the existence of God troubles you. It once troubled me but no longer. You wrote, "God is in all of us" and, "God is a spirit and they that worship Him must worship Him in spirit." This seems like conventional theology and incomprehensible to me.

    The difficulty I have in reaching any sort of understanding is not helped by the clergy of my church, an Anglican one. We have a vicar, also a retired ordained priest, born in Jamaica and a truly delightful bloke. Two curates. A young chap of about 40 years and the other a mature chap of 70 plus who took early retirement from ICI and was ordained. It was he who was on duty at last week's 08:00 Communion service. He preached quite a good sermon but went on too long so that his later ramblings obscured his early good points. It always happens. After the sermon comes prayers. "Let us pray," says Dick, standing in front of the altar... With eyes closed, he begins – "Let's pray for the world!" How does one pray for the world? Who does one pray to? Fifteen minutes later, after calling to mind all the news at 06:00 that morning we finished with, "Lord, hear our prayer and let our cry come unto thee." After the service a friend of mine would sometimes stroll up to me and say "Wilfrid, he forgot to pray for the Battersea Dogs' Home!"

    Such is the contrast. The "God within me" and the God "out there," to whom, presumably, our curate was sending his prayers and hoping that someone (something) will pick them up like a radio beacon. Perhaps my antenna is defective!

    Sincerely
      Wilfrid

148.

1 January 2004.05.12

The Reply to Wilfrid's S O S

Dear Wilfrid

Your 'communication' received on the last day of 2003, merits a reply penned on the first day of 2004 – as we face... the coming days with its uncertainties, hopes and fears! We try to anticipate the future – pretty hopeless! – but as the Eastern Sage remarked – "The moth of curiosity will always flutter around the lamp of circumstance." My favourite quotation from John Ruskin, the great Victorian, is, "As far as knowledge is concerned, we are forever as children gathering pebbles on a boundless shore!"

I think it was a gentleman poet with the surname of Clough who said, "New occasions teach new duties; time makes ancient good, uncouth." We are told that life moves from the relative to the absolute – the latter we never reach perhaps, one day, the secret of life and the purpose of living will be revealed to us; perhaps the end of this early life may not be a terminus; but a station for call, on the journey of the soul – whatever the soul may be!

Two thousand years ago we believed in a flat earth, with Heaven above the clouds and Hell below our feet, with 'our planet' the centre of the Universe, and the sun revolving around 'our world'. Now we know that 'our little world' is, compared to the Universe, like a speck of dust floating in the immensity of St Paul's Cathedral! – and we measure distance in light years – with light travelling at nearly 186,000 miles per second!

In this latter part of my lifetime it is obvious that there has been a progressive decay in Christian belief. Two World Wars, subsequent wars and the present situation worldwide, have seen the destruction and non-observance of Christian values. Leslie Weatherhead said many years ago, "that a church, true to the mind of Christ, would be prepared to lose itself in saving the world!" There is bad religion as well as good religion. Today, so many churches are self-centred and inward looking – self-preservation is the rule – churchanity not Christianity. There are too many pernicious 'holy wars' – witness Ireland and Palestine, also the African problem of poverty and neglect by so-called Christian countries; we fail to practice what we preach, individually and collectively and the USA which claims to be 90% plus Christian, shares in the hypocrisy of "ONE WORLD" – which is a misnomer in present circumstances.

Your comment that you no longer believe in the existence of God troubles me, and your reference to Auschwitz is relevant. Dostoevsky said that the death of a single child could make God unacceptable, and it is a fact of history that the reason why many, once orthodox Jews have relinquished their faith, is due to what happened in Auschwitz, and elsewhere, during World War II. They can no longer subscribe to the Biblical idea of a God who manifests Himself so forcefully in Old Testament history; who they say, for them, died in Auschwitz. The idea of a personal God, like one of us, creates problems!

149.

If this God is omnipotent, he could have prevented the Holocaust. We could say – he gave us free-will – the power to choose ourselves what we do – good or ill – but one would expect a Loving Father to intervene in these circumstances. If He was unable to stop it, He is, we could argue, impotent and useless. If He could have stopped it, and chose not to, then He must be a monster, and not a Loving God. Could this be the reason why so many Jews, and others, no longer perform religious observance? – believing that the Holocaust, and so many recent tragedies, have been the demise of conventional theology and belief.

What is my position as a Christian Agnostic? Well, I believe in a personal God, but not in God as a person. In other words God is in all of us – Jesus, in John's Gospel, speaking to the woman at the well said, "God is a spirit, and they that worship Him must worship Him in spirit and in truth." The Kingdom of Heaven is within you, and whoever shall know himself shall find it (Luke 17 v 21). I read the Bible, not to learn history, geography, philosophy or religion. Most of it is outdated – myth, legend and story, illustrating great truths, but not to be taken as literal facts. I read the Bible to try to understand and appreciate better, the mind and teaching of Jesus Christ. Voltaire reminds us that the only Christian died on the Cross, and as Prof. Herbert Butterfield said in his book 'Christianity & History' – "Hold on to Christ, and for the rest – be totally uncommitted."

Some thoughts with reference to After-Life-What-Next! Both Isaac Newton and Albert Einstein, great physicists and thinkers, believed in a Powerful Force they called God, giving us an ordered and controlled Universe. Marcel Proust (1891-1922) who died aged 51, spent the last twenty years of his life, as a recluse, writing his famous auto-biography in 15 volumes – in it he said "There is nothing in the condition of life on this earth to make us think ourselves obliged to do good, to be sensitive, polite, kind. The praise it may evolve matters little to an earthly body sooner or late to decay and return to the dust. These feelings and aspirations are not part of our physical body; they have no sanction in our present life; they belong to a different world, a world from whence we came as human minds, souls and personalities, a world founded on goodness and love, to which, one day we return" – Great thoughts!

EXORCISM is, I understand, practised in the Catholic church to deliver from the influence of evil spirits, etc. In my ministry, quite unexpectedly, I have been twice involved in different retirement homes to 'perform this function' and in each case, beyond my understanding, the results have been achieved! Again, looking back over a long life, certain coincidences that have happened border on the miraculous! So, my friend, as Jesus commands "Be of good cheer – the best is yet to be!"

As ever, yours sincerely
Eric

A Thought

We are such stuff as dreams are made on
and our little life rounded with a sleep.
(Shakespeare: The Tempest, 1V:156)

CONVERSION FACTORS

POSTCRIPT Age shall not whither
A certain lady went into a Marks & Spencer's in Manchester to purchase some greetings cards. Four floors, the largest M & S in the World. She searched diligently, rack after rack for what she required. There were engagement cards, wedding, bar-mitzvahs, retirement, get-well, anniversary, passing the driving test, extending sympathy, congratulation cards, etc, etc. She scoured the shelves in vain for a suitable card for a septuagenarian and finally sought the help of an assistant:- " I'm looking for a card for a 70-year-old" says she. "Sorry madam" came the polite reply "We only go up to 65! We don't have much call for 70s, – There are not many of them about"!!". As George Santayana reminds us. "There is no cure for birth and death, save to enjoy the interval in between".

Conversion Factors

To Convert	Into	Multiply By
1 inch	millimtres (mm)	25.4
1 foot (ft)	metres (m)	0.304
1 yard	metres (m)	0.914
1 mile	kilometres (km)	1.64

As a brief guide for all oldies (70'plus)

¼ lb (4oz) = 113 grams   100 grams = 3.5 oz
½ lb (8oz) = 227 grams   500 grams = 1.1 lbs
1 lb (16oz) = 454 grams   1 kilogram = 2.2 lbs

What is a senior citizen?

A SENIOR Citizen is one who was here before television, the pill, penicillin, polio jabs and anti-biotics. We were here before frozen food, plastic bags, radar, fluorescent lights, credit cards and ball point pens. For us 'timesharing' meant togetherness, a chip was a piece of wood or potato, 'hardware' you bought at the ironmongers and 'software' wasn't even a word.

We were here before tights, drip-dry clothes, dishwashers, tumbledryers, freezers and electric blankets;before men wore long hair or earrings and before women wore dinner-jackets.

We were here before yogurt, the 40 hour week and the NHS.

We got married first and then lived together afterwards, how quaint can you get?

We were here before girls wore Peter Pan collars and thought 'cleavage' was something the butcher did.

In our day, smoking was fashionable; grass was for mowing, coke was something you burnt in the stove and pot was something you cooked in.

A 'gay' person was a person who was the life and soul of the party, while 'AIDS' meant beauty lotion or help for people in trouble.

> I made hay while the Sun shone,
> my work sold.
> Now, if the harvest is over,
> and the world cold.
> Give me the bonus of laughter,
> as I lose hold.
>
> John Betjeman

The Wisdom of Solomon (Chapter 2)

'Our life is short and tedious, we are born to adventure and in death there is no remedy, and there is no returning - let us enjoy the good things that are present - let no flower of the spring pass us by, let us crown ourselves with rosebuds, before they be withered - let us leave tokens of our joyfulness in every place, for this is our portion and our lot is this.'

> 'So with the wild waste grasses on my spear
> I ride forever seeking after God.
> My hair grows whiter than my thistle plume
> and all my limbs are loose; - but in my eyes
> the star of an unconquerable praise:
> For in my soul one hope forever sings,
> that at the next white corner of the road
> My eyes may look on Him.

ADDENDUM

A miscellany, unlike a novel of fiction, does not require to be read consecutively from cover to cover, with it, there is always a random choice of selections. This particular miscellany spans some 30 years in time, recording observations and events covering those years.

It can be "picked up" at random and read with interest and enjoyment on any page, according to the interest and inclination of the reader. The author realises that inevitably, sometimes there are a number of duplications, but suggests that in spanning a period of 30 years this is a pardonable intrusion!

All life is a pilgrimage, and on the journey we are influenced by others along the way. This applies to the written word, Blaise Pascal, one of the wisest of men, expressed it well when he said, "Certain authors, speaking of their works, say "my book," "my commentary". They would be better to say "our book," "our commentary" – because there is in them more of other peoples work than their own!" In this volume the observant will note a change in emphasis and outlook over the years. This is due to the influence of personalities such as the late Bishops, Barnes (Birmingham) and Jenkins (Durham) plus the later views of the departed Leslie Weatherhead of blessed memory.

I realise that in my old age I have become something of a Christian Agnostic – in youth I knew all the answers, now I have many doubts and queries. I take comfort in the fact that consistency is not regarded as an absolute virtue. On the authority of none other than Winston Churchill (who should know) who observed – those that never change their opinions, love themselves more than they love the truth.

Looking back, in memory over some 80 years, when I was a callow youth in my early teens, it was in the local village library that I became, in a way beyond my comprehension; a life reader of John Ruskin, the great Victorian, coming under the influence of "Sesame & Lilies," "Unto This Last," "Time & Tide" etc. and his works on art and architecture. Since then I have tried, not always successfully, to follow his "Golden Rule":– "Let every dawn of morning be to you, as the beginning of life, and every setting sun as its close; then let every one of these short lives leave the sure record of some kindly deed done for others , some goodly store of knowledge gained for ourselves."

E. C. May 2004